Preserving the Sixties

Preserving the Sixties

Britain and the 'Decade of Protest'

Edited by

Trevor Harris
Professor of British Studies, University of Tours, France

and

Monia O'Brien Castro
Senior Lecturer in British Studies, University of Tours, France

Foreword by Dominic Sandbrook

First published 2014 by
PALGRAVE MACMILLAN

Palgrave Macmillan in the UK is an imprint of Macmillan Publishers Limited,
registered in England, company number 785998, of Houndmills, Basingstoke,
Hampshire RG21 6XS.

Palgrave Macmillan in the US is a division of St Martin's Press LLC,
175 Fifth Avenue, New York, NY 10010.

Palgrave Macmillan is the global academic imprint of the above companies
and has companies and representatives throughout the world.

Palgrave® and Macmillan® are registered trademarks in the United States,
the United Kingdom, Europe and other countries.

ISBN 978–1–137–37409–7

This book is printed on paper suitable for recycling and made from fully
managed and sustained forest sources. Logging, pulping and manufacturing
processes are expected to conform to the environmental regulations of the
country of origin.

A catalogue record for this book is available from the British Library.

A catalog record for this book is available from the Library of Congress.

Contents

Tables and Figures

Tables

Figures

Contributors

Alexis Chommeloux is Senior Lecturer at the University of Tours, France, where he is Head of the Law and Languages Department. His fields of research include labour history and labour law, and he is interested in looking at various issues pertaining to British studies from a legal perspective.

Raphael Costambeys-Kempczynski is Senior Lecturer at the Sorbonne Nouvelle, Paris, where he lectures in Radio Journalism, Cultural Studies and English literature. His research interests focus on the performances of the figures of post-modernity and their availability as signifying codes in music, journalism, literature and other forms of cultural manifestation. These analyses attempt to tackle the politico-cultural and semiotic dimension of text, the aim being to understand how the fictions behind commonplaces are inscribed within contemporary cultural production and communication systems.

Mark Donnelly is Senior Lecturer in History at St Mary's University College, London. His research interests include theory of history, memory and the politics of historiography. His most recent books are *Sixties Britain: Culture, Society and Politics* (2005) and *Doing History* (co-authored with Claire Norton, 2011). His next book, *Liberating Histories: Truths, Power, Ethics* (also co-authored with Claire Norton) will be published by Routledge.

Trevor Harris is Professor in British Studies at the University of Tours, where he teaches nineteenth- and twentieth-century British political and intellectual history. His publications include (with Richard Davis and Philippe Vervaecke), *La Décolonisation britannique: perspectives sur la fin d'un empire 1919–1984* (2012), *Art, Politics and Society in Britain (1880–1914): Aspects of Modernity and Modernism* (ed., 2009) and *Une Certaine idée de l'Angleterre* (2006).

Matthew Leggett lectures in English at the University of Burgundy, France, specializing in contemporary British politics. His doctoral thesis was a study of the career of Harold Wilson as Prime Minister and Leader of the Labour Party, based on the memoirs of his colleagues and aides. He has published work on race relations, on the role of insults in politics, on the British media and British political institutions. He is currently working on working-class eating habits in the UK, both past and present.

R. J. Morris is Emeritus Professor in Economic and Social History at the University of Edinburgh. He has written extensively on the British middle classes, on urban history in industrial England, in Scotland and in Ireland. He has contributed a wide range of essays on associational culture to a variety of publications. He was president of the European Urban History Association in 2000–2002, and is currently President of the Economic and Social History Society of Scotland. He has now turned his attention to the visual, and to photography of the urban.

Monia O'Brien Castro lectures in British studies and translation at the University of Tours, France. She also works as scientific advisor for the La Villette Exhibition Centre in Paris. Her doctoral research explored the decline and renovation of inner cities from 1960 to the end of the Conservative era. She has published academic papers on urban policy, and urban social and ethnic exclusion.

Martine Pelletier is Senior Lecturer in Irish Studies at the University of Tours, France. Her publications include *Brian Friel: Histoire et 'histoires'* (1997); she has contributed chapters to *The Cambridge Companion to Brian Friel* (ed. Anthony Roche, 2007), *The Book in Ireland* (eds Fabienne Garcier, Jacqueline Genêt and Sylvie Mikowski, 2006) and *Irish Literature since 1990* (eds Scott Brewster and Michael Parker, 2009). She has also prefaced Alan Delahaye's translations into French of Brian Friel's plays (published by Les éditions l'Avant-scène).

Sylvie Pomiès-Maréchal has written a thesis on the domestic and professional roles of women in British society during the twentieth century, and has studied, in particular, the historical construction of female identity through an analysis of gender relations in both the public and private spheres. Her work deals mainly with eugenics, women and maternity, but she is also interested in the impact of the two world wars on the social role of women and the consequent readjustment of social relations. She has recently produced a work on British women in the French Resistance.

Judith Roof is Professor of English at Rice University, Texas, US. She has worked on comparative modernisms, drama and performance studies, film studies, theories of sexuality, as well as contemporary British and American fiction and the relationship between science, literature, and culture. She has published on feminist narrative, and gay theory (*Come As You Are: Narrative and Sexuality*, 1996, and *All About Thelma and Eve: Sidekicks and Third Wheels*, 2002), as well as works on key concepts and trends in contemporary culture – *Reproductions of Reproduction* (1996) and *The Poetics of DNA* (2007).

Dominic Sandbrook is one of Britain's best known historians. Born in 1974, he was educated at Oxford, St Andrews and Cambridge. Formerly a lecturer in history at Sheffield and a senior fellow of the Rothermere American Institute, Oxford University, he is now a prolific writer, columnist and broadcaster. He is the author of four bestselling volumes of British history since the 1950s, most recently the top ten bestseller *Seasons in the Sun*. Outside the academy, he is probably best known for his BBC television series on the 1970s, the British car industry and the Cold War, and he has also presented numerous programmes on BBC Radio Four. He is also a book critic for the *Sunday Times* and a columnist for the *Daily Mail* and *BBC History Magazine*.

Jeremy Tranmer is Senior Lecturer in British Studies at the University of Nancy, France. Since his PhD (on the British Communist Party in the 1970s and 1980s), he has published numerous articles about the radical left and social movements such as anti-fascism. He is also interested in the relationship between the left and popular music and has written about 'Rock Against Racism', as well as the role of musicians in the 1984/1985 miners' strike. He is a member of the IDEA (Interdisciplinarité dans les Etudes Anglophones) research group.

Peter Vernon began teaching at University College London, and then worked on contract for 16 years as Lecturer, then Visiting Professor with the British Council in various parts of the world. He was appointed to the English Department, University of Tours, France, in 1991 and retired in 2007. He has published over 40 articles on nineteenth- and twentieth-century English and American literature, and has edited two volumes: *Seeing Things: Literature and the Visual* (2005) and *L'Allusion et l'accès* (2005). He was elected Fellow of the English Association in 2005.

Ben Winsworth is Senior Lecturer in English Literature at the University of Orleans, France. He has published a variety of articles on the work of James Joyce, John Fowles, Graham Swift, Julian Barnes, Kazuo Ishiguro, Nick Hornby, and on psychoanalytical approaches to the study of literature. Among his current teaching commitments is a Master's class on Popular Music in the UK from 1960 to 2000.

Foreword

In June 1966, a new nightclub held a private party just off Piccadilly Circus. For its grand opening, Sibylla's could hardly have attracted a more glittering line-up. All four Beatles were there, as well as their wives and girlfriends; so were Mick Jagger, Keith Richards and Brian Jones, accompanied by Chrissie Shrimpton and Anita Pallenberg. David Bailey was there, accompanied by the model Sue Murray, and his great friend Terence Donovan was there too, with his muse Celia Hammond. Mary Quant and Alexander Plunket-Greene were there, of course; so were Cathy McGowan, John Barry, Michael Caine, Julie Christie and Andrew Loog Oldham.

This was what one of the club's founders, the property dealer Bruce Higham, called 'the new boy network... people who were doing things in finance, architecture, press, pop and films... the kind of people the colour supplements write about'. Sibylla's, agreed his colleague Kevin MacDonald, would be the crucible of a new social order: 'We're completely classless. We're completely integrated... It's the greatest, happiest, most swinging ball of the century.'

Half a century on, it is hard to read accounts of Sibylla's grand opening without picturing Mike Myers's splendid Sixties parody, Austin Powers, who would almost certainly have been the first onto the dance floor. But with its overwrought invocation of glamour, modernity, classlessness and youth, the Sibylla's story captures the enduring myth of the swinging Sixties. In fact, the club did not even survive the decade, while MacDonald, who had been its chief cheerleader, killed himself only four months after it opened.

But the image of the Sixties as a period of unprecedented excitement – and in particular, as an age of reckless, liberating change – has become embedded in our national historical consciousness. Looking back, liberals mourn the passing of a golden age, while conservatives typically see the Sixties as the key moment in Britain's moral and cultural decline. During this decade, Margaret Thatcher told a Conservative meeting in March 1982, 'fashionable theories and permissive claptrap set the scene for a society in which the old virtues of discipline and self-restraint were denigrated'. As it happens, the statistics for divorce, abortion, crime and illegitimacy were far higher during her time in office than they had been in the age of Macmillan, Home and Wilson; indeed, many historians now argue that Thatcherism was a natural political development of the self-gratification they associate with the Beatles' decade. But the Sixties remain one of modern history's great litmus tests. Tell me what you think of the Sixties, and I will tell you who you are.

The irony, though, is that the pop-cultural stereotype of the Sixties bears little resemblance to the experiences of millions of people – young and old, rich and poor, black and white, Labour, Liberals and Tories – who lived through the decade. Only a tiny and very rich minority enjoyed the kind of lifestyle that the Beatles, David Bailey and Julie Christie came to take for granted. Most people led longer, healthier, better educated and more comfortable lives than ever, yet outside the more affluent areas of London and the leafy enclaves of university towns, the pace of change often seemed gentle and gradual. When the writer Brian Jackson visited Huddersfield to investigate how working-class life had changed, he found that 36 brass bands were still competing for recruits within a 15-mile radius, while the town's most popular sport was Crown Green bowls, with 33 clubs and five thousand regular players. 'It was a long time before minis made it up North,' one woman later remembered – talking about the skirts, not the cars. 'In fact, I think it was about 1966 or 1967 before they reached our village. They may have worn them in Newcastle before that, but not in Sunderland.'

As for the stereotype of the Sixties as an age of extraordinary moral change, the facts do not bear this out. In December 1969, NOP asked respondents: 'If you could pass one law, what would it be?' The biggest proportion, 26 per cent, chose the return of hanging, followed by 25 per cent who chose to bring back the birch, 5 per cent who wanted the government to tighten welfare benefits, and 5 per cent who wanted an immediate halt to immigration. There was little generation gap: in survey after survey, young and old alike often deplored immigration, the liberal reforms of the 'permissive society', student protest and the commercialization of sex. And as the journalist Anthony Sampson wrote in his *New Anatomy of Britain* at the end of the decade, the newspapers might talk all they wanted about sex, drugs and rock and roll, but for millions of ordinary people, the real pleasures of the time were very different. Britain, he remarked, was 'the greatest nation in Europe for handymen and potterers-about', its people devoted to 'mowing lawns and painting walls, pampering pets, listening to music, knitting and watching television'. If one thing symbolized contemporary life in Britain, he thought, it was not the nightclub, the boutique or even the record player. It was the potting shed.

All of this, as the current volume shows, makes the Sixties irresistible territory for the historian. One way of thinking about the period, of course, is to invoke Arthur Marwick's idea of a 'long Sixties', marked by unprecedented consumerism, the visibility of young people and the steady liberalization of moral attitudes. But this does not strike me as completely convincing. Popular accounts often cast the Sixties and the Seventies as diametrical opposites: optimistic, sexy and swinging, on the one hand; miserable, dreary and confrontational, on the other. But from the perspective of the 2010s, it is increasingly hard to distinguish the two. It was in the Sixties, not the Seventies, that commentators began asking 'What's wrong with Britain?'; that the British motor industry began to fall behind its European competitors; that relations between the government and the trade unions began to break down; that violence broke out in Northern Ireland; and that a mood of fractiousness and confrontation seeped into the newspapers. And it was in the Seventies, not the Sixties, that many single women began taking the Pill; that the feminist and gay rights movements really gained momentum; that most working-class people started taking foreign holidays and drinking wine regularly; that attitudes to sex and morality really began to shift; and that ordinary families bought their first colour televisions, deep freezers and central heating.

The truth, I suppose, is that the further away we move in time from the 1960s, the muddier and more confusing the concept 'the Sixties' becomes. To those who lived through it, the period has a flavour all its own. In his massive and deservedly successful histories of post-war Britain, the historian David Kynaston has a lovely trick of inserting long, strangely poetic lists of brand names and catchphrases from a particular moment, from long-vanished sweets and crisps to quiz-show patter and playground jokes. To readers who remember them, these are the equivalent of Proust's madeleines. But to readers born in the 1980s and after, they must be meaningless. So it is with the distinctions between the Fifties, the Sixties and the Seventies: to a student born in 1990, they probably seem a criminally old-fashioned and murkily incomprehensible blur.

Yet all of that said, the idea of the Sixties still has an enduring historical resonance. What gave this period a kind of distinctiveness, I think, was the experience of affluence and the expectation that it would continue indefinitely. People in the mid-1950s were still living in the shadow of the Second World War. Their cities were still scarred by bomb damage, while the longevity of rationing made it impossible to forget the economic (and military) sacrifices that Britain had demanded to defeat the Nazis. As for the mid-1970s, the mood felt very different once the impact of the OPEC oil shock, the two miners' strikes and the three-day week had sunk in. For all that most people were more comfortable than ever, optimism was in very short supply.

But that was not quite true of the mid-1960s. When all is said and done, this *was* a unique and distinctive historical moment. There was, of course, plenty of anxiety at the social, economic and cultural changes of the day. But there was also a palpable sense of confidence that life was getting better, transformed by full employment, mass education, new technology and rising living standards. Perhaps it is inevitable that television producers and commissioning editors will always remember it as the decade of clubs like Sibylla's. For my money, however, there is a much better symbol of the world the Sixties made. From Piccadilly Circus, head east and then north along the A400, turn left on the Marylebone Road, and then strike north on the A5 and the M1. Keep going for an hour or so, and then you will see it. The 'North Bucks Monster', newspapers called it at the time – a temple to the car, the shopping centre and the brand-new home. But you and I know it as Europe's fastest-growing town, Milton Keynes.

Dominic Sandbrook
King's College London

Acknowledgements

The editors would like to thank Tony Harcup, former member of the Leeds Other Paper Workers' Co-Operative, for permission to reproduce a front page from 'Leeds Other Paper'.

Introduction

Trevor Harris and Monia O'Brien Castro

Watching the Queen's Diamond Jubilee celebrations in June 2012, it was difficult not to be struck by the obvious scale and durability of commitment to the British monarchy. A reign which had begun in the austerity of the early 1950s was once again, 60 years later, generating national festivity against a background of economic uncertainty, albeit relative to a vastly increased standard of living for the majority of the population, compared to that of Britain in 1952. And, just as at the time of Queen Elizabeth II's coronation, witnessed by millions, lining the routes followed by the royal procession, or crowded around impossibly small television screens, peering at a very low-resolution black and white image – and again in September 1982, when huge crowds had welcomed home the task force following Britain's successful recapture of the Falkland Islands – here was clear evidence of an unwavering and unapologetic sense of national community, an obvious desire to be part not only of that community, but of a national communion. The community, of course, may have been 'imagined', and the crowds may well have contained large numbers of tourists, as well as many British people who were not remotely aware of, or even interested in, the political or constitutional significance of the monarchy. Yet there was no getting away from the fact that participation was important, a sense of belonging to history in the making, the right to say afterwards, 'I was there.'

The 'Sixties'[1] have generated their own parody of this notion, since, according to the famous quip, if you can remember the Sixties, you were *not* there. This is, of course, a neat one-liner to imply that the main participants in the Sixties were so constantly affected by various hallucinogenic substances that little retrievable memory of the period, for those people at least, remains intact. Yet the joke, in spite of itself, also conveys a very apposite historiographical commentary. The counter-culture of the 'swinging' Sixties – as Peter Vernon points out in Chapter 7 in this volume – was highly exclusive, only ever affecting directly a small proportion of the population. The poet Roger McGough, in an interview in March 2012, for example, probably summed up the experience of many when he admitted that for him, 'The 60s were something that happened elsewhere, at parties I wasn't invited to.' True, participation was greater than it would have been just 10 or 20 years earlier; access to the media or to musical events rose steeply throughout the 1960s. But being 'in with the in-crowd' was something which, for the vast majority of Britons in the Sixties, was limited to watching some of the more fashionable television programmes, or buying a much-coveted article of clothing, or dancing to the current hit records (usually in front of a small 'gramophone' or 'record player' in one's own 'front room'). As a result, the Sixties – in the sense of *avant-garde* or innovative set of political, aesthetic, social and sexual practices – were experienced by relatively few people, were, indeed, not experienced by most of the people who were actually there.

And yet, everyone would have liked to be there. So the Sixties which are remembered today are something which the majority of people alive at the time did not actually know. Many people who lived through the Sixties, that is, as they remember them, are actually giving personal value to, and attempting to experience in the present, something which they did not experience in the past. In short, for many people today, the relationship with the Sixties is dominated by nostalgia: the desire to re-create the past, or an idealized version of it, from extant materials in the present which are used to generate – in the case of the Sixties – a cosy, flattering fiction of a 'moment' drenched in revolutionary behaviours, oozing with self-fulfilment and individual pleasure.

But it is clearly a gross exaggeration to suggest that the Sixties were dominated by youth culture or that voyages of personal discovery were the stuff of everyday life. For every liberated inhabitant of Sixties Britain, there were many more who remained stuck inside their oppressive shell of laborious, repetitive daily routine. The very modernity which was meant to free individuals only served the better to trap them in what was, much of the time, a reconfiguration of past oppressions. The Britain forged in what Harold Wilson proudly billed as 'the white heat of [the] technological revolution', turned out to be – as R. J. Morris shows in Chapter 2 in this volume – an oppressive regime after all; and science, conceived once more as an energizing, liberating force – just as it had been during the Enlightenment or the mid-Victorian age – seems often to have acted once again as hand-maiden to the ruling class.

Yet, if the idealized vision of the Sixties which has grown up around the nostalgic 'swinging' and 'counter-culture' motifs is undoubtedly well wide of the mark – a restrictive, unrepresentative view – the inverse propensity to empty the Sixties of all their radical aspects, to see them as dominated only by conservatism, is surely just as untenable. There was clearly a radical dimension there. One would have to be unusually impervious to the signs of social change, for example, not to agree that modes of dress evolved rapidly and, in some cases, provocatively during the Sixties. During that (chronological) decade, popular music entered an exponential phase of development in which the amplification of sound, for example, and the sheer scale of performances, fundamentally changed the nature of the music and its reception and consumption. Britain's major social institutions were clearly also going through a period of reorganization which had far-reaching consequences: not least education, with the highly contested application of Circular 10/65 and the move to the comprehensive system in many schools. The legalization of abortion and homosexuality in 1967, the lowering of the voting age from 21 to 18 in 1968, the abolition of capital punishment or the establishment of the Open University in 1969, and reforms of divorce and equal pay in 1969 and 1970: all these, also, were bold decisions and certainly make a good case for considering Harold Wilson's Labour governments of 1964–70 as reforming and modernizing administrations.

But does this mean that the Sixties were a 'radical' decade? The Labour hiatus, sandwiched between the Conservative governments of 1951–64 and the re-election of the Conservatives under Edward Heath in 1970, was very much part of a broadly conservative century. There was, indeed, a solid core of conservatism at the very heart of Labour itself: just as the first majority Labour administration, elected in July 1945, had stopped short of reforming some of the central institutions of the country – the City, public schools, the Church – so the Wilson governments of 1964–70 held firm to a vision of Britain as a proud, independent state. Hugh Gaitskell, at the Labour Party Conference in 1962, had already emphasized that joining the 'Common Market' would mean 'the end of a thousand years of history'.[2] Wilson himself was to emphasize various aspects of a nationalist economics, officially endorsing, for example, the brief 'I'm backing Britain' campaign of 1967–68, with the Union Jack omnipresent to force home, if need be, the patriotic message. And, with his conservative instincts in international affairs, and his 'Atlanticism', Wilson made no secret of the fact that he, too, would cling to the 'special relationship' with the United States and that he considered Britain to be a world power, famously insisting that 'Britain's frontiers extended to the Himalayas'.[3] Wilson also engaged in a number of grand diplomatic gestures: for example, meeting Rhodesia's Premier Ian Smith on board HMS *Tiger* in December 1966, and again, in October 1968, aboard HMS *Fearless*, anchored off Gibraltar. Indeed, the Labour government elected in 1964 'showed an essential continuity with the previous Conservative administration on the key questions of British foreign policy', and, in general, 'between 1966 and 1970, there was little open conflict between the main parties over the major issues of foreign policy'.[4]

The social and, in some respects, the political conservatism of the British Labour Party – and of the British labour movement in general, as Jeremy Tranmer argues in Chapter 5 in this volume – tends to show that attempts to account for the major developments in Britain's political culture during the Sixties with reference to a party-political paradigm, are likely to be unsuccessful, since there was considerable common ground between the two main parties. This is not to argue that Britain did not have its share of ideological conflict: clearly, the range of political approaches, from the left of the Labour Party to the right of the Conservative Party, was wide. But this tended to be more visible in the context of domestic policy, where issues of social justice, the role of representative institutions, or an enduring belief in the perfectibility of the citizen, tended to divide Labour from the Conservatives along predictable, recognizable lines. Where external (foreign, imperial and Commonwealth) policy was concerned, or questions of public and private morality, the frontier between the two main parties was much more permeable. Where Britain's national interest, or national self-image was concerned, especially, it was the continuities between the parties, rather than the differences, which were more in evidence. Labour, it was true, presided over a sizeable chunk of the decolonization process. But this was not the result of a deep-seated, anti-imperialist conviction. It was the previous Conservative government which had felt, and reacted to, the 'wind of change', and Labour continued something which was already underway, Harold Wilson being only too well aware of the economic imperatives which Britain faced. Similarly, on the question of joining the EEC, both Macmillan and Wilson were convinced Atlanticists, yet both guided their parties, in the face of significant internal opposition from well-organized minorities, towards acceptance of EEC membership. And it was Wilson, again – back in government from

1974 – who adroitly confirmed Britain's presence inside Europe, by way of the June 1975 referendum.

Although there are arguments, therefore, for seeing the Sixties as defining a radical moment in British political, social or even cultural development, they do not necessarily dominate. The 'great labour unrest' on the eve of the First World War, the General Strike of 1926, the National Hunger March of 1932, the publication of the Beveridge Report in 1942: all of these, and many other incidents, mean that a case might be made for any (chronological) decade preceding the 1960s to be seen as every bit as radical. From a cultural perspective, one of the most forward-looking and innovative developments in Britain was undoubtedly the emergence of the group of outspoken young playwrights and novelists who became known as 'angry young men' – a phenomenon which was generated by the antagonistic effects of the rapid development of consumerism, on the one hand, and the persistence of cultural conformism, on the other. But this creative collision was very much a characteristic of 1950s Britain, not of the 1960s. Unless, of course, one argues that the Sixties in fact began, say, on 8 May 1956 – the opening night of John Osborne's *Look Back in Anger*, a play which quickly came to be seen as typifying a rejection of Britain's fusty, deferential, middle-class values.

And here we come up against one of the most important difficulties, perhaps the main difficulty, raised by the Sixties and any attempt to understand how one can begin to define their significance: the problem of periodization. It is common – in everyday conversation, in journalism – to talk in terms of decades. But to what extent can the same approach be used when defining historical processes? The divisions in a diary, a calendar or a chronology bear little relation to events 'on the ground'. True, some events – a declaration of war and the signing of an armistice, for example – can provide us with convenient start and finish times for a 'period'. But even a statement as apparently unproblematic as 'the Second World War began in 1939 and ended in 1945' will not do: if only because it depends on which side of the Atlantic Ocean one is speaking from. The problems become all the more apparent if one asks a question like 'When did the Industrial Revolution begin?' In our own case, can one sensibly argue that the process of women's liberation, for example, started, and still less finished, during the period 1960–69?

The remark about the Industrial Revolution, however, and that concerning the Sixties, are perhaps of two different orders. Most people can see the obvious necessity to talk about the past in convenient chunks – the Cambrian period, the Stone Age, the Renaissance. But as the perspective shortens, many would agree that it becomes increasingly difficult to separate defining characteristics from convenient numerical boundaries: the 'age of Pitt the Younger' or 'Victorian England' are good shorthand, but 'eighteenth-Century Britain' or 'England in the nineteenth century' do not bother us unduly: until, that is, we try to define exactly what we mean by 'the nineteenth century' – historians often feel the need to posit a 'long' eighteenth century, for example (1688–1815), a 'long' nineteenth century (1783–1914), or a 'short' twentieth century (1914–91), giving us new chronological units which sometimes overlap.

This is difficult enough, but the difficulty with the Sixties is a different one. It would probably not occur to most historians to write a book devoted entirely to, say, 'Britain in the Fifteen-Tens'... Although extant sources might well be in sufficient quantity to provide for a study of the 1510s, the precision seems incongruous because of the distance which separates us from the early sixteenth century. Our current perspective, and the questions we are likely to want to ask about the early sixteenth century, makes such an undertaking appear eccentric, if not flippant and rather pointless. The perceived unity of 'the Roaring Twenties', on the other hand, or 'the 1930s' seems to most of us to be of a different order: their relative proximity to us seems to authorize the numerical label. Even here, though, the illusory nature of the precision created can quickly become apparent with a change of geographical perspective: the French tradition, for example, refers not to 'the Roaring Twenties', but to *les Années folles*.

So proximity is not everything. And our difficulties are confirmed when we attempt to apply the same 'decadist' reasoning to the Sixties. On the one hand, a convenient, numerical approach (1960–69) clearly will not do, unless one is simply listing events. On the other hand, if one allows an overflow beyond the limits of the decade, according to which criteria does one then introduce new limits which are necessarily, in some way, bespoke, customized for the purpose of the discussion in hand?

In one way or another, that search for when to begin and when to end the Sixties runs through all publications on the subject: and the current volume is no exception. But while a more or less arbitrary decision is usually taken, it is one of the recurring realizations of the chapters here that no single definition will do: any more than it will do for 'the nineteenth century', or even for something as apparently hermetic as 'the Thatcher years'.

In practice, although some historians have made a good case for one set of dates (Arthur Marwick prefers 1958–73, for example), others make an equally convincing case for different pairs of dates: R. J. Morris in Chapter 2 in this volume, for example, chooses to begin his Sixties in 1953 and closes them at 1970. Other contributors propose their own dates according to criteria which appear appropriate in their case. What is certain is that none of the contributors conceive the Sixties as beginning in 1960 or ending in 1969: and this is surely something which should give us pause for thought. If a 'decade' can be defined in many different ways, are we not in fact saying that it cannot really be defined in any satisfactory way? If a 'decade', in order to be characterized, has to be elongated to the point where it spans nearly two chronological decades, is there any point at all in using the 'decade' as an object of study? In other words, it becomes necessary to distinguish between the 1960s – a purely numerical expression – and the Sixties – the shorthand for a period in post-war (British) history. This does not get 'decadism' off the hook completely. Nor does it make it straightforward to find the right questions to ask. But clearly we need to ask about the 'what' rather than simply the 'when'.

Carol Hanisch claimed in 1969 that 'the personal is political'. She might well have added that the personal was economic – to the extent that the Sixties involved a form of personal emancipation and individual expression through the medium of consumption. She might also have added that the personal was historical. It was during the Sixties, after all, that oral history achieved real prominence: the personal account, individual experience as an indicator of general trends which could be used to document the period. Taking oneself – one's self – as a viable object of study while doing 'one's own thing', became a legitimate practice. In such a self-regarding, self-obsessed environment, where the image, the self-image, the 'look' and the moment were so important, the impact of the passage of time on 'the young ones', on the 'beautiful people' of the Sixties, was bound to generate anxiety about the loss of that moment, about the loss of that beautiful image: 'What a drag it is getting old', sang the Rolling Stones, in their 1965 song, 'Mother's Little Helper'.

Such anxieties find a natural expression in the desire to record, to preserve. But to preserve what exactly? In many cases it was a question of conserving the output of a society in thrall to its own capacity to produce and consume, but afraid of its inability to prevent the aging process. And this is perhaps the point at which the radical Sixties meet the conservative Sixties. Not only because it brings together youth and the fear or rejection of change, but also because it brings together the sense of modernity and one of the most recurrent tropes of the creative spirit: the desire for eternal youth. The Sixties, consequently, far from being a radical innovation, are at this important level a restatement of a long-standing human conundrum: how to conserve ourselves, but also what we perceive to be beautiful, from the inevitable ravages of time. This has been read as a sense of impending decline, a sense of scepticism about the possibly dystopian future. The Kinks' 'village green preservation', explored here by Raphael Costambeys-Kempczynski in the final chapter, Chapter 10, returns us to the theme of the management of the land, to town-planning, to architecture, but also to the theme of the rural idyll and the past. The real question that arises here is how we can reconcile the Sixties 'youthquake' with an evident fascination for the past. There are indications – in the village green preservation society, but also elsewhere in these chapters – that one of the realizations in the Sixties was that the 'man from Whitehall' did *not* know best, that technocratic encroachment was un-English, and that what was needed was the preservation of one's 'negative' freedom, one's ability – precisely – to do one's own thing, even if the means used to make that point were highly innovative.

The aim of the chapters in this volume, then – which begins with an historiographical essay by Mark Donnelly, who explores in some detail attitudes to the 1960s, the way historians have written about them, and the meanings which have then been attributed to the period – is neither to condemn the Sixties as the root of all present evil in British society, nor to present the period as the embodiment of the most impeccable credentials of liberalism and freedom. What the chapters here attempt to do, rather, is to neutralize that contradiction, and ask in what way the notion of the Sixties is still relevant and useful: why, in short, it is worth preserving. As Mark Donnelly makes clear, it is not so much the 'burden of history' from which we are attempting to escape, but the 'burden of historians', the accumulated impact of historical interpretation. This seems to be particularly acute and polarized where the Sixties are concerned. The chapters here seem to suggest that rather than pitting radical against conservative, something may be gained by attempting to see how the two represent opposite sides of the same problem.

Notes

1. Written afterwards without quotes.
2. He went on: 'You may say: let it end. But, my goodness, it is a decision that needs a little care and thought' (Gowland *et al.*, 2010).
3. Gowland *et al.* (2010), p. 224.
4. Sked and Cook (1993), pp. 210, 237.

Bibliography

Gowland, D., Turner, A. and Wright, A. (2010) *Britain and European Integration Since 1945: On the Sidelines*, London: Routledge.

Sked, A. and Cook, C. (1993) *Post-War Britain: A Political History*, 4th edn, Harmondsworth: Penguin.

1

Sixties Britain

The cultural politics of historiography

Mark Donnelly

This chapter provides a critical survey of recent historical accounts of Sixties Britain, particularly those texts that intersect with wider memory discourses about the Sixties as being a 'decade of protest'.[1] Its primary function is to provide a framing historiographical analysis for the book's subsequent chapters, each of which problematizes a more specifically defined aspect of Sixties British culture, social change or political activism. Its secondary function is to discuss possible ways in which readers can orient themselves in relation to a field of historical writing where interpretive disputes have become more than matters of purely academic interest. These disputes, of course, have a transnational rather than purely British focus of attention, and some important writing about Sixties Britain is to be found in texts whose approach is internationally comparative, or at least multi-national in scope. Fifty years on, the Sixties (whichever precise periodization is preferred)[2] remain a productive site of research for scholars from different disciplinary backgrounds – particularly within North American and (some) European academies. Indeed, the potential for continuing research work on the Sixties is deemed sufficiently important for the decade to warrant its own academic journal.[3] Sixties histories continue to proliferate in a variety of genres and cultural forms – audio, visual and written, with texts that range from review articles to rock star memoirs – and they still generate an unusually high degree of interpretive partisanship.[4] The Sixties have frequently polarized commentators into the 'pros' (who might discursively construct the decade as being a high point of affluent, socially progressive, liberalized modernity, and as a period that produced radical challenges to various social, sexual and political norms), and 'antis' (who might imagine the Sixties to be the decade that legitimized personal and social irresponsibility, radical posturing, cultural infantilism, uncritical endorsement of the 'new', and so forth).

Historians – notwithstanding their claims about professional integrity, the primacy of disinterested archival research, and their ability to generate secure knowledge of the past – simultaneously feed off and help to sustain these wider cultural skirmishes about what the Sixties 'meant'. Historians contribute to a wider social knowledge of the Sixties, but they also research and write their accounts from within a culture in which that social knowledge circulates and has a purchase. As Patrick Finney has stated, 'historical writing is a product not merely of empirical factors but also of context-grounded aesthetic, ideological and moral choices' – and this is why, he argues, we should think in terms of a 'cultural politics of historical knowledge' (pp. 6, 10).

This chapter seeks to explore such a cultural politics of historical knowledge within the field of writing about Sixties Britain. It refuses the still dominant way of conceptualizing the Sixties as a referent that can be subject to positivist forms of historical evaluation and audit – 'what was Sixties Britain *really* like?'. Instead, it proceeds by recognizing at the outset the 'doubleness' of historical writing – history is a genre that, on the one hand, invokes disciplinary protocols of empirical research and source criticism, and which, on the other, has always relied on poetic (fictive) techniques of composition and figuration to construct an imagined world within a text for readers to encounter. As Docker and Curthoys understood, it is this doubling that creates the space within historiography for uncertainty, disagreement and creativity. My argument here will be that we should welcome the unavoidable pluralism and uncertainty generated by historiographical practices; moreover, we should recognize that our reading of history texts is as perspectival and context-bound as the act of writing those texts. Therefore, the task of textual surveys such as this is to move beyond conventional historiographical analysis and towards a more fundamental set of 'meta' questions about historical practices. Such questions would be ontological rather than methodological: what is historical enquiry, what are its goals, whose interests are served by contemporary productions of historical knowledge, and how do we justify continuing to think historically about subjects like the Sixties?

In his major comparative survey, *The Sixties: Cultural Revolution in Britain, France, Italy and the United States, c.1958–c.1974* (1998), Arthur Marwick directly answered questions of both a methodological and ontological type. In the opening section of this book,

Marwick reaffirmed the epistemological assumptions that stood behind his work:

> My methods are those of the professional historian, a scientist, I have said, rather than a poet or novelist...We need a history supported by evidence and based on dispassionate analysis. We need a history which tells it, as nearly as humans can, as it was. We do not need a history which goes on and on about the wickedness of the bourgeoisie, or which is merely designed to support predetermined theories about language, ideology, narratives, and discourse as agents of bourgeois hegemony.
>
> (ibid., p. 20)

However, it is hard to recognize what followed this opening discussion of sources and methods as 'dispassionate analysis'. Instead – and this is not intended as a criticism *per se* – Marwick weaved a personalized and idiosyncratic path through his own selection of source materials. In effect, *The Sixties* became an extended vehicle for Marwick to articulate his own liberal-humanist ideology, and to rebut what he termed 'the Great Marxisant Fallacy'. He used the term 'fallacy' throughout the text to reference (and disparage) all manifestations and variants of Sixties Marxist theory – which he believed had been shown to be 'simply incorrect' (ibid., p. 14). These variants included the work of 'cultural theorists' and 'postmodernists', who may have thought that they were challenging the normative conceptual categories and vocabularies that underwrote existing political and social arrangements in the Sixties, but who, in Marwick's terms, were metaphysicians whose theories warranted a 'full frontal exposure' (ibid., pp. 20–1, 809). He referred specifically in this context to writers such as Marcuse, Lévi-Strauss, Barthes, Lacan, Althusser, Derrida and Foucault, whose ideas were variously dismissed on ideological and/or *ad hominem* grounds. The problem with Marxists in the Sixties, argued Marwick, was that they were 'so busy looking for a revolution which could not happen' that they missed the one that did – the 'cultural revolution' (ibid., pp. 14–15). Indeed, Marwick's primary aim in *The Sixties* was to substantiate and elucidate his progressive reading of the period, which he saw as being characterized by widespread increases in personal and social freedoms (at least in the four countries discussed).[5] The most important of these freedoms were what Marwick described as the related phenomena of entrepreneurialism, individualism, and 'doing your own thing'; 'massive' material improvements in consumption; a general sexual liberation; emancipation from the old canons of fashion, which in turn helped to set the body free; and – contrary to the dominant ideology critique of Herbert Marcuse and Theodor Roszak – a liberal, progressive presence within institutions of authority that enabled the extension of freedoms to occur.[6] The irony of Marwick's account of a period that was apparently defined by its enabling of increasing freedoms, however, was the extent to which that account was itself so intolerant of dissenting or alternative viewpoints. By mistaking empiricism for a coherent epistemology rather than a research method, Marwick believed that his work in the archives – valuable though it undoubtedly was – had taken him towards the goal of producing a singular, true account of the Sixties, one in which the 'cultural revolution' of the period 'established the enduring cultural values and social behaviour for the rest of the century' (ibid., p. 806).

Despite the weight of the book, the breadth of Marwick's erudition and the cultural authority of the publisher (Oxford University Press), *The Sixties* had a mixed critical reception.[7] Indeed, it was fashionable for a time among contemporary British historians – at least among those who attended the Institute of Contemporary British History's 2001 conference – to cite approvingly James Obelkevich's negative review of the book. It might have been expected that Marwick had left himself open to the charge that his empiricism-as-epistemology was intellectually untenable in the wake of postmodernism and the linguistic turn. But the principal point of Obelkevich's critique was that Marwick had not been attentive enough to archival sources, and that only by consulting *more* primary documents could historians clear away the 'myths' about the Sixties (2000, p. 333). According to this line of interpretation, Marwick had been overly concerned with the 'trendy' Sixties – the Arts Labs, experimental theatres, 'swinging' scenes, rebellious students and psychedelic music. But the 'ordinary' Sixties, claimed Obelkevich, the lives of people in suburbs, provincial towns and villages, who watched *Coronation Street* and liked Cliff Richard records, had disappeared from view in Marwick's account. Obelkevich wanted a history that wrote such people back into the story, and one that 'above all' used the 'sources' to capture the 'all-too-human-realities' of the Sixties (ibid., p. 336). Dominic Sandbrook's two-volume history of the decade, *Never Had It So Good: A History of Britain from Suez to the Beatles* (2005) and *White Heat: A History of Britain in the Swinging Sixties* (2006), is perhaps the most self-conscious attempt yet to provide the kind of general 'demythologizing' account of the Sixties that Obelkevich apparently had in mind. In the Preface to the first volume, Sandbrook adapted

E. P. Thompson's oft-quoted line from *The Making of the English Working Class* (1963) and announced that he would rescue from the condescension of posterity the lives of the 'kind of people who spent the 1960s in Aberdeen or Welshpool', and whose memories of the Sixties were likely to be of 'bingo, Blackpool and Berni Inns' (2005, p. xix). Sandbrook went on to argue that many people who lived through the Sixties never embraced social and cultural change with much enthusiasm. In any case, he tells us, the media version of the Sixties – mini-skirts, Mini cars, Swinging London, psychedelia – was only experienced by a young, privileged and educated minority. In places like Hull or Wolverhampton, DIY was more popular than LSD, *The Black and White Minstrel Show* was more important than *avant-garde* cinema, and more people watched the average Second Division football match than attended the Albert Hall's counter-cultural Poetry Reading of June 1965.[8] Such historical 'truths', Sandbrook believed, have long been overlooked because of the metropolitan snobbery of historians. This was why, he argued, historians have never shown much interest in writing about places like Basildon and Stevenage – derided by commentators in the Sixties as exemplars of soulless New Town aesthetics – even though they were generally popular with their inhabitants.

None of this is to suggest, however, that Sandbrook wrote a particularly unorthodox historical account of the Sixties. Despite having an apparently different perspective on the period from Marwick – a difference that Sandbrook attributed to the fact that he was too young to have experienced the Sixties at first hand – both writers agreed that affluence and new consumer freedoms were defining features of the decade. According to Sandbrook, high-street fashion was one of the main signifiers of Sixties 'new times' – recalling the kind of modernist commentary that threaded together Piri Halasz's observations on 'London: The Swinging City' in *Time* magazine in April 1966. Moreover, one of the 'heroes' of *White Heat* was Terence Conran, the entrepreneur behind the designer furniture store Habitat, whose 'idealised ethos of economic wealth, artistic effervescence and technological sophistication … pointed the way to a better tomorrow in Harold Wilson's Britain'. Sandbrook believed that Habitat, which opened in May 1964, was the most important retailing institution in Britain since the Second World War, its presence on the high street marking out mid-Sixties Britain as a pinnacle of design innovation and consumerism (2006, p. 80). This was a reading of Sixties mass-market aesthetics that was shared by others, and it featured strongly in a Victoria and Albert Museum exhibition, 'British Design 1948–2012: Innovation in the Modern Age' (2012).

The 'long Sixties' section of this exhibition began with a display about the Whitechapel Art Gallery's 'This is Tomorrow' show in 1956, and it went on to reference key features of the Sixties art-design-commerce interface: Mary Quant and Bill Green fashions, style magazines *Queen* and *Nova*, poster designers Martin Sharp and Michael English, fabric designer Shirley Craven from Hull Traders, the Cramer Saatchi advertising agency, and David Hockney.[9] Meanwhile the film *Blow-Up* (1966) silently played on a loop, with the David Bailey-esque fashion photographer lead character perhaps subliminally referring visitors to their own status as tasteful but passive gazers. Neither the V&A exhibition nor *White Heat*, it should be said, offered uncritical endorsements of the culture they described. Sandbrook acknowledged that the core constituency for Conran's designs was limited to a predominantly young, affluent, 'with it' middle class (2006, pp. 62–5). Meanwhile, the V&A's ordering of its exhibits suggested that a growing sense of unease with the rational modernism of high-Sixties design produced a counter-aesthetic in the form of late-Sixties, anti-technological romanticism. Nonetheless, it is fair to use these two 'texts' as exemplars of a particular perspective on one aspect of Sixties British culture: the idea that the period saw a 'democratic' reconfiguration of the relationship between the worlds of elite art and mass commerce.

Curiously perhaps, given that he devoted two lengthy volumes to the decade, Sandbrook's overarching thesis about the Sixties was that continuity and tradition ultimately proved to be the dominant forces. By 1970, he concluded in *White Heat*, Britain was largely the same country that it had been 40 or even a hundred years before – in fact in his next book, *State of Emergency. The Way We Were: Britain, 1970–1974*, he went on to argue that there was also much more continuity between the 1970s and 1960s 'than we commonly remember' (2010, p. 10). Citing Orwell's *The Lion and the Unicorn* in support of his analysis, Sandbrook invoked the trope of an unchanging British 'national character' that would always endure, like an 'everlasting animal stretching into the future and the past' (2006, p. 749). Sixties social and cultural change, he argued, was a 'halting, fragmentary and bitterly contested' process, and by the time that the decade was over, the instinctive conservatism of middlebrow British culture had reasserted itself as a necessary antidote to the country's 'moral decay' (ibid., p. 747). The popularity of *Dad's Army* – the comedy TV series set in southern England in 1940 – was read here as proof that the national mood had grown tired of change, and instead had become nostalgic for that time of imagined social cohesion known as 'the people's war'. Sandbrook's history of Sixties Britain, therefore, was written from a conservative perspective – politically and culturally. In some respects, *Never Had It So Good* and *White Heat* can be read as an exercise in filling out earlier narrative and interpretive templates that had been left by writers who shared similar ideological ground. One thinks here of Christopher Booker's *The Neophiliacs*, which argued that a worship of novelty and innovation in late-fifties and early-Sixties Britain gave way after 1966 to a cultural climate of 'aftermath, disillusionment, exhaustion, even of reaction' (1969, p. 292), and Bernard Levin's *The Pendulum Years*, which described the Sixties as 'shaken and ambiguous years', and a 'credulous age' in which irrationalism held sway and charlatans posing as gurus were gullibly accepted (1970, pp. 332, 9–10).

Sandbrook's recent attempt to debunk a generalized 'myth' of the Sixties can be seen as part of a recent trend within the historiographical field – a trend that Frederic Jameson summarized as attempts to 'trash the Sixties generally' (2008, p. 494). The early years of the twenty-first century have seen a sustained critique of the Sixties, commonly grounded on a version of the theory that cherished Sixties notions of 'personal freedoms' and 'self at the centre' have proven to be socially corrosive in the longer term. A populist articulation of this thesis was rehearsed in a BBC television programme in 2004: *Why I Hate the Sixties: The Decade That Was Too Good To Be True.*[10] The programme's script was occasionally tongue-in-cheek, but nonetheless commentators such as Peter Oborne, Peter Hitchens, Anne Atkins, Mike Phillips, Christina Odone and David Aaranovitch capitalized on their opportunity to criticize Sixties architecture, social policies, pop music and much else besides. Oborne provided the programme's unifying trope when he said: 'Everything was supposed to have got better in the Sixties, but actually almost everything got worse.' Although it never descended to such a crude dismissal of the period, Gerard DeGroot's *The Sixties Unplugged: A Kaleidoscopic History of a Disorderly Decade* (2008) is a recent historiographical analogue of this form of interpretive debunking. DeGroot acknowledged at the beginning of his text that 'meaning and structure' did not inhere in the historical record of the Sixties in itself, but that these properties were constructed in the historian's act of writing about the period. As such, DeGroot explained, he had sought to avoid imposing a false linearity and order in his account and to provide instead what he called an 'impressionistic wandering through the landscape of a disorderly decade' – hence the reference to a 'kaleidoscopic history' in the book's title (ibid., p. 3). However, DeGroot remained sufficiently historicist to believe in what he called a 'law of historical continuity – the fact that everything develops from that which precedes it' (ibid., p. 450). According to his reading of this 'law', DeGroot concluded that the Sixties left a profoundly damaging historical legacy. In his final audit of the decade he itemized what he saw as malign Sixties phenomena – murder, greed, drugs, ethnic cleansing, a 'warped sense of equality' and a 'bizarre notion of freedom' – and calculated that these outweighed the more benign Sixties embrace of 'flowers, music, love, and good times'. Bearing all this in mind, he reasoned, 'the decade should seem neither unfamiliar nor all that special' (ibid., p. 450).

Sheila Rowbotham (2000) and Jenny Diski (2009), each of whom wrote memoirs about their experiences of being young, female and politically active in the Sixties, share some aspects of DeGroot's antagonism. Although Rowbotham and Diski remained sympathetic to the spirit of Sixties radical utopianism, they also believed that the main legacies of the Sixties were socially and politically negative. Rowbotham was a prominent intellectual and activist on the radical left in 1968 and 1969. After becoming disillusioned with the ideological orthodoxies and revolutionary vanguardism of the International Socialists and International Marxist Group, she switched her attention to the then developing Women's Liberation Movement. From a vantage point in the late twentieth century, Rowbotham described the 'radical dream' of the Sixties as 'stillborn'. In place of the cooperative and egalitarian society that was the left's ideal, she believed, 'the Sixties ushered in an order which was more competitive and less equal than the one we had protested against' (2000, p. xv). In somewhat similar vein, Diski's *The Sixties* recounted her involvement in some of London's overlapping countercultural scenes – she watched Jean-Luc Godard films at the Academy Cinema, waitressed at the Arts Lab, lived in a commune, helped to set up a free school. She described the Sixties as being like the 'longest gap year in history', but regretted that her generation failed to anticipate how their ideals of 'doing your own thing' would morph so easily into the neo-liberal nostrums of 'rabid individualism and the sanctity of profit' (2009, pp. 4, 9). A burgeoning drugs culture contributed to the interiority of the late Sixties which, Diski argued, 'didn't achieve anything very much... No new ideas, no great books or paintings or poetry come to mind from those late Sixties days – just an album cover or two' (ibid., p. 44). Much of the period's popular music was no doubt 'remarkable', she conceded, but any counter-cultural associations this music might have invoked were undercut by the fact that it was mixed by sober technicians and distributed by multinational companies. Diski's reading of the radical political legacies of the Sixties is as downbeat as

Rowbotham's. She had hoped that when her generation of Sixties youth came to hold political power, things would be better. Instead, she concluded, nationalism and capitalism had triumphed by the early 2000s, and everywhere nations continued to chase the economic growth of old despite warnings about the environmental catastrophe that this would produce (ibid., p. 94).

Phillip Blond's critique of the Sixties in *Red Tory: How Left and Right Have Broken Britain* (2010) was developed from a different ideological starting point to Rowbotham and Diski, but his analysis relied on some shared assumptions with them about the period's apparent social and political failings. Blond – who helped British Conservative Party leader David Cameron to develop his 'Big Society' theme, and who arranged for Cameron to deliver the opening remarks at the launch of his think tank, ResPublica in 2009 – argued that twenty-first-century Britain was suffering from a social crisis that was caused in part by Sixties political and cultural experiments. Governments at that time, he believed, had failed the British working class by turning millions of people into passive recipients of centralized welfare benefits. Before the introduction and extension of the modern welfare state, the working class had relied on family and local and workplace mutual organizations to support them through hard times. But the growth of a bureaucratic welfare state in the Sixties, Blond argued, 'began to destroy the extended family' and thus 'shattered the vivid communal life of the urbanized white working class' (ibid., pp. 15–16). Moreover, he charged that the New Left's discourse of personal pleasure as a route to 'public salvation' in these years (what Blond called a 'politics of desire') proved to be lethal to the working class, because it dissolved the social bonds that had kept families together through the hardships of the 1930s and the war years (ibid., pp. 16–17). Finally, the New Left's turn towards identity politics in the late Sixties meant that it disengaged from the political concerns of the working class.

> The great tragedy is that, in the unleashing of the freedom of the 1960s, it is those at the bottom who have suffered most acutely. A neo-liberalism in part generated by the Left has torn through the social fabric of those communities least able to cope with the unfortunate consequences
>
> (ibid., p. 284)[11]

Blond's arguments here relied on a particular reading of the significance of the New Left in Sixties Britain, a reading that was at odds with some contemporary commentators. In a collection of essays and pamphlets on *The Left in Britain* (1976), David Widgery and his fellow contributors focused mainly on 'traditional' Left issues of low pay, social deprivation and social exclusion, and on the continued importance of the trade unions in both the workplace and the wider political sphere. In fact, Widgery expressed his regret that the pre-1968 British Left had shown a 'complete lack of interest' in what later came to be called the identity politics of race and gender (ibid., p. 14). Moreover, Blond's description of an over-reaching welfare state that trapped people into benefit dependency ran counter in some respects to the findings of studies by Brian Abel-Smith and Peter Townsend (1965), and Ken Coates and Richard Silburn (1970), both of which emphasized the welfare state's deficiencies in tackling poverty among citizens who were unable to work. According to these writers, more state resources should have been directed towards the poorest in Britain, not less. Blond, of course, was pursuing a different agenda. We should not exaggerate the contemporary political significance of *Red Tory*. But equally we should recognize that it played some part at least in a wider project of intellectual and infrastructural preparatory work for major reforms of Britain's welfare arrangements in the wake of the 2008 global financial crash. Blond denied any party-political affiliations – and, in fairness, politicians from all the main UK political parties expressed interest in attempts by Blond's think tank, ResPublica, to reconceptualize the 'common good'. Nonetheless, *Red Tory* and the various media appearances where Blond publicized his ideas were strands of a public discourse that sought to challenge the view of the post-war welfare state as a benign provider of material support, pedagogy and affordable access to culture. In the language of Coalition ministers such as Iain Duncan Smith and George Osborne, Britain's contemporary welfare system was bloated and unaffordable, it offered disincentives for people to seek paid employment, and it was milked by idlers, scroungers and cheats. The political culmination of this discursive shift has been the Welfare Reform Act (2012), which the Department of Work and Pensions described as 'the biggest change to the welfare system for over 60 years'.[12] Ironically, if not unpredictably, the Coalition government's welfare reforms – and what has been perceived as their attacks on the public realm more generally – have been criticized by the very charities, housing associations, voluntary groups and churches that were meant to form the organizational core of the 'Big Society' supplement to a leaner welfare state.

An alternative way to explore how contemporary political imperatives have had a shaping influence on historical thinking about the Sixties is to consider how the global revolts of 2010–11 have refocused critical attention on the decade's confrontational reputation – the Sixties as a 'decade of protest'. Some of the resulting studies have sought to question whether historical thinking about the trans-national protest movements of the Sixties might provide inspiration, ideas or encouragement for the global protestors of the early twenty-first century. Paul Mason's extended journalistic account of these revolts, for example, began by referencing the first student protest at Berkeley, California, in 1964, thus positioning contemporary global activism as being analogous to campaigns that were fought in the Sixties (2012, p. 4). Mason went on to draw repeated parallels between the two periods of confrontational political activity (ibid., pp. 38, 45–7, 129–30, 133, 140, 144–5, 149, 173). Similarly, contributors to Bryn Jones and Mike O'Donnell's *Sixties Radicalism and Social Movement Activism: Retreat or Resurgence?* (2010) argue that many of the values and sensibilities of the 'radical Sixties', as well as some of its organizational techniques and strategies, continue to inform how protest groups operate in the present (ibid., p. 238). Jones and O'Donnell offer their collection of essays in part as a counter-reading to those histories – by writers such as Marwick, Sandbrook and DeGroot – that have dismissed Sixties cultural and political rebellion as being 'ephemeral, politically inconsequential or absorbed into the mainstream' (ibid., p. 225). Far from failing, they argue, Sixties activists showed how collective action could challenge normative thinking and thus generate momentum for political change. Sixties activists, they point out, successfully opened up a series of previously non-existent or only embryonic social spaces, such as improved rights for women and minorities, greater sexual freedoms, and establishing the legitimacy of environmental campaigning. Moreover, the authors regard the international anti-war and anti-capitalist movements of the Sixties as harbingers of current global protests (ibid., p. xii). Not only were these protest movements – separated by almost fifty years – mobilized around similar values and grievances, they say, but each had to contend with a substantial increase in the capacity of states to use surveillance and aggressive policing methods against protestors (ibid., p. xiv). One is reminded here of accounts that detailed the state's ability to harass protesters and keep them under surveillance in the earlier 'decade of protest' (see Nuttall, 1968; Thompson, 1970; Miles, 2010). Understandably, Jones and O'Donnell were reluctant to use historical comparisons with the Sixties as a basis for predicting how current global protests might affect relationships between states, markets, civil society and the natural environment. They were equally wary of being seen to distil simple 'lessons' for contemporary protestors from their reading of the Sixties. However, they did argue that one of the weaknesses of Sixties protest movements was that they frequently relied on an old Marxist language (usually of a Cuban or Chinese variant) as their principal political vocabulary. This language, they believe, proved to be inadequate as a discursive vehicle for sustaining radical energies across different countries, and therefore a central task for contemporary social movements was to find new forms of discourse that could adequately respond to the unfolding crises of war, recession and environmental crisis (ibid., pp. xiv–xv).[13]

Writing about a specifically British context, Bryn Jones argued against 'culturalist' ways of interpreting the Sixties 'radical upsurge', which saw its effects as being confined to the apolitical realms of life styles, art, personal relationships and sub-cultural institutions (2010, pp. 3, 5). According to Jones, such culturalist interpretations were produced from a 'historico-empiricist perspective' that only wanted to evaluate revolt or rebellion quantitatively – how many marchers, how many student occupiers, how many members of a revolutionary group or organization?[14] But in the 'cultural hothouse' of the late Sixties, argued Jones, the important shift that occurred was among people's sensibilities – a phenomenon that was difficult to describe empirically, but which some qualitative data suggested continued to have a resonance among workers in voluntary and community sector organizations as late as 2008 (ibid., pp. 6–8, 17). Fundamental socio-cultural change, he believed, arose 'less from the conscious and articulate propagation and pursuit of clearly defined values than from shifts in a more general and deeper set of emotional and cognitive "sensibilities" ' (ibid., p. 6). In effect, people could be 'counter-cultural' while stopping short of deciding to live in a commune or join the International Marxist Group. The libertarian and solidaristic ethos of the counter-culture, said Jones, was sufficiently flexible to include anyone from 'office-working festival goers and weekend drug trippers to anarchistic artists and radical welfare professionals' (ibid., p. 7). But crucially, this did not mean that counter-cultural values were necessarily diluted and transformed into a lifestyle adornment.[15] Rather, insisted Jones, they were at the centre of a 'libertarian micropolitics' whose impact was experienced not in the institutions of the state, but along the contours that existed between state and civil society. Jones's thesis was that the spirit of Sixties libertarianism was often most prevalent among those social groups who were subsequently able to propagate this sensibility – higher education graduates, and those in (or about to enter) professions in the fields of arts, media, politics, education and welfare. It was people within these social and occupational groups – working in community and campaign groups, charities, and various non-governmental organizations – who became the key defenders of civil society against the worst effects of an increasingly powerful free market ethos in the post-Sixties decades (ibid., pp. 4–5). Moreover, as Christopher Moore suggested in a study of the National Council for Civil Liberties, pressure groups of this type helped to define and facilitate a new type of politics from the 1960s onwards – drawing on 'old' and 'new' political models and institutions, and mediating between the views of 'experts' and 'do-it-yourself' activists (2009, p. 560).

Michael Hardt and Antonio Negri wrote *Empire* (2000) some years before the global revolts of 2010–11, but parts of their analysis are relevant to the current discussion of Sixties protests. According to Hardt and Negri, it was the multiple social struggles of the 1960s that produced a crisis and transformation in the paradigm of capitalist production – resulting in the post-Fordist, postmodern, globalized economy that is the focus of contemporary anti-capitalist protests (ibid., pp. 275–6). If it had not been for the protests caused by the Vietnam War, the worker and student revolts, 1968, second-wave feminism and anti-imperialist struggles, they argue, capitalism would have maintained its then 'disciplinary' paradigm of production. But the various forms of Sixties activism, or people's refusal to co-operate with existing social and cultural arrangements, constituted the expression of a radically new mode of subjectivity, and it was this new subjectivity that was crucial to the destruction of an old regime of capitalist production. To understand this, they say, we must appreciate '*the profound economic power of the cultural movements*' of the Sixties (original emphasis, ibid., p. 275). The restructuring of production to a post-Fordist model was anticipated by the rise of a new subjectivity (the 'merely cultural' in the Sixties proved to have profoundly 'materialistic' consequences), and it was driven from below (ibid., p. 276). As they explained:

> The enormous rise in the social wage (in terms of both working wages and welfare) during the period of crisis in the 1960s and 1970s resulted directly from the accumulation of social struggles on the terrain of reproduction, the terrain of non-work, the terrain of life.

> The social struggles ... forced a change in the quality and nature of labor itself. Particularly in the dominant capitalist countries, where the margin of freedom afforded to and won by workers was greatest, the refusal of the disciplinary regime of the social factory was

accompanied by a re-evaluation of the social value of the entire set of productive activities. The disciplinary regime clearly no longer succeeded in containing the needs and desires of young people. The prospect of getting a job that guarantees regular and stable work for eight hours a day, fifty weeks a year, for an entire working life, the prospect of entering the normalized regime of the social factory, which had been a dream for many of their parents, now appeared as a kind of death.

(ibid., pp. 273–4)

In Hardt and Negri's analysis, therefore, the Sixties 'revolution in the head' (MacDonald, 1997; Green, 1999) was not about a personal reordering of lifestyle, but instead it was seen as the necessary precursor to the kind of praxis that Herbert Marcuse termed the 'Great Refusal' – or, 'the protest against that which is' (1991, p. 63).

Of course, arguments that the Sixties were responsible for the development of contemporary political conditions (for good or ill) risk confusing temporal sequence with a relationship of historical cause-and-effect – much as Gerard DeGroot did when he invoked his 'law of historical continuity'. Also, as an explanatory strategy it requires that we regard the Sixties not as a discursively constructed object of knowledge – a useful but nonetheless arbitrary way of assigning cognitive shape to a mass of now absent phenomena – but as some*thing* that possessed both form of its own (separate from one's preferred ways of putting the Sixties under a description) and agency in its own right. It was this kind of conventional thinking about history as a discourse that the metahistorian, Hayden White, critiqued in a series of publications from 'The Burden of History' ([1966] 1978) onwards – most specifically in a series of essays that he published between 1966 and 1973 (White, 1966, 1969, 1971, 1972, 1973). White is important here less as a writer whose work had an affinity with the ideals of the Sixties cultural Left – undoubtedly true though this was. Rather, his significance derives from the innovative contributions he has made to modern debates about historical practices. White above all has challenged the assumption that the meaning of the past inheres in the historical record itself. In the final section of this chapter, I want to use White as a critical guide who can help us to negotiate the ways in which we interact with the contested and often contradictory historiography of Sixties Britain. In more specific terms, White will be used to support the argument that we can legitimately evaluate Sixties histories not in terms of their putative correspondence to the past 'as it was', but by the extent to which they help us to reflect upon socio-political challenges in our present – and perhaps to imagine more democratic and politically emancipatory futures as a consequence. Two strands of White's thinking are particularly relevant here. First – and using an argument that he developed at greater length in *Metahistory* (1973) – White believed that historians should let go of the mistaken assumption that their accounts of historical events or an era corresponded 'to some preexistent body of "raw facts"' (ibid., p. 47). The 'facts' were not a 'given' in the historical record itself, he argued, but were constructed by the questions that the historian asked of their empirical data, and by the problem that was implied by the choice of metaphor that the historian used to order their account (ibid., p. 47). White was not an anti-realist. He accepted that historians' discourse referred to 'real' events in the past. But against those who assumed that histories were objectivist descriptions of the past as it had occurred, White argued that historiography was (and always had been) a poetic mode of composition – one in which historians employed the same kind of figurative techniques, narrative models and tropes as fiction writers in order to assemble their empirically-derived data into an account that had a story form. As a consequence, there could be no singularly definitive or 'true' account of any past event in textual form; instead, there were as many possible (and equally plausible) narrative versions of an event as there were culturally available plot structures for endowing stories with meanings (Jenkins, 1999, p. 198).

The second aspect of White's thinking that has salience here is his belief that historians should recognize and *act* upon their present-day ethico-political obligations. As he wrote:

> The contemporary historian has to establish the value of the study of the past, not as an end in itself, but as a way of providing perspectives on the present that contribute to the solution of problems peculiar to our own time.
>
> (1973, p. 41)

This was an appeal for historians to use historical enquiry as a means to inspire new political imaginaries, and as a way of reminding readers in the present that human choices ultimately determine the course of history – thus empowering people to see themselves as the architects of their own lives, rather than as products of impersonal historical processes (ibid., pp. 48–9). Only by doing so, argued White, could humans free themselves from the 'burden of history', and instead use the study of the past as a means to help them accomplish 'an ethically responsible transition from present to future' (ibid., p. 49).

Hardt and Negri's approach to historical thinking is similar in important respects to Hayden White's. Towards the beginning of *Empire* they explained how they wished to emphasize both the power of the multitude to 'make history', and the political potential of a praxis that was grounded in social hope (2000, p. 46). To achieve these ambitions, they employed a methodology that had two main elements. The first element was critical and deconstructive, aimed at subverting hegemonic languages and normative social structures. Hardt and Negri summarized this as a process of deconstructing the *historia rerum gestarum* of the 'reign of global capitalism', in ways that would subvert the idea that its development was a historical necessity, and which would point towards the possibility of alternative social organizations. The second element was constructive and ethico-political, working to create subjectivities that opened towards social and political alternatives. Here the focus was on *res gestae*, the subjective forces acting in historical contexts that produced not a 'new rationality' but a 'new scenario of different rational acts – a horizon of activities, resistances, wills, and desires that refuse the hegemonic order...and forge alternative constitutive itineraries' (ibid., p. 48). The Sixties, they had argued, demonstrated the power of human agency to resist and reshape practices that were integral to a dominant mode of capitalism. Hardt and Negri's historical consciousness, therefore, was ideologically attuned and politically oriented – a mode of comportment towards the past that Hayden White advocated most forcefully of all in his essay, 'The politics of contemporary philosophy of history' (1973). In this manifesto for activist historiography, White observed that historians – viewed across the long span of culture – had usually conceded that there were ideological motivations behind their writing. The exception to this general rule occurred during a brief period between the mid-nineteenth and mid-twentieth centuries, when intellectual and political fashions required that historians should profess their belief in 'disinterestedness and objectivity' (ibid., p. 140). By the 1970s, however, White was attempting to reposition the way in which historiographical practices were understood, arguing that historians should seek to provide a 'socially innovative historical vision', and encouraging them to work using the activist rather than the dianoetic voice (ibid., pp. 144, 151). Of course, to write politically engaged history was to invite a charge of unprofessional conduct from objectivist historians. But, as White argued, to state that historians should not let ideology intrude into their work was itself an expression of ideology, not its negation (Paul, 2011, pp. 53–4). White summarized the case against writing activist history in the following terms:

> It seems to me that the objection to using a vision of a desirable future to give the form to one's account of past and present would bear weight only for those to whom the present is basically satisfactory as it is. And by the 'present', I mean the *social* status quo.
>
> (emphasis in original, 1973, p. 144)

For those who wished to challenge features of the status quo, White showed that the past could be a source of inspiration and imagination. History, according to Hayden White – and so too for Hardt and Negri, Jones and O'Donnell, Mason and others who have written on the Sixties – was not about external and impersonal forces (the 'hidden hand' of history). What mattered in history, they agreed, was what people decided to do – and in the context of writing about the Sixties, it was possible to produce valid accounts of the period that demonstrated how people's collective actions had brought about meaningful socio-economic and cultural change. This does not mean of course that we should uncritically endorse all aspects of Sixties activism, or only write about the period using inspirational language. Rather it means that we can use our historical enquiries into the Sixties as a means of fashioning new communal identities, and of challenging entrenched ways of thinking that serve to reinforce the social status quo. Part of the 'burden of historians' now is to recognize their ethico-political obligations to the cultures of which they are a part; not to study the past as it 'really' or 'essentially' was, but to use their thinking about the past to challenge what present-day cultures regard as real, essential or unavoidable (Paul, 2011, p. 53).

Notes

1. I focus largely here – but not exclusively – on recent historical accounts. I previously surveyed an older historiography of Sixties Britain in Donnelly (2005), pp. 1–14.
2. For a useful discussion of this issue, see Jameson (2008), pp. 483–515.
3. *The Sixties: A Journal of History, Politics and Culture*, has been published by Taylor and Francis since 2008.
4. Recent examples of continued cultural interest in the Sixties include: the popularity of films such as *Factory Girl* (2006) and *Made in Dagenham* (2010); BBC Radio 2 programmes 'Sounds of the Sixties', 'Mark Lamarr's Alternative Sixties', and the station's programming of a Beatles Season in 2012; the BBC

World Service four-part series on '1968: The year that changed the world?' (2008); BBC TV's adaptation of Jake Arnott's Sixties London crime novel *The Long Firm* (2004); BBC4's 'Black Power Salute' (May 2010); BBC Parliament Channel's 'Harold Wilson Night' (February 2013); Yesterday TV channel's 'Spirit of the Sixties' season in 2011; the popularity of Rolling Stone Keith Richards' memoir *Life* (2010); Tate Britain's exhibition 'Art & The Sixties: This was Tomorrow' (2004); the opening of York Castle Museum's 'The Sixties Experience' exhibition in March 2008; the release of a re-mastered Beatles Box Set (2009); and press reports in 2013 which suggest that Andrew Lloyd Webber's next musical will be about the 1963 Profumo affair.

5. For a less progressive and rather more complex account of Sixties change in the sexual sphere see Mort (2011, pp. 269–98); and on the contradictory impulses of sexual attitudes in the early Sixties as evidenced in the Profumo affair, see Davenport-Hines (2013).

6. Marwick restated this thesis in the first and final chapters of Aldgate, Chapman and Marwick (2000).

7. See, for example, Robert Taylor, 'Doing One's Own Thing', *Spectator*, 11 July 1998; Roger Scruton, 'Dispatches from a Turbulent Decade', *New Statesman*, 16 October 1998; Ellen Willis, 'On the Barricades', *New York Times*, 8 November 1998; Christopher Hitchens, 'Where were you in the long Sixties?', *Times Literary Supplement*, 13 November 1998; Luisa Passerini's review (1999) *The American Historical Review*, 104(5); James Obelkevich's review (2000) in *Twentieth Century British History*, 11(3), pp. 333–6.

8. An alternative perspective on the value of avant-garde art as a stimulus for the political imagination can be found in Nuttall (1968) and Whiteley (2011).

9. For a fuller discussion of these subjects, see Metzger (2012).

10. *Why I Hate the Sixties*, BBC4/BBC2 (BBC Bristol: dir. Gerry Dawson), June 2004.

11. Holding Sixties New Left-inspired individualism to account for the corrosion of public values in contemporary political debate is also a key strand of the analysis in Judt (2010), pp. 85–91, 94.

12. UK Department of Work and Pensions website, www.dwp.gov.uk/policy/welfare-reform/legislation-and-key-documents/welfare-reform-act-2012/ (accessed 28 March 2013). The Coalition government's principal welfare reform measures involved a sharp reduction in housing benefit, the introduction of a cap on the total amount of benefit working-age people can receive, and the replacement of the disability living allowance scheme.

13. For an interesting contemporary discussion about the relevance of Marxist discourse to Sixties British radicals, see Eagleton and Wicker (1968). These essays argued that Marxism was inadequate in the revolutionary moment of the late Sixties, and suggested that Christian social teaching could go 'beyond' Marxism – enabling the Catholic Church to act as a revolutionary opposition to neo-imperialism, racism and nuclear violence. On a similar theme, see MacIntyre (1968). For a defence of the idea that Marxism-Leninism remained relevant in the Sixties, see Woodis (1972), who argued that Fanon, Debray and Marcuse were well intentioned but ultimately wrong. Their thinking, he concluded, was elitist and thus anti-working class. See also Widgery (1978) and Bouchier (1978).

14. For an example of this type of method, see Thomas (2002).
15. There is a good, recent collection of essays on the Sixties counter-culture as a focal point of Peter Whitehead's film-making in (2011) *Framework: The Journal of Cinema and Media*, 52(1) and 52(2).

Bibliography

Abel-Smith, Brian and Townsend, Peter (1965), *The poor and the poorest: a new analysis of the Ministry of Labour's Family Expenditure Surveys' of 1953–4 and 1960*, London: Bell.

Aldgate, Anthony, Chapman, James, and Marwick, Arthur (eds) (2000) *Windows on the Sixties: Exploring Key Texts of Media and Culture*, London: I. B. Tauris.

Blond, Phillip (2010) *Red Tory: How Left and Right Have Broken Britain*, London: Faber and Faber.

Booker, Christopher (1969) *The Neophiliacs: The Revolution in English Life in the Fifties and Sixties*, London: Collins.

Bouchier, David (1978) *Idealism and Revolution: New Ideologies of Liberation in Britain and the United States*, London: Edward Arnold.

Cronin, Paul, Riley, James, and Stutesman, Drake (2011) 'Peter Whitehead Issue', *Framework: The Journal of Cinema and Media*, 52(1) and 52(2).

Davenport-Hines, Richard (2013) *An English Affair: Sex, Class and Power in the Age of Profumo*, London: Harper.

DeGroot, Gerard (2008) *The Sixties Unplugged: A Kaleidoscopic History of a Disorderly Decade*, London: Macmillan.

Diski, Jenny (2009) *The Sixties*, London: Profile.

Donnelly, Mark (2005) *Sixties Britain: Culture, Society and Politics*, Harlow: Pearson.

Eagleton, Terry and Wicker, Brian (eds) (1968) *From Culture to Revolution: The Slant Symposium 1967*, London: Sheed and Ward.

Finney, Patrick (2011) *Remembering the Road to World War Two: International History, National Identity, Collective Memory*, London: Routledge.

Green, Jonathon (1999) *All Dressed Up: The Sixties and the Counterculture*, London: Pimlico.

Hardt, Michael and Negri, Antonio (2000) *Empire*, Cambridge, MA: Harvard University Press.

Hardt, Michael and Negri, Antonio (2009) *Commonwealth*, Cambridge, MA: Harvard University Press.

Hitchens, Christopher (1998) 'Where were you in the long Sixties?', *Times Literary Supplement*, 13 November.

Jameson, Frederic (2008) 'Periodizing the Sixties', in *The Ideologies of Theory*, London: Verso, pp. 483–515.

Jenkins, Keith (1999) 'On Hayden White', in *Why History? Ethics and Postmodernity* London: Routledge, pp. 85–98.

Jones, Bryn (2010) 'All along the watershed: sixties values as defence of community lifeworlds in Britain, 1968–2008', in Bryn Jones and Mike O'Donnell (eds) *Sixties Radicalism and Social Movement Activism: Retreat or Resurgence?*, London: Anthem, pp. 3–21.

Jones, Bryn and O'Donnell, Mike (eds) (2010) *Sixties Radicalism and Social Movement Activism: Retreat or Resurgence?*, London: Anthem.

Judt, Tony (2010) *Ill Fares the Land: A Treatise on Our Present Discontents*, London: Allen Lane.

Levin, Bernard (1970) *The Pendulum Years: Britain and the Sixties*, London: Cape.

MacDonald, Ian (1997) *Revolution in the Head: The Beatles' Records and the Sixties*, London: Fourth Estate.

MacIntyre, Alasdair (1968) *Marxism and Christianity*, London: Duckworth.

Marcuse, Herbert (1991) *One-Dimensional Man: Studies in the Ideology of Advanced Industrial Society*, London: Routledge.

Marwick, Arthur (1998) *The Sixties: Cultural Revolution in Britain, France, Italy, and the United States, c.1958–c.1974*, Oxford: Oxford University Press.

Mason, Paul (2012) *Why It's Kicking Off Everywhere: The New Global Revolutions*, London: Verso.

Metzger, Rainer (2012) *London in the Sixties*, London: Thames and Hudson.

Miles, Barry (2010) *London Calling: A Countercultural History of London Since 1945*, London: Atlantic.

Moore, Christopher (2009) 'The progressive professionals: the National Council for Civil Liberties and the politics of activism in the 1960s', *Twentieth Century British History*, 20(4): 538–60.

Mort, Frank (2011) 'The permissive society revisited', *Twentieth Century British History*, 22(2): 269–98.

Nuttall, Jeff (1968) *Bomb Culture*, London: MacGibbon and Kee.

Obelkevich, James (2000) 'Review of Arthur Marwick *The Sixties: Cultural Revolution in Britain, France, Italy, and the United States, c.1958–c.1974*', *Twentieth Century British History*, 11(3): 333–6.

Passerini, Luisa (1999) 'Review', *The American Historical Review*, 104(5): 725–48.

Paul, Herman (2011) *Hayden White: The Historical Imagination*, London: Polity.

Richards, Keith (2010) *Life*, London: Weidenfeld & Nicolson.

Rowbotham, Sheila (2000) *Promise of a Dream: Remembering the Sixties*, London: Allen Lane.

Sandbrook, Dominic (2005) *Never Had It So Good: A History of Britain from Suez to the Beatles*, London: Little Brown.

Sandbrook, Dominic (2006) *White Heat: A History of Britain in the Swinging Sixties*, London: Little Brown.

Sandbrook, Dominic (2010) *State of Emergency. The Way We Were: Britain, 1970–1974*, London: Allen Lane.

Scruton, Roger (1998) 'Dispatches from a turbulent decade', *New Statesman*, 16 October.

Taylor, Robert (1998) 'Doing one's own thing', *Spectator*, 11 July.

Thomas, Nick (2002) 'Challenging myths of the 1960s: the case of student protest in Britain', *Twentieth Century British History*, 13(3): 277–97.

Thompson, E.P. (ed.) (1970) *Warwick University Ltd: Industry, Management and the University*, Harmondsworth: Penguin.

White, Hayden ([1966] 1978) 'The burden of history', in *Tropics of Discourse: Essays in Cultural Criticism*, Baltimore, MD: Johns Hopkins University Press, pp. 27–50.

White, Hayden ([1969] 2010) 'The tasks of intellectual history', in Robert Doran (ed.) *The Fiction of Narrative: Essays on History, Literature and Theory, 1957–2007*, Baltimore, MD: Johns Hopkins University Press, pp. 80–97.

White, Hayden ([1971] 2010) 'The culture of criticism – Gombrich, Auerbach, Popper', in Robert Doran (ed.) *The Fiction of Narrative: Essays on History, Literature and Theory, 1957–2007*, Baltimore, MD: Johns Hopkins University Press, pp. 98–111.

White, Hayden ([1972] 2010) 'What is a historical system?', in Robert Doran (ed.) *The Fiction of Narrative: Essays on History, Literature and Theory, 1957–2007*, Baltimore, MD: Johns Hopkins University Press, pp. 126–35.

White, Hayden ([1973] 2010) 'The politics of contemporary philosophy of history', in Robert Doran (ed.) *The Fiction of Narrative: Essays on History, Literature and Theory, 1957–2007*, Baltimore, MD: Johns Hopkins University Press, pp. 136–52.

Whiteley, Gillian (2011) 'Sewing the "subversive thread of imagination": Jeff Nuttall, *Bomb Culture* and the radical potential of affect', *The Sixties: A Journal of History, Politics and Culture*, 4(2), 109–33.

Widgery, David (1976) *The Left in Britain 1956–68*, Harmondsworth: Penguin.

Willis, Ellen (1998) 'On the barricades', *New York Times*, 8 November.

Woodis, Jack (1972) *New Theories of Revolution: A Commentary on the Views of Frantz Fanon, Régis Debray and Herbert Marcuse*, London: Lawrence and Wishart.

Part I
Politics

2
The 1960s

Days of innocence

R. J. Morris

This chapter interrogates the 1960s through two simple questions. When did they begin and when did they come to an end? The decade is examined as a very specific and intense experience of modernity. This setting of boundaries will provide a framework for an examination of the contradictions of freedom and oppression present in the modernity of that decade and its many strands of cultural and material change. There were three dates which signalled the social, cultural and economic processes which set the framework for the decade.

On 5 February 1953, sweets came off rationing. Overnight thousands of children were thrown into the market economy where they could make choices in that desirable and sensual world of sugary sweetness. Within a year all food rationing had come to an end. The British entered a world in which each year would be better than the one before. There was a sense of limitless material resources. By 1960, those children who looked for pocket money rather than ration coupons would be entering their teens and twenties.

The demographics of the 1960s deserve careful attention. The population of Britain increased from 53 to 55.7 million. The 15–29 age group rose from 10.3 to 11.8 million. The 30–59 groups fell in size but the over-65s increased.[1] The generational contrast was not only one of size but in experience. The older generations claimed authority from the experience of two world wars and the economic depression and poverty of the 1930s. This was increasingly irrelevant to the twenty-somethings of the 1960s.

The year 1956 was dominated by the Suez Crisis in which the British and French invaded Egypt in response to Nasser's nationalization of the Suez Canal. It was a complex crisis but it brought to an abrupt and effective end any sense that the British Empire could compete with the world authority of the United States. Among the actions taken by the USA was a threat to sell their holdings of sterling bonds and a refusal to allow the International Monetary Fund to assist the British. Empire and the sense of standing alone against fascism were crucial to the British sense of self and the authority of their rulers. Suez set questions for Empire, creating confusions over the meaning of Britain as an imperial power which provided a backdrop to much of the 1960s. Issues of justice, citizenship and racial superiority were all debated in the shadow of Empire. Those who administered the Empire were more likely to be mocked than be regarded as heroes of Kipling or John Buchan novels.

4 September 1957 saw the publication of the Wolfenden Report, *The Report of the Departmental Committee on Homosexual Offences and Prostitution*. It was an important event in 'gay' culture although the law was not changed until 1967 and even then left many unresolved issues around the age of consent, prejudice and the potential for blackmail. The Report was important because it set the terms of the debate over the nature of freedom, especially freedom before the law and the relationship of individual freedom to society as a whole. The concept of 'consenting adults in private' became central to these debates. In the words of the Report, 'unless a deliberate attempt be made by society through the agency of the law to equate the sphere of crime with that of sin, there must remain a realm of private morality and immorality which is, in brief and crude terms, not the law's business'.

Embedded in the Report and in many of the assertions of freedom identified with the 1960s was a concept of freedom which went back to John Stuart Mill and central ideas of English liberalism. An action was morally valid if it was the result of the free and informed choice of the individual, just so long as it did not harm others. The concept of self involved here had an important universality and lacked national identity, race, class or gender with implications that would take several decades to become evident. The concept of 'adult' provided an ill-defined age limit which formed a boundary to be fought over. What followed was a crucial debate over the nature of law, freedom and popular morality.

Patrick Devlin, a senior judge, argued that popular morality should have an important influence on law-making (Devlin, 1965). He argued that society's existence and cohesion depended upon shared political and moral values. Actions which challenged these values, however private, threatened society with disintegration. He produced the idea of the 'reasonable man'. When his 'limits of tolerance' were reached and the intensity of 'intolerance, indignation and disgust' over the mere presence of certain actions rose, then the law was entitled to take action. H.L.A. Hart, Professor of Legal Philosophy at Oxford University, replied with almost pure John Stuart Mill: the law had no business interfering with private acts that harm nobody. Disputed notions of public/private distinctions, of the reasonable, of harm and adult littered the 1960s while the 'reasonable woman' had yet to intervene. The key texts of this debate rapidly became a staple of university philosophy courses, providing a stock of understandings for those who would become decision-takers in politics, the civil service, the Church and corporate business in the following decades. At the same time, Isaiah Berlin's (1958) inaugural lecture, *Two Concepts of Liberty*, was a reminder that the 'negative' concept of freedom as freedom from interference by the law and the state was on its own an inadequate basis for understanding.

Alongside Wolfenden and perhaps more important in terms of its wider public impact was the trial, in 1960, of *Lady Chatterley's Lover* or rather of Penguin Books for publishing a paperback edition of the D.H. Lawrence novel of that name. British courts had a long list of successful prosecutions against books which might 'deprave and corrupt'. The 1959 Obscene Publications Act was designed to allowed publication if it could be shown that a work had literary merit. The case brought by the Crown laid stress on the adulteries of the main characters and laboriously counted out the rude words: there were apparently 30 'fucks', 14 'cunts' but only 13 'balls'. The jury were required to read the book but not allowed to take it home. They took only three hours to agree a not guilty verdict. As a result of the trial publicity, the book was to sell some three million copies (Robertson, 2010). The themes of personal integrity, the crossing of class barriers, sensuality and sexual fulfilment ran through the 1960s. The trial emphasized two processes of the 1960s. The first was the failure to assert class authority. The prosecution famously asked: 'Is it a book that you would even wish your wife or your servants to read?' The jury probably had no servants and three were qualified by gender to be wives. In the eyes of the Crown Prosecution, the real crime of Penguin books was to publish it at 3/6d, making the book accessible to an enormous range of people.

The second feature was the decisive impact of the authority of experts: Helen Gardner, literary critic and fellow of St Hilda's College, Oxford, promoter of John Donne, the seventeenth-century poet whose work embodied all the sensuality and spirituality of the metaphysical poets, T. S. Eliot, 'Eliot the church' premier modernist was a supporter, as was Richard Hoggart, a lecturer at Leicester University and developer of the new discipline of cultural studies. The Sixties were to explore the boundaries of literary merit and obscenity, as well as the meaning of class and fulfilment. Despite the claims of Philip Larkin, that 'Sexual intercourse began in 1963 (which was rather late for me) – Between the end of the Chatterley ban and the Beatles first LP', the processes highlighted by the trial worked their way slowly through the 1960s. Crude birth rate and fertility both fell while illegitimate births and divorce both rose, all signs of choices being made and the disciplines of 'society' being ignored. The trial exemplified the manner in which London became a theatre which was to educate the United Kingdom in the possibilities of social change not just in matters of sexuality and individual autonomy, but also in matters of class, race and what came to be called gender. The streets, the law courts, the media, Parliament and a variety of clubs and revue bars projected themselves as a national stage undermining the authority of the ruling class, as well as questioning the assumptions of the 'reasonable man' who had inhabited Lord Devlin's polemic (see Irving *et al.*, 1963; Mort, 2010; Rycroft, 2002).

Alongside the drama and excitement of *Lady Chatterley* was a more subtle literature which validated cultures which had been ignored, denigrated, treated with contempt or as vaguely amusing. Alan Sillitoe's *Saturday Night and Sunday Morning* (1958) was about Nottingham and the repetitive work of the cycle factory lathe. There was drink, which meant beer, casual violence often linked to the culture of national military service, male-centred sex and occasional moments of calm. John Braine's *Room at the Top* (1957) made the less than happy transition from working class to the white-collar middle classes. The novel traversed sexual possibility, class cultural superiority and motor-car culture. It validated something later to be called 'northernness', though its author celebrated literary success by moving to London. Stan Barstow's *A Kind of Loving* (1960) was another morality play of life in the white-collar clerical classes and the confused fumbles of sex and gender. Keith Waterhouse's *Billy Liar* (1959) was a study of working-class males let loose in the new world. These novels placed the internal colonies of the industrial provincial working class and the borderlands with clerical white-collar respectability at the centre of literature, which had often been the preserve of the respectable and metropolitan. Equally important was an intellectual culture which validated, rather than simply studied, these subordinate cultures. Richard Hoggart's *Uses of Literacy* (1957) created a central place for the meanings of working-class language and literature through an account of the culture of the working-class industrial suburb of Hunslet in south Leeds (see Hall, 1990; Hall and Hoggart, 2007).

Thus far (1960), this was an intensely male literature. One exception was Sheila Delaney, *A Taste of Honey* (1958), a play and then a film. It was a so-called kitchen-sink drama in which race and sexuality competed for attention with class and the northern setting. The assertive maleness of this literature was not always a happy one. The pregnant bride, the abortion scenes in *Saturday Night and Sunday Morning* and *Billy Liar*, the restrictive disciplines of class were part of a world out of control, full of contradictions and full of sensuality, but lacking the fulfilment promised by the *Lady Chatterley* trial.

The 1960s, as a cultural experience, presented a world of limitless material possibility, a world which valued the free, informed decision-taking individual, which sought fulfilling sensuality, especially in sexual matters, and which accepted the widespread literary discussion of such matters. Difficulties and dissatisfactions were debated mainly in class terms: gender and race were left in the margins. Cultural change was marked by the authority of the United States marked by Jazz and Elvis, and the long contest between Hollywood and British film studios for the attention of a vibrant cinema. The influence of Empire on culture evaporated to be replaced by new European strands, notably the attention to Sweden where it was believed they had better sex, well-designed modern cutlery and more intelligent films. There was a cult of much-watched Ingmar Bergman films and the influence of Swedish design involved everything from buildings to teaspoons (see Shaw, 2003). The 1960s were to mark the high noon of the modern, of the morality of self-fulfilment, and a faith in science and technology. There was a confident search for solutions through science, technology and experts. The latter competed for attention in a world which forgot Empire and for a moment ignored any sense of the past. Standard interpretations of the 1960s might follow this in terms of birth control and 'the pill', though it should be noted that the pill became available on the NHS in 1961 only for married women and was not more widely available until 1967. Some of the subtleties and contradictions inherent in these processes of modernity can better be followed through the fate of the planner and the motor car.

The motor car was central to the manner in which technology came to dominate, mediate and transform all aspects of social life. In 1961, there were 5.5 million cars in the UK. In 1971, there were 11.3 million. That meant in 1961, one car for every 5.5 adults and one per 2.8 adults in 1971. In 1961, some 18 per cent of adults owned a car. In 1971, it was 35 per cent. By 1991, it was to be over 50 per cent. In 1961, there were 48 cars for every mile of road. It 1971, it was 72. Modes of transport

Table 2.1 Percentages of miles travelled in
mode of transport

	Bus	Car/van	Rail
1961	28	49	14
1971	14	75	9

measured in terms of percentage of miles travelled indicated the same
centrality of motor transport (Table 2.1).

The change since 1951 was even greater. Then, there had been one
car for every 13 adults. The same story could have been written for
other technologies – telephones, televisions and photography. The percentage of homes with televisions had risen from 36 per cent in 1956
to 75 per cent in 1961 and 93 per cent in 1971.[2] The numbers were
compulsive, indeed, the quantity of numbers was itself an aspect of
the changing quality and quantity of accumulation. The government
publication, *Social Trends*, began in 1970, drawing together in table
and commentary the accelerating quantity of information, an attempt
through the technology of numbers to comprehend and perhaps control an increasing pace of change. Of these changes, the motor car was
pervasive and dominant. It moved from being the rich man's toy to an
elite middle-class privilege and working-class ambition. In *Room at the
Top*, John Braine used the motor car as an easy-to-understand indicator of social class: the Daimler was the established wealth of the rich
manufacturer, whilst the Austin Eight served the ordinary middle-class
couple. The car was an icon of masculinity but also central to the gender
contest. In Braine's novel, the character of Alice Aisgill represented the
choice-making, rule-breaking female, manipulative, assertive, and ultimately a victim. Her ownership of a small Fiat 500, a foreign car no less,
provided the reader with a clear warning of danger and excitement.

The motor cars and the roads they used were not only important
because of their centrality to the cultural experience of the 1960s,
but also because they exemplified the manner in which that decade
represented the high noon of modernity with all its freedoms and
contradictions, and because of the confidence and processes which
were brought to respond to the opportunities and problems of the car.
Congestion, traffic jams and parking problems were not new in the late-
1950s, but they were experienced on a new scale. At the same time they
brought a response based upon expert analysis and technology together
with new forms of authority. The first parking meters appeared in 1958

and parking wardens were empowered to levy fines in 1960. The parking meter and the wardens were a perfect symbol of the oppression and freedom embedded in modernity. The 'freedom' of choice offered by the motor car came to depend upon an increasingly complex system of rules, regulations, prohibitions and authorities which limited choice in a manner that was deeply resented and seen as oppressive. The key document was *Traffic in Towns* by Colin Buchanan, published in 1963.[3] The report accepted the dominance of the new technology of the motor car. The problems caused by growing motor car use and ownership were identified – noise, pollution and congestion. These problems were to be solved by scientific analysis and the engineering solutions of the experts. The first motorways for long distance travel had already arrived. Seventy miles of the M1 were opened in 1959. The towns were to be re-engineered and made fit for the motor car. The massive authority of the state was used to deliver the future. Small towns like Newbury, west of London, were offered a bypass and parking restrictions. Larger places like Leeds and Newcastle saw substantial demolitions of property in order to provide space for inner-city motorways. The technologies of movement were given priority over residential needs. Working-class communities were destroyed to provide the freedoms of the motor car. There were two key features to this: one was the confidence that whatever problems were caused by the car, these could be solved by science and technology; the second was the variety of restrictions and oppressions essential to the freedoms of the car. These might vary from the parking meter and speeding fines to the demolition of housing.

In the long term, this was to result in major changes in attitudes to space and time. In the first scene of Alan Sillitoe's novel *Saturday Night and Sunday Morning*, the central character, young Arthur Seaton, wakes up late, puts his head under the cold tap, pulls on his shirt and trousers, grabs breakfast and runs down the street to the engineering works, which was at the other end of the street. Here he was just in time to have his card stamped by the timekeeper at the gate (see Daniels and Rycroft, 1993). This was an organization of space and time characteristic of the early 1960s. It was one which had been in place for over a century. Families lived within sight and sound of the workplace and were able to walk to their work. Other accounts might have added shops, often at the corner of the terraced streets. Most neighbourhoods would have a variety of chapels and churches. There were public houses and meeting places for lodges of trades unions and friendly societies, with names that hinted at the mystic of mutuality as well as exclusion: Masons, Foresters, Gardeners and the Royal Order of Buffaloes.

The street was as likely to be used for recreation and drying washing as it was for circulation. Work, residence, leisure, circulation, consumption, all shared the same space. In these respects there was almost no specialization of area. The divisions of space, set out with care in *Room at the Top*, were in terms of social class and the complex contests of gender. A more considered account came from Richard Hoggart's *Uses of Literacy* with his description of working-class space and culture in Leeds. Hoggart became a major literary and cultural critic but his account of Hunslet, published in 1957 and derived from memories of childhood in the 1930s showed the narrow completeness of the world in which he grew up. He had a detailed knowledge of streets and people. There was the prestige of the end house in the terrace and the identity of the person who would help filling in the forms from the growing bureaucracy of the state. His initial ambitions were located in the local grammar school and then the walk or cycle across the city to the university on the hill above the north bank of the river. Social life was based upon the local chapel and the cycling club associated with it (Hoggart, 1988).

A very different account came from Caryl Phillips (2002, 2005), a novelist who grew up in exactly the same bit of space in the 1970s. In his essays he gave an account of being 'integrated into cobbled streets' and the uncomfortable experience of being a black Leeds United Football Club supporter among an intensely racist crowd culture. In different ways, both Hoggart and Phillips became major international figures, both spending part of their life in New York. Phillips goes to university in Oxford. His novels take in Africa, the Caribbean and move across space and time. Hoggart began with a detailed account of the culture around him in Hunslet in order to explore the tensions of social class and to evaluate that culture. It was a culture both narrow and secure, located in its speech patterns and literature. Hoggart and Phillips were clearly exceptional people who used the processes of the educational meritocracy to 'escape'. The generational difference was more than a move from social class to race as the focus of creative tension: it was a move from inward-looking neighbourhood spaces to a sense of space which was global and unbounded.

In the 1950s world of neighbourhood, of the mixed spaces of work and residence, even the holidays tended to be collective. Whole neighbourhoods closed down and families moved for a week or a fortnight to the same seaside resort, during an appointed local holiday. Some communities would choose Blackpool, others Morecambe, both on the Lancashire coast. Individual families would show their superiority by going to Southport or Prestatyn, the latter in north Wales. In the 1980s,

Hunslet was visited by the inevitable team of sociologists to ask how it had changed since the days reflected in *Uses of Literacy*. The terraced house and cobbled streets had been demolished and replaced by Hunslet Grange, a damp-ridden, socially dysfunctional, systems-built, housing complex. This in turn had been demolished and replaced by cottage housing and wasteland. More significant were changing holiday and friendship patterns. Many families took their holidays in Spain each year. They went to the same places and met the same people, naming friends who came from the English Midlands and other regions.

A key aspect of change in neighbourhoods like Hunslet was a fundamental reorganization of the built environment. The 1960s were part of a great rebuilding in Britain. This started in the 1950s with an expansion of local authority house building. In the 1960s the local state was joined by massive private enterprise contributions. Part of this was the destruction of large areas of nineteenth-century housing and the mass movement of working-class populations to the outskirts of great cities. Here, there was no more walking to work. There were several key features to this specific aspect of modernity. Local authority housing was subsidized in various ways. Thus many families were lifted away from the poverty of rents and unfit housing. In return, they accepted the discipline of the local authority housing department. Most authorities had long waiting lists for 'council houses' and hence discipline could be enforced. At the same time, most big urban housing authorities were controlled by active Labour Party branches and trades union lodges. Tenants gained internal sanitation, toilets, hot and cold running water: there were stories of women running up and down stairs turning taps and light switches on and off in celebration, something they had never been able to do before. Others felt uncomfortable. They washed children standing in the sink as they had always done, rather than in the new bath.

Control could be quite subtle. For example, most houses had three bedrooms, announcing a preference for a man and wife with children and the separation of sleeping for children of different sexes. The provision of bathrooms and 'living' rooms as well as kitchens demanded cleanliness and an increased expenditure on furniture. The private sector prospered on a vision of freedom and choice-making dependent on house ownership. Both right- and left-wing parties promoted a 'property-owning democracy'. This vision fixed a middle-class and to some extent skilled working-class life cycle in which mortgage debt was paid off over a working lifetime. Building societies, many with origins in nineteenth-century artisan culture, expanded rapidly to become key features of middle-class finance. In the north-east of England, much of the compensation paid for the nationalization of coal mines in the 1940s found its way into financial institutions such as the Northern Rock Building Society.[4] Low unemployment and a rapidly expanding professional and white-collar sector of the economy supported this life cycle. In return for regular payments to a variety of financial institutions, the private house-owners/mortgagees gained a flexibility of movement limited by the market rather than the rules of local authority bureaucracies. They gained space in which they could make choices, filling this space with new furnishings and domestic white goods. It was a space for the display of wealth and taste. The television was added to the wireless and gramophone (now renamed the radio and the record player). The home asserted itself as the family entertainment centre.

Housing made several contributions to the enthusiastic modernity of the 1960s. It was a key feature of class relationships. The middle classes, who for this purpose included many skilled working-class people, bought their own house through a mortgage and the building society. The working classes were council tenants. The 1960s began as a society which understood and interrogated itself in terms of social class. Working-class 'communities' and affluent workers were observed and encapsulated in questionnaires. Hidden by this were Caribbean and Asian populations growing in size – 'the empire coming home'. As new arrivals often in male-led migrations, they fell into the margins of local authority waiting lists. For Labour Party and trades union-led local authorities, the houses were for 'our people' and points in the waiting list were scored for waiting, at times for a generation. Added to this was scarcely concealed prejudice, and black and Asian people were moved to what remained of the private rented sector, forming what John Rex called a 'housing class' (Rex and Moore, 1967). It was one indication that the British, especially the English, tendency to think about their society in class terms alone simply would not do.

The changing experience of housing, especially local authority and other forms of state housing was increasingly driven by technology and a faith in the ability of technology to deliver political objectives. In order to increase the output of new local housing an increasing variety of factory-produced and systems-built housing was created. Little attention was paid to sound and heat insulation. Many houses like those at Hunslet Grange rapidly became known for damp and mould. Local authority politicians were attracted to spectacular demonstrations of their status as housing providers. Tower blocks and deck-access housing on a monumental and often inhumane scale were central to the provision of the 1960s. There was a major re-ordering of space. Work was separated from home and home from entertainment. Social provision – shops, bars and clubs – were limited. Equally serious was the manner in which the 'points' system for the allocation of local authority housing divided generation from generation. Families with young children gained priority, separating them from older people left behind in the inner cities, This meant that 'mother' was no longer within easy reach of her daughter with young children. They were separated by a bus fare rather than living in the same street. The mortgage-paying middle classes were also separated by career structures which became less local, but for them technology in the shape of the telephone and motor car helped bridge distance.

There was a much wider re-organization of space implied by the total area planning which was increasingly involved in the remaking of cities in the 1960s. The concept of planning dated to the late-nineteenth century as a response to the squalid and congested conditions of the great towns. The concept reached its confident peak in the 1960s, often based upon surveys and reports made in the 1940s and the 1950s. Men like Patrick Abercrombie saw the war of 1939–45 as an opportunity and an inspiration, and saw themselves as wise and benevolent experts using their skills and knowledge to solve problems for the benefit of others. Wartime destruction was to be followed by demolition and the re-organization of urban space. The scale, confidence and assumption of power in their imagination were breath-taking. During the war, Abercrombie wrote:

> The whole of the first stage of over one million people and the first movement of industry to correspond could be done in ten years … if the present wartime powers were continued sufficiently long.
>
> (Abercrombie, 1945, p. 1)

Their planning encapsulated many cultural features of modernity. The gathering of measurable information was followed by the identification of problems, and then came the analysis of experts using their special skills. Solutions were proposed with little sense of negotiation with the populations concerned. They were solutions with all the features of categorization and rationality required by 'modern' cities. The planners thought in terms of zones separating residential from industrial and motor traffic from pedestrians. The problem of reducing the density of inner cities while containing the spread of the urban was solved by green belts in which building and development were restricted. Movement was crucial in the form of ring roads, inter-city motorways, as well as new urban roads. Style was to be modern: clean lines, the new materials of glass, concrete and steel were to replace the disorderly, over-decorated built environment of the Victorians. In Edinburgh, Princes Street – the main shopping street – a chaotic product of every style the nineteenth century could devise, was to be replaced by a three-decker motorway and 'modern' properties which, it was believed, would replicate the order of the original eighteenth-century landscape (Abercrombie and Plumstead, 1949). In the eyes of the planners and the politicians who supported them, these interventions would produce the freedoms which enabled people to make choices.

Ronan Point was a 23-storey system-built tower block in the borough of Newham in east London. In May 1968, a gas explosion in one of the higher flats triggered a progressive collapse and four people died (see Crawford, 1975). This event became a symbol of the reaction against modern industrial solutions, especially in housing and architecture. It was part of a social reaction against high-rise living which rapidly spread to much of the local authority housing management and stock. In part this was due to poor quality control and a failure to carry out repairs. Working-class politics began to be expressed in tenants associations and anti-dampness campaigns (see Figure 2.1). Ironically, the 'enemy' was often the Labour Party-controlled local authority, which had become increasingly distanced from its members and constituents. At the same time, the career paths of local authority officials began to be referenced not to the locality but to national paths of promotion and recognition. As a result, within the space of a few years 'the planners' moved from being heroes to villains.

Ronan Point was one of many developments which marked the end of the innocence and optimism of the 1960s. It was one example of the manner in which the 'modern' solution had become the problem. It was part of a general loss of faith in the expert and the 'scientific' solution. Atomic energy had entered the 1960s as a source of clean, inexhaustible energy. Atomic weapons were much feared but recognized as the means of bringing a world war to a rapid end and saving many allied lives. But by the end of the 1960s, these developments were being increasingly rejected as a source of dangerous waste and threatening military confrontation.

The most brutal punctuation mark for the 1960s was in the north of Ireland where a civil rights movement morphed into a complex civil war. Detailed analysis can be found elsewhere, but two points need to be made. Events in Belfast and Derry marked out a broader change in which identities and political mobilizations moved from

Figure 2.1 'Leeds Other Paper'. Tenants groups became the new working-class politics

universals to the particular. Citizens, middle- and working-class people became members of nations, ethnic groups, racial and religious groups. In the late-1960s and early-1970s, the English-led Westminster government and their intellectuals, lawyers, academics and journalists, found themselves in major difficulties trying to understand what was happening. They thought in terms of class and citizenship, perhaps even human rights, and failed to respond to the anxieties of race, religion and nationality.[5]

Another warning appeared in 1972 with the publication of the Club of Rome's study, *The Limits of Growth*. It was the first of now familiar accounts of the limits of the world's resources. It was full of predictions of population growth and carbon dioxide concentrations in the atmosphere. There were tables showing when key resources would run out, copper in 36 years, oil in 31 years, and so on. Malthusian thinking was back and the 1960s assumptions of unlimited resources were challenged. The Labour governments of the 1960s had looked to growth and technological change as ways of resolving class conflict without conflict, as a way of eliminating poverty without taking from the wealthier parts of society (Meadows *et al.*, 1972). The change in perception that marked the end of the 1960s was reinforced in 1974 when Arab members of OPEC forced a fourfold increase in the price of oil. For a brief period, price inflation in Britain rose to 24 per cent a year. Mild inflation had long been a way of resolving class conflict and ensuring near full employment. But the early 1970s brought an end to the so-called Keynesian underpinning of the Sixties.

The final punctuation mark for the 1960s which has been chosen for this chapter was a more benign one; namely, the return of 'history'. A key aspect of the 1960s was the rejection of the past. The past was seen as dirty, oppressive and inefficient. It was there to be improved upon and reformed. Housing, health services and working conditions were only some aspects of this. The end of Empire was celebrated as a gain, as was the replacement of steam engines and railways with roads and the internal combustion engine. The sense of the rejection and abolition of a past identified with poverty, war, conflict and oppression was part of the sense of freedom central to the 1960s. This rejection of the past was clearest in attitudes to the built environment (Esher, 1981). Planning strategies were key to the destruction of the past and its replacement by the modern. The Euston Arch stood outside one of the major London railway stations. It was a celebration of Victorian engineering and achievement. Its demolition, like the destruction of working-class homes in the industrial towns, was a symbol of this rejection of the past. Change came in 1973–74 as part of the re-development of Covent Garden Market in Central London. This had long been the wholesale fruit and vegetable market for the capital. It was a major source of traffic congestion, frequently illustrated in planning literature as 'a problem'. It was vacated in the late-1960s. A major area of real estate became available for the developers. The first published plans were very 'modern'. The major historic buildings, such as the seventeenth-century church and the Georgian market buildings were to be retained but they were to be enveloped like toys in a mass of steel, glass and concrete. Tower blocks, slabs, underpasses and overpasses were all there. It was an environment fit for the motor car and the corporate market economy. This met opposition from an unholy alliance of heritage organizations, radical groups and local community associations. Radical and heritage organizations often overlapped with the officers of the historic building division of the Greater London Council which was key in formulating opposition. The planning application went to the relevant government department, which decided that development must preserve not just the few buildings of major historic importance but over 200 others (*Covent Garden Local Plan*, 1974; Thorne, 1986). In other words, the total and varied environment became the object of preservation and not just a few trophy buildings. The outcome was significant. It was a world of variety. It was a world which emphasized small units of consumerism. Above all, it was a world to be valued simply for the experience of being there – to drink coffee, to display juggling and musical skills – or just sit in the sun (Figure 2.2). It was a sign of the early moves towards what

Figure 2.2 Covent Garden was 'saved' to become an environment of variety valued for the quality of its experience

was to be called the 'post-modern' in which individuals began to judge success in terms of the quality of experience rather than the quantity of accumulation (Harvey, 1990). The historic content of the built and visual experience was one aspect of that experience.

There were many other punctuation marks which could have been chosen here. There was the radical feminist attack on the Miss World Contest in 1970: leaflets, ink and flour bombs as well as tomatoes were thrown. At the same time the *Sun* newspaper began the regular page three publication of semi-naked women. A long contest changed focus. The 1960s notion that the contraceptive pill, miniskirts and a modest extension of female access to higher education and the job market were an adequate definition of freedom came to a contested end.

The 1960s was more than a decade. These years were marked by a sense of limitless possibilities and resources. They were marked by the many contradictions of freedom (Bauman, 1993). The parking meter was as much a symbol of this as the contraceptive pill. These were the years of the rise and fall of the experts, of science and of faith in the universals of class, citizenship and human rights.

Notes

1. See *Social Trends*, No.16, 1986 edition, London: HMSO.
2. See the website of the Broadcasters Audience Research Board (BARB). Available at: www.barb.co.uk/facts/tv-ownership-private.
3. A cheaper version was published by Penguin Books, making the Report's ideas widely available. Buchanan himself warned that long-term problems would remain; see Delafons (1998) and Gunn (2011).
4. The best accounts of the cultural fortunes of housing were produced by the Community Development Projects of the early 1970s, notably *The Making of a Ruling Class*, Benwell Community Project Final Report Series, no. 6, Newcastle upon Tyne, 1978; *Whatever Happened to Council Housing*, London, 1976; *Private Housing and the Working Class*, Benwell Community Project Final Report Series, no. 6, Newcastle upon Tyne, 1978.
5. There are many academic accounts but the struggle to record and understand from a variety of perspectives can be found in The Sunday Times Insight Team (1972), McCann (1974), Purdie (1990), Ó Dochartaigh (1997), and O'Doherty (2007).

Bibliography

Abercrombie, Patrick (1945) *Greater London Plan 1944*, London: HMSO.
Abercrombie, Patrick and Plumstead, Derek (1949) *A Civic Survey and Plan for the City and Royal Burgh of Edinburgh*, Edinburgh: Oliver and Boyd.

Bauman, Zygmunt (1993) *Modernity and Ambivalence*, Oxford: Polity Press.

Berlin, Isaiah (1958) *Two Concepts of Liberty: An Inaugural Lecture Delivered Before the University of Oxford on 31 October 1958*, Oxford: Clarendon Press.

Buchanan Report (1963) *Traffic in Towns: A Study of the Long-Term Problems of Traffic in Urban Areas. Reports of the Steering Group and Working Group Appointed by the Minister of Transport, 1963*. London: HMSO.

Crawford, David (ed.) (1975) *A Decade of British Housing, 1963–1973*, London: Architectural Press.

Daniels, Stephen and Rycroft, Simon (1993) 'Mapping the modern city: Alan Sillitoe's Nottingham novels', *Transactions of the Institute of British Geographers*, 18(4): 460–80.

Delafons, John (1998) 'Reforming the British planning system, 1964–5: The Planning Advisory Group and the genesis of the Planning Act of 1968', *Planning Perspectives*, 13(4): 373–87.

Devlin, Patrick (1965) *The Enforcement of Morals*, Oxford: Oxford University Press.

Esher, Lionel (1981) *A Broken Wave: The Rebuilding of England, 1940–1980*, London: Allen Lane.

Greater London Council (1974) *Covent Garden Local Plan: Report of Survey, 1974*, London: Greater London Council.

Gunn, Simon (2011) 'The Buchanan Report: environment and the problem of traffic in 1960s Britain', *Twentieth Century British History*, 22(4): 521–42.

Hall, Stuart (1990) 'The emergence of cultural studies and the crisis of the humanities', *October*, 53 (Summer issue, 'The Humanities as Social Technology'): 11–23.

Hall, Stuart and Hoggart, Richard (2007) 'The uses of literacy and the cultural turn', *International Journal of Cultural Studies*, 10(1): 73–84.

Hart, H.L.A. (1963) *Law, Liberty and Morality*, Stanford, CA: Stanford University Press.

Harvey, David (1990) *The Condition of Postmodernity. An Inquiry into the Origins of Cultural Change*, Oxford: Blackwell.

Hoggart, Richard (1957) *The Uses of Literacy*, London: Chatto and Windus.

Hoggart, Richard (1988) *A Local Habitation: Life and Times, 1918–1940*, London: Chatto and Windus.

Irving, Clive, Hall, Ron, and Wallington, Jeremy (1963) *Scandal '63. A Study of the Profumo Affair*, London: Heinemann.

Marwick, Arthur (1984) '*Room at the Top, Saturday Night and Sunday Morning*, and the "Cultural Revolution" in Britain', *Journal of Contemporary History*, 19(1): 127–52.

McCann, Eamonn (1974) *War and an Irish Town*, London: Pluto Press.

Meadows, Donella *et al.* (1972) *The Limits to Growth. A Report for the Club of Rome's Project on the Predicament of Mankind*, London: Potomac Associates.

Mort, Frank (2010) *Capital Affairs: London and the Making of the Permissive Society*, New Haven, CT: Yale University Press.

Ó Dochartaigh, Nial (1997) *From Civil Rights to Armalites: Derry and the Birth of the Irish Troubles*, Cork: Cork University Press.

O'Doherty, Malachi (2007) *The Telling Year: Belfast 1972*, Dublin: Gill and Macmillan.

Phillips, Caryl (2002) 'Leeds United, life and me', in Caryl Phillips, *A New World Order*, London: Vintage.

Phillips, Caryl (2005) 'Northern soul', *The Guardian*, 22 October.

Purdie, Bob (1990) *Politics in the Streets: The Origins of the Civil Rights Movement*, Belfast: Blackstaff Press.

Rex, John and Moore, Robert (1967) *Race, Community and Conflict: A Study of Sparkbrook*, London: Oxford University Press for the Institute of Race Relations.

Robertson, Geoffrey (2010) 'The trial of *Lady Chatterley's Lover*', available at: http://www.guardian.co.uk/books/2010/oct/22/dh-lawrence-lady-chatterley-trial/ (accessed 24 July 2013).

Rycroft, Simon (2002) 'The geographies of Swinging London', *Journal of Historical Geographies*, 28(4): 566–88.

Shaw, Richard (2003) 'Through a glass darkly: Bergman as critical and cultural bellwether', *Bright Lights Film Journal*, 40 (May).

Sunday Times Insight Team (1972) *Ulster*, London: A Penguin Special.

Thorne, Robert (1986) *Covent Garden Market, its History and Restoration*, London: Covent Garden Development Team.

3

The Abortion Act 1967

A fundamental change?

Sylvie Pomiès-Maréchal and Matthew Leggett

In the 1960s, Great Britain underwent a series of profound changes in both social and cultural terms. For some, these changes were the result of a growth in liberal values and individual freedom, while critics saw this as the rise of a permissiveness which was destroying national values and morals. Politicians' sexual peccadilloes were now being revealed, while satirical publications and television programmes were daring to challenge and ridicule both politicians and the Establishment, a thing previously unheard of, just not quite the done thing. The 'Celtic fringe' was making its voice heard far more, either through civil rights demonstrations or nationalist calls for independence, or at least some form of cultural autonomy. Though not removed altogether, literary and theatre censorship became more tolerant. Young people were expressing themselves defiantly and a youth culture was born, as shown through music and fashion. Certain minorities, including women, homosexuals or Commonwealth immigrants, saw their status change more or less radically. Apparently, Britain was no longer the staid, conservative place that had emerged from the post-war consensus. Several factors account for this transformation, among them a series of social reforms passed while Harold Wilson's Labour governments were in power from 1964 to 1970. Labour had been elected in 1964 on its radical manifesto pledges, which offered a transformation of Britain. Indeed, during the period, four major pieces of legislation were passed, in turn legalizing homosexuality, simplifying divorce law, ending capital punishment and reforming the abortion laws.

We would like to focus on just one of these laws, namely, the Abortion Act of 1967. Drawing on the verbatim reports of Parliamentary debates, official statistics, political interviews, ministerial memoirs, diaries and biographies, TV documentation, newspaper articles and reports, we shall study the 1967 Act from the point of view of the government's stance and role in the passage of the legislation through Parliament, while seeking to answer two interconnected questions: 'The Abortion Act, a fundamental change?', a question put in 2010 by its original sponsor, David (now Lord) Steel, to describe the Act; we will also try to explain, if it was such a key piece of legislation, why was it not government-sponsored legislation? To answer both points, we begin with a brief historical introduction to place the legislation in its context. Then we shall study briefly the legislation itself, in terms of its content, before examining the manner in which it was carried through Parliament, taking into consideration the role and attitude of the government both on a collective and individual basis. Finally, we assess the impact it had, both on British women and women's rights in particular, as well as on British society.

Legislation on abortion in Britain in the latter half of the twentieth century was based on precedents set in the Victorian period. In a recent newspaper article, David Steel, the sponsor of the 1967 legislation, described these laws as 'harsh and archaic' (Steel, 2004). Indeed, for a brief period in the 1820s and 1830s, any attempt to abort a pregnancy was a capital offence, and, following the Offences Against the Person Acts in 1837 and 1861, it was redefined, though any person using poison or any other method to induce a miscarriage, be it the woman herself or a third party, was still guilty of a felony and faced the death sentence.

In 1929, *The Infant Life (Preservation) Act* prohibited the destruction of a child capable of being born alive, unless it could be proved that the act, which could not be carried out before a 28-week term, had been performed in good faith to preserve the life of the mother.[1] This meant that the law was totally unclear as to what exactly could and could not be done, since abortion as such remained illegal, while certain forms of operation could be carried out.

In 1936, the Abortion Law Reform Association was founded by members of the legal profession and leading feminist figures such as Alice Jenkins and Stella Browne. This association adopted a radical stance, demanding the removal of all restrictions on abortion. In particular, it advocated the right to abortion in cases involving a risk to the mother's physical or mental health, the risk of severe handicap in the child, pregnancy following a rape and where a mother's ability to bring up a child was in serious question.

If we turn to the question of the growth in support of some kind of reform to the existing system among public opinion, strong backing would seem to have emerged in the 1930s. This was highlighted in a famous case when a woman was arrested after she had illegally operated on a mother of three children. The mother subsequently died, and the woman who performed the termination stood trial for murder. In the words of the judge, Mr Justice McCardie, such a prosecution showed what was wrong with the existing law and how out of touch with public opinion its supporters were:

> The law on abortion as it exists ought to be substantially modified. It is out of keeping with the conditions that prevail in the world around us... It is plain to me that many of those who seek to uphold this law of abortion are wholly ignorant of the social problems which menace the nation... I cannot think that it is right that a woman should be forced to bear a child against her will.
>
> (HC Deb, 22 July 1966, vol. 732 cc1071–1072)

As a result of this verdict, McCardie was ostracized by the legal profession and when he committed suicide in 1933, this was seen as a contributing factor in some quarters (Potts, Diggory and Peel, 1977, p. 286). Nevertheless, together with the campaign by the Abortion Law Reform Association (ALRA) and, to a lesser extent, the statements of the British Medical Association, these views led to the setting up of a Government Interdepartmental Committee on abortion in 1938. The Committee, chaired by Lord Birkett, turned out to be favourable to a liberalization of the law. Nevertheless, the outbreak of the Second World War abruptly brought things to an end and deferred plans for reform for more than a decade. Regretting the fact that the outbreak of hostilities had naturally diverted national attention away from such an important issue, the report stressed:

> the urgency of the problem of the misery and heartbreak which at present prevail, of the need for clear thinking on the problem, and of the strong necessity for making the law clear and intelligible and in accordance with public opinion – the only ultimate sanction of the law.
>
> (HC Deb, c1072)

This status quo was, however, challenged in various ways: by open medical defiance, legal objections, public opposition and parliamentary initiatives. If we take the first instance, there were various cases, but the most famous became, in the words of Dr David Owen – a strong supporter of reform and one of the MPs who sat on the 1967 Bill Committee – a 'cause célèbre' (Owen, 1991, p. 102). While the Birkett Committee was still sitting, the 1861 Act was severely put to the test by the Bourne case. In June 1938, Aleck Bourne, a London-based gynaecologist, carried out an abortion on a 14-year-old girl who had been raped. Bourne reported himself to the police on his own initiative and was tried at the Old Bailey in July. According to Owen, Bourne did this to attract attention to the absurdity of the situation that existed at the time, namely that in such a case the young future mother was obliged to keep the baby. The defence argued that the gynaecologist had acted responsibly and rightfully, having judged the girl's mental and physical integrity in danger:

> Life depends on health, and it may be that if health is gravely impaired, death results.... If the doctor is of the opinion that the consequences of the continuation of the pregnancy would indeed make the woman a physical or mental wreck, then he operates, in that honest belief, for the purpose of preserving the life of the mother.
>
> (see Potts, Diggory and Peel, 1977, p. 289)

Aleck Bourne was found not guilty. Mr Justice Macnaughton furthermore stated that the use of the term 'unlawful' in respect of abortion implied that some abortions could be lawful. This set a precedent that was to be followed in many cases over the next 30 years, though David Steel would have preferred the judge to have ruled on the circumstances of the pregnancy and whether the doctor was right to have carried out the operation, rather than just on the potential effects on the victim.

Alongside ALRA, in the 1950s, several associations like the National Association for Child Welfare or the Women's Co-operative Guild started to campaign for the reform of the law (Rowbotham, 1999, p. 306). At the same time, the need to educate and support the population in terms of sexual matters was given greater credence when the Family Planning Association was given official charitable status in 1955. Several hundred family planning clinics were opened within the next few years, offering help and advice on contraception, sexually transmitted diseases and abortion. This enabled people to understand the issues at stake better and encouraged them to actually think about and discuss sexually related matters.

As far as political parties are concerned, none ever really embraced the cause of abortion. Between 1952 and 1966, six attempts were made to amend the law. All of them were hindered by religious opposition, filibustering and the over-cautiousness of governments. In the early 1960s, ALRA entered a new phase of activism, coinciding with the thalidomide tragedy which reopened the debate over therapeutic abortion.[2] Several contemporary sets of figures and poll findings exist to show that the status quo was no longer acceptable in many people's minds. Various sources give different figures, for example, in his critique of the Wilson government, Clive Ponting refers to the tremendous popular support that abortion reform had now acquired: 'an opinion poll in 1965 showed that 72% favoured reform' (Ponting, 1990, pp. 264–5); a Gallup poll taken in 1966 showed a similar picture, with 79 per cent in favour of abortion in cases where the mother's health was in danger, and 71 per cent supporting termination in cases where the 'child may be born deformed' (Charlot, 1998, p. 58).

In September 1965, Lord Silkin introduced a Bill including clauses on rape-related pregnancies and on the social condition of the pregnant woman.[3] As opposed to the previous attempts in the Commons, the Bill was discussed at length. Though harshly criticized and revised, the 'social clause', as it came to be called, was passed at the House of Lords Third Reading in early 1966. Quite significantly, two bishops voted in favour of the termination of pregnancy on the sole ground that the mother was under 16, demonstrating the open-mindedness of the Church of England on this matter (Lord Brain, 1966 Family Planning Association [FPA] conference, 1966, p. 2). Nevertheless, the general election which was held at the time somewhat disrupted the parliamentary agenda and the Bill failed to go through the House of Commons. Its extensive media coverage had, however, fostered discussion in medical and religious institutions as well as in society at large (Marsh and Chambers, 1981, p.14).

The 1966 general election resulted in the re-election of the Labour Party, while introducing generational change with the influx of open-minded young MPs more attuned to the expectations of 1960s Britain. Among the tiny Liberal minority was David Steel, MP for Roxburgh, Selkirk and Peebles, a Church of Scotland minister's son and 28-year-old lawyer. The 'Baby of the House', as he became known, came third in the ballot for Private Members' Bills (Potts, Diggory and Peel, 1977, p. 292).[4] He was then wooed by several pressure groups but when approached by ALRA, Steel eventually set his mind on the cause of abortion. At that time, several options were thus open to women, essentially: to proceed under the system allowed by the 1929 legislation and in rulings like that in the Bourne case (but this would depend heavily on where the future mother lived, the opinions of doctors in that area, and the woman's financial resources – points that Steel was to underline in his speech concluding the Second Reading of his Bill); or to proceed by other means which were all illegal (self-inflicted means, recourse to a friend or to a private individual by a cash payment, which Steel categorized as the most risky in health terms). Finally, by paying between 100 and 200 guineas, a considerable sum of money at the time, a woman could hope to obtain a termination from a surgeon or doctor. This therefore meant that *de facto* a two-tier system existed, in which the poorer sections of society, who often could not afford another child, were forced to risk all the dangers of a back-street abortion, while the upper- and upper-middle classes were able to use all the financial means at their disposal to obtain a medically and legally safe termination. This was a situation that advocates of reform utterly deplored, as Steel made clear in his 1966 speech: 'Any law which means one law for the rich and another for the poor is in itself unsatisfactory and should be examined' (Steel, 1981, p. 50). Back in 1960, Alice Jenkins's (1964) *Law for the Rich* had brought this situation into the open.[5] It was also this social iniquity that David Steel intended to address.

This discrepancy was heightened by the number of illegal operations thought to take place each year. According to an opinion poll commissioned by the ALRA in July 1966, the figure stood at 40,000 operations per year at least, while a figure approaching five times that amount also circulated at the time. Steel argued that the true figure must have been somewhere between the two, yet he added the proviso that this was surely 'the tip of the iceberg' (interview with Lord Steel). When introducing his Bill to reform abortion, Lord Silkin, mentioned above, placed the figure between 100,000 and 300,000. Added to this was the number of deaths caused by such 'botched operations', as Steel qualified them, which he estimated at around 50 per year, once again, describing this as 'the tip of the iceberg' (Ward, 2007).

Another indicator of the widespread recourse to abortion (or rather, attempted abortion) was the extensive sale of 'abortifacients', discreetly referred to as 'female pills'. In 1965, the Birmingham branch of ALRA had conducted an inquiry into the extent and nature of this lucrative trade. Two women and one man from the association had visited 40 establishments in Birmingham and London and had been able to purchase 'remedies' from 12 out of 15 pharmacies, 17 out of 22 drug stores and rubber-goods shops, and two out of three herbalists. Those pills contained either purgatives like castor oil or hazardous substances thought to give 'relief' from 'irregularities'.

In June 1966, David Steel introduced his Bill. Largely based on the Bill sponsored by Lord Silkin,[6] *The Medical Termination of Pregnancy Bill, An Act to Amend and Clarify the Law Relating to the Termination of Pregnancy by Registered Medical Practitioners*, allowed abortion in four cases: (1) if the future mother's physical or mental health were at risk; (2) if there was a major risk that the child would suffer from serious physical or mental handicap; (3) if the future mother's capacity as a mother would be overstrained if she had another child; (4) finally, if a woman was considered defective, became pregnant either under the age of 15 or as a result of being raped.

Provided medical agreement was granted, the operation was to be performed within an NHS hospital or in a registered nursing home. Section 1 (a) of the Bill was basically a clarification of the existing law as it merely codified a practice which had tacitly been accepted by case law since the Bourne case. The main difficulty in drafting a Bill on such a sensitive issue was to 'decide how and where to draw the line'. As David Steel declared, 'We [want] to stamp out the back-street abortions, but it is not the intention of the Promoters of the Bill to leave a wide open door for abortion on request' (HC Deb, c1075). However, for the critics of the Bill, clause 1 (c), the so-called social clause, was tantamount to abortion on demand. Religious groups, and more particularly Catholics, fiercely opposed any form of legalization, though Norman St John-Stevas, at the head of the 32 Catholic MPs, asserted: 'The voice of theology can be raised, although I should be the first to agree that it should not be imposed.'[7]

Generally speaking, the parliamentary debates on abortion did not follow traditional party lines. By the time Steel came third in the annual ballot for Private Members' Bills, the view of the majority in Parliament was certain, as Steel put it himself in his memoirs: 'There was a proven all-party support' (Steel, 1981, p. 50). This support was particularly strong among government ranks and not just for the legislation in question, but also for capital punishment, homosexuality, and divorce. The question that arises, therefore, is why were such popular causes taken up by backbench MPs like Steel, rather than as command legislation? After all, the government had been elected on a socialist programme of reform that would forge a New Britain in 'the white heat of a technological revolution'. One answer might be the economic crisis that the government found itself in when it took office faced with a record balance of payments deficit. However, we are not here to judge the Wilson government's economic record: so could the government have been less radically inclined than it had claimed, or did it lack the political courage required to take up such delicate social issues? Opinion is divided on these questions; for critics, the Prime Minister was conservative by nature and had no real appetite for such major changes. For example, for Clive Ponting, the position of the premier on the matter, as well as that of the First Secretary of State, George Brown, himself a Catholic, was manifest, namely, he just wanted the Bill to go away: 'Wilson and Brown originally wanted to leave the Bill uncompleted and recess as planned at the end of July 1967.' Ponting goes on to claim that Wilson's reluctance to see the Bill progress was based on electoral considerations: 'Wilson was worried by the number of Catholics in his constituency of Huyton' (Ponting, 1990, p. 266). This view is shared by two of Wilson's biographers, Ben Pimlott and Austin Morgan, the latter, more critical of his subject than the former, who argued that Wilson did not wish to 'antagonise' his Catholic constituents (Morgan, 1992, p. 303; Pimlott, 1992, p. 487).

However, electoral considerations work two ways, and in this instance apparently may even have worked in favour of Steel's Bill, with the Leader of the House of Commons, Richard Crossman, calculating how it could benefit the government, since it would 'be a pretty popular measure, especially among working-class women' (Morgan, 1992, p. 303). Such cynical considerations cannot detract from the fact that this measure, as well as the one involving homosexuality, had the backing of many members of the Cabinet and government from all political wings of the Labour Party, including Richard Crossman, Barbara Castle, John Silkin (the Government Chief Whip and son of Lord Silkin), Tony Crosland, Gerald Gardiner, the Health Minister Kenneth Robinson, and Tony Benn, who greeted the 223 to 29 majority in favour of the Bill in the vote at the end of its Commons' Second Reading as 'a notable victory' (Benn, 1988, p. 460).

Polarization between advocates and opponents quickly emerged. The debates were thus marked by a dichotomous phraseology where the emotional dimension ran up against the rational and pragmatic spheres in an 'Enlightenment v. Obscurantism' debate. According to Roy Jenkins, 'The existing law on abortion [is] uncertain and [is] also, and perhaps more importantly, harsh and archaic and... [is] in urgent need of reform' (HC Deb, c1141). Opponents regarded abortion as the first step towards euthanasia, as demonstrated by Jill Knight's speech:

> If we agree that we should have abortion because a mother feels she cannot cope with caring for her child, what about the other end of

the scale?... Plenty of sons and daughters who are grown up and married feel they cannot cope with their elderly parents. Should they be put down too?... It is an utterly inhuman doctrine, yet it would be a perfectly logical next step after this Bill.

(HC Deb c1101)[8]

By questioning the sanctity of life, the Bill was denounced as inconsistent with the founding principles of British society and the abolition of the death penalty passed by Parliament in 1965, as leading critic Norman St John-Stevas made clear in Commons debate:

> The Bill is fundamentally flawed because it rests on denial of the sacred character and value of human life. The principle was recently reaffirmed by the House when it voted for the abolition of the death penalty... It rests upon the moral principle, all but universally accepted, that human life has an intrinsic value in itself and that innocent human life should never be taken.
>
> (St John-Stevas, HC Deb, c1155)

The proponents of the Bill and of the social clause in particular counteracted, highlighting the principle of human dignity and the right of individuals to develop in a decent environment.

The ethical debate focused mainly on foetal abnormalities. Renée Short, MP for Wolverhampton, quoted a National Opinion Poll according to which 91 per cent of the British women surveyed were favourable to abortion when there was a substantial risk of the child being born seriously handicapped, whether mentally or physically (HC Deb, c1161). Though abortion in such cases was approved of by the BMA Gerrard Commission and the Conservative Political Centre, many MPs, including W. Wells, raised concerns about the destruction of potentially healthy foetuses. The eugenic nature of the clause was another bone of contention, sparking heated reactions, with opponents even making references to Nazism: 'There is something utterly repugnant to me here, because it so reminds me of Hitler's conception of a race of perfect physical specimens. Is it right that only the physically perfect should be allowed to survive?' (Jill Knight, HC Deb, c1103).

The 'social clause' allowing abortion on social grounds turned out to be a major sticking point. On Steel's own admission, it represented the most contentious section of the Bill. During the House of Commons debates, the BMA and the Royal College of Gynaecologists (RCOG) published articles considering that all factors affecting the pregnant woman's health had to be taken into account. These included age, social difficulties and the circumstances under which the pregnancy had started, recognizing the vital role of the socio-economic background as a constituent part of mental and physical health. Beyond purely medical aspects, this clause thus put the social dimension at the heart of the legal framework and formed the backbone of the Bill. One of its objectives was to relieve practitioners of the legal burden. As a matter of fact, a generous and liberal interpretation of the existing law left a certain degree of discretion to surgeons who could claim that the patient's mental health was jeopardized. For Steel, it was, however, important to set a clear framework and lessen doctors' responsibility. According to W. F. Deedes, MP for Ashford, 'doctors today are confronted with a choice between humanity and illegality' (HC Deb, c1091).

As the large majority of Members supported the Bill, all pro-life pressure groups joined forces against it. In September 1966, the Society for the Protection of Unborn Children (SPUC) was set up, three years before 'Life'. SPUC fiercely militated against the Bill and embarked upon a fiery war of attrition and influence against ALRA (Marsh and Chambers, 1981, p. 19). SPUC was made up of humanists, agnostics, Christians, but also of several renowned gynaecologists, including Aleck Bourne, whose membership was highly symbolic. After his acquittal, Aleck Bourne had been praised by ALRA and other pro-choice associations. Yet, he had remained very wary and strict regarding the interpretation of the law. Tired of the 'abortionist' image, he joined SPUC to openly assert his opposition to abortion on request which he considered to be a disaster (Hindell and Simms, 1971, p. 168).

With passion often prevailing over reason, several eminent medical professors went so far as to display bottled foetuses at public meetings or to play tape-recorded foetal heartbeats in order to describe the pain felt by the foetus during the operation. These rather unorthodox methods obviously aimed to strike a chord and prompt guilt and shame among the most ardent advocates of abortion. As a result of this fierce opposition, some MPs decided to withdraw their support for the Bill for electoral reasons (Potts, Diggory and Peel, 1977, p. 294). In this matter, we have already mentioned Harold Wilson's over-cautiousness. As the chief parliamentary lobbyist during the passage of the 1967 Act through Parliament, Alastair Service, later declared:

> It was clear that we were not going to get strong positive support from the Government in the way that Harold Wilson had supported the ending of capital punishment. Wilson never mentioned any of the other social law reforms in his memoirs; quite

extraordinarily he thought Private Member's Bill reforms to be of no importance. However, we had in Roy Jenkins, Dick Crossman, Douglas Houghton, Tony Crosland and Barbara Castle formidably strong cabinet supporters.

(Furedi and Hume, 2007, p. 28)

In his memoirs, Steel acknowledges the 'coincidence of support' of the senior ministers cited above, which, in his words, was to prove 'decisive' for the success of his Bill (Steel, 1981, p. 53). He stresses that among them, one Cabinet Minister stands out 'notably' in terms of his contribution to the successful passage of the Abortion Act, namely, Roy Jenkins, appointed Home Secretary in 1965. This support was to prove vital as the comparatively simple success of the Bill's Second Reading was to be followed by what Steel qualified as a 'protracted and sometimes bad-tempered Committee stage of the Bill', when amendments could be discussed (ibid., p. 52).

Perhaps the best way to appreciate Jenkins' role and the methods he adopted to facilitate the Bill's passage through Parliament, is to return to the question why the government did not itself undertake to introduce these reformist Bills. To begin with, once Steel came third in the ballot mentioned above, it was Jenkins who convinced him to sponsor one of the major pieces of legislation. In the 1966 election campaign, Steel had openly supported what he classed as 'the touchy subjects of homosexuality and abortion' (ibid., p. 50). Initially, Jenkins wished the young Liberal MP to introduce a Bill to decriminalize homosexuality, but Steel feared that such a measure would be highly unpopular among his own constituents. Steel acknowledges the part luck played in his ending up sponsoring abortion reform, first, with a long parliamentary session due to the State Opening of Parliament in April 1966, which would allow more time for debate of any Private Members' Bill, and his third place in the ballot (ibid., p. 49).

These issues provoked strong feelings and controversy not only within the Cabinet, the government, and all of the political parties, but in society in general. As we have seen, there was strong backing for the four different major reforms undertaken, but within the ranks of the government, certain ministers were fiercely opposed to one or all of the major reforms proposed. George Brown, as we have seen, objected categorically to both abortion and the decriminalization of homosexuality, and he was joined by the Scottish Secretary, Willie Ross. Some in the government found themselves in the paradoxical position whereby they expressed the same strong support for one Bill, and disapproval of the other. This was the case particularly of Lord Longford, an outspoken backer of the Sexual Offences Bill and a fierce critic of any reform of the abortion law. Similarly, outside the government, but in the majority ranks, Leo Abse, the backbench Labour MP who steered the Sexual Offences Act through Parliament, bitterly opposed Steel's Bill. At the same time, several other ministers were indifferent and felt the government should focus on other priorities. Furthermore, the fact that seven previous attempts to reform the abortion laws showed that any government initiative on the matter could become bogged down in debate with the result that precious parliamentary time would be lost, at a time when the government desperately needed such time to devote to its various emergency economic measures. These legislative failures would also have caused any government to have had second thoughts about embracing reform officially and starting the legislative wheels in motion in their favour in the form of command legislation. Jenkins makes this point eloquently in his memoirs, citing the problems given above: 'I could not have got the Cabinet to agree that they should bear the *imprimatur* of the Government' (Jenkins, 1991, p. 208). Richard Crossman, the Lord President at the time, also took an active part in elaborating the tactics put in place by Jenkins. In 1970, he reflected in his diaries on the risks such legislation posed and how the decision to grant a free vote had helped avoid irreparable damage to the government: 'We have got away with changes which were long overdue and which no Cabinet would ever make before because these matters of conscience would cause a Government split' (Crossman, 1991, p. 681).

Jenkins adopted a stratagem of government neutrality while at the same time allowing Labour MPs a free vote on the Bills. This meant that no party whip was placed on the votes over the Bills.[9] Allowing a free vote on these measures meant that backbench MPs and ministers alike were able to act according to their personal convictions on major social issues without having to take partisan obligations into consideration, as Richard Crossman noted in his diaries: 'The Government remains technically neutral, so that the consciences of people like George Thomas and Willie Ross and, in the case of abortion, Shirley Williams, can be squared' (ibid., p. 681).

We have mentioned that the Bills were not Government Bills, but were rather Private Members' Bills. In Parliament, around 95 per cent of all legislation introduced is official government legislation. Among the remaining Bills, a certain amount is introduced by backbench MPs, usually backing a cause they firmly believe in or have been lobbied to support, or which they wish to introduce into public debate, knowing full well that it will fall at the first parliamentary hurdle: hence the title Private Members' Bills as opposed to Government Bills. Such legislation often stands little chance of success, as the time allocated to its debate is minimal and such Bills often fall victim to such time-wasting tactics as filibustering or constant interruptions and questions on the part of opponents. On top of the free vote given to MPs, Jenkins therefore also opted to give the sponsors of the Bills a greater chance of success in the form of the allocation of Parliamentary time:

> The Government, while nominally neutral, would free the backbench sponsors of these measures of the normal bane of Private Members' Bills, which is a shortage of time. The Government would allow the House to sit for as long as was necessary to get the Bills through.
>
> (Jenkins, 1991, p. 208)

The Lord President and Leader of the House, Richard Crossman, aided the cause of Steel's Bill even further, by accepting to grant Steel two extra night sittings for the committee stage to run its course in July 1967. Steel recalls going to see Crossman in his office to ask him for extra time and having to drink a disgusting mixture of whisky and brandy poured absent-mindedly into his glass by the Lord President as a sacrifice well worth making (Lord Steel, BBC).

The Home Secretary also enhanced further the likelihood of the Bills gaining sufficient votes in a division, by offering the services and expertise of the Home Office ministerial machine and staff. Nevertheless, although the Sexual Offences Act passed its Report Stage and Third Reading in an eight-hour, one-night sitting, the latter stages of the passage of the Abortion Bill were different altogether. Indeed, in the words of Jenkins, it 'was a higher fence', ostensibly because 'it had more skilful opposition', especially on the part of Leo Abse, the Conservative MP Jill Knight and, in particular, her fellow Tory, Norman St John Stevas, a staunch Roman Catholic (Jenkins, 1991, p. 209). Jenkins and Crossman made it clear to opponents, however, that they were prepared to continue to the bitter end, even if that meant extending debate into the weekend. Whether or not this was true or a bluff, the tactic worked, as debate finally came to an end on 14 July, a division was held and the Bill was approved by a majority of 167 votes to 83. For Jenkins, this was the crowning moment of a long struggle: 'It was indeed the liberal hour' (ibid., p. 209).

The Bill that was passed did not, however, contain the same clauses as at the Second Reading, several amendments having been accepted. The agreement of two doctors was still required for an abortion to be sanctioned. Furthermore, the legislation still legalized termination in the case of any threat to the mother's well-being or the risk of serious handicap to the child. However, the references to rape, to a defective mother or a girl aged below 15 becoming pregnant were dropped. A conscience clause was added, allowing medical staff opposed to abortion not to perform it against their will. This concern had often been voiced, especially by the Catholic Doctors Guild. Jointly drafted by Norman St John-Stevas and David Steel, the clause states that:

> No person shall be under any duty, whether by contract, or by any statutory or other legal requirements, to participate in any treatment authorized by this Act to which he has a conscientious objection. However, if the pregnant woman's life is endangered, this clause does not apply.
>
> (The 1967 Abortion Act)

Much to ALRA members' dismay, David Steel had had to yield to the pressure from the BMA, the RCOG and the Church of England and the social clause was withdrawn. This had, however, been the only way of safeguarding the Bill altogether, as Diane Munday, the then vice-chair of ALRA later admitted: 'Our legislation, being the first, had to have limits to get through; it was that or nothing...I think we had to do what we did. If we had not accepted compromise, we would have achieved nothing' (Furedi and Hume, 2007, p. 12). In the same spirit, Madeleine Simms, author of *Abortion Law Reformed* (with Keith Hindell) and founding trustee of the Birth Control Trust declared: 'I was unhappy about the absence of a straight social clause, but we had to settle for what we could – in this case the "medico-social" clause as it came to be called' (Furedi and Hume, 2007, p. 16). Thus, after some bitter debate, the social background could still be taken into account at the doctor's discretion. Subsection (2) reads:

> In determining whether the continuance of a pregnancy would involve such risk of injury to health as is mentioned in paragraph (a) of subsection (1) of this section, account may be taken of the pregnant woman's actual or reasonably foreseeable environment.
>
> (The 1967 Abortion Act)

Despite Roy Jenkins' satisfaction at the legislation's passage through the Commons, the Bill was still not law, having to pass through the House of Lords. This proved to be 'another tortuous process', according to Steel (1981, p. 54). Indeed, a stand-off occurred between proponents and opponents over two amendments passed in the upper house. While one called for the presence of a specialist to decide whether each individual abortion was appropriate or not, the other sought to remove the terms 'family' and 'children' from the text. After public outcry and a media campaign, along with further debate in the Lords, the amendments were overturned. Steel's Bill finally received the Royal Assent on 27 October 1967 and came into effect as of 27 April the following year. The whole legislative process, particularly during the committee stage, had been sometimes bitter and acrimonious, becoming personally dangerous for the sponsor and his family who even received several death threats, as Steel noted somewhat ironically:

> I received huge quantities of mail, some of it abusive and some obscene. Some even went to Judy [Steel's wife], who was pregnant twice during the long passage of the Bill. I could not help reflecting that those who were trumpeting the highest moral tones were associated with some of the lowest tactics.
>
> (Steel, 1981, p. 53)

The Abortion Act legalized abortion up to 28 weeks' gestation 'if two registered practitioners are of the opinion, formed in good faith that':

> (a) The continuance of the pregnancy would involve risk to the life of the pregnant woman, or of injury to her physical or mental health or that of any existing children, greater than if her pregnancy were terminated; or
>
> (b)There is a substantial risk that if the child were born it would suffer from such physical or mental sub-normalities as to be seriously handicapped.
>
> (The 1967 Abortion Act)

The logical result of the enactment of the Bill was a net increase in the recorded number of terminations carried out. Figures for England and Wales show that 22,332 were carried out in 1968, mostly among single women. This figure more than doubled the following year to 49,829, which was hardly surprising given that the Act only came into force on 27 April 1968, while the figures released for each year thereafter covered a full calendar year. Figures rose and occasionally stabilized, but peaks were reached in 1973 with 110,568 recorded: 1980 saw 128,900 abortion operations performed and 156,200 in 1987 (Butler and Butler, 1994, p. 340). According to the latest Department of Health statistics, the figure for 2010 was 189,000, 8 per cent up on the 2000 figure of 175,542. These figures have led many to argue that an abortion can now be obtained very easily, a point made in the BBC TV documentary on the Abortion Act cited above: 'today, despite it being stricter than in other countries, abortion is, *de facto*, on demand' (Lord Steel, BBC). When introducing the Bill in 1967, Steel had stated that his intention was in no way to bring about such a situation where abortions could be obtained on request, but rather to eradicate the horrors of back-street abortions. When questioned on this point recently, his view was clear: the answer is not to tinker with the abortion law, but to improve sexual education and knowledge about contraception (Lord Steel, BBC).

The Act does not extend to Northern Ireland which continues to enforce the unamended 1861 *Offences against the Person Act*. In 1967, Northern Ireland had its own parliament and the issue of abortion was left for it to decide. Nevertheless, it did not take up the issue and when Direct Rule returned, Westminster never extended abortion rights to the women of Northern Ireland. According to Abortion Rights, the national pro-choice campaign resulting from the merger of ALRA and NAC (National Abortion Campaign), over 54,000 women have been forced to make the difficult journey to Britain since the 1967 Abortion Act was passed. Furthermore, their abortions can be performed only in private nursing homes at a minimal cost of £450.[10]

Several attempts were made to amend or to repeal the Abortion Act in the years that followed. In February 1970, a Conservative MP proposed an amendment to the Abortion Act calling for a gynaecologist to be present at each operation. It was defeated in a free vote in the Commons, but only after the Wilson Cabinet debated the ins and outs of the amendment and what strategy to adopt. This shows that feelings still ran high two and a half years after the passage of the Act, and underlines the continued influence of the anti-abortion lobby.

In the early 1970s, following further intensive lobbying, the recently elected Heath government set up a committee of enquiry under Justice Lane to establish the merits of the Act. The main objective of the proponents in setting up the committee had been to find the arguments or evidence that would show the reform had been a failure or had not brought any benefits, medically or otherwise, so that it should be removed. However, such hopes were dashed when the Lane Committee's report was published, concluding as follows: 'We have no doubt that the gains facilitated by the Act have much outweighed any disadvantages for which it has been criticized' (Steel, 1981, pp. 54–5).

This does not mean that the rules governing abortion have not been changed in any way. The Abortion Act was amended by the 1990 Human Fertilisation and Embryology Act which lowered the time limit and permitted the termination of pregnancy up to 24 weeks' gestation, as a result of advances in neo-natal medicine, leading to the survival of very premature babies. In cases where there is a grave risk to the woman's life or a grave threat to her mental or physical health or if the foetus shows signs of severe abnormality, an abortion is allowed after 24 weeks. Debate in recent years has included calls to reduce the time limit to 22 weeks or even less, while supporters of abortion want to make procedures easier and quicker, mainly by removing the requirement that women obtain the agreement of two registered doctors, thereby allowing abortion to be carried out as early as possible. In 2010, 91 per cent of the abortions performed in England and Wales were carried out at under 13 weeks' gestation. Some 77 per cent were at under 10 weeks compared to 58 per cent in 2000 (ONS figures for 2010).

If we now turn to the question of the impact of David Steel's Act, the first obvious observation, is that thanks to the legislation, all women, whatever their social status or financial situation, could have access to a free medical termination of an unwanted pregnancy in an NHS hospital or state-approved clinic. This ended the hypocritical two-tier system that had existed beforehand. More importantly from a health and safety point of view, the whole squalid, dangerous practice of illegal or back-street abortions had been removed. As the social historian Arthur Marwick noted, women no longer faced the 'attendant horror and danger' that this presented (Marwick, 1988, p. 152). It is interesting to compare the attitude of David Steel towards the reform that he fought so hard to defend. At the time he referred to the Bill he was sponsoring as a 'relatively minor but significant social reform in our country' (O'Grady, 2007). In a BBC TV documentary made in 2010, Steel reiterated this view while acknowledging with hindsight that, despite his initial view, the Abortion Act did have a significant impact on the health and well-being of women in Britain: 'I didn't realize at the time that people 40 years on would be looking back and saying this was a fundamental change, but it was' (Lord Steel, BBC).

Conclusion

The 1967 Abortion Act is a product of its time, reflecting and codifying the concerns of 1960s Britain. As encapsulated in Lord Brain's opening speech to the Family Planning Association conference a few months before the introduction of David Steel's Bill, Britain was then marked by fast-changing notions of society[11] where what had once been held as immutable was unrelentingly challenged:

> One outstanding feature of this age is the speed with which ideas change...The current rate of change of ideas is unprecedented. It is very apparent in the realm of sexual ethics...Ideas which were proclaimed as embodying natural law, and therefore quite immutable, are dissolving under our eyes. We must therefore be prepared to look at all our ideas afresh; and it is in that spirit that we are meeting today.
>
> (FPA conference, 1966, p. 1)

Yet, in spite of this favourable background, as in most moral matters, British attitudes to abortion were ambivalent and there existed quite a sharp contrast between social attitudes of condemnation and evidence of a widespread resort to abortion. The polarization of the parliamentary debates is a reflection of the ambiguity within a society torn between a yearning for emancipation from the Victorian moral code and the preservation of social conservatism. The issue of abortion on request was rarely broached but the twofold objective of the 1967 Abortion Act was met, while setting a middle-of-the-road framework. The Act above all meant to legalize what had before been a widespread, hazardous and tacitly accepted practice, by placing it in the hands of professionals. The second objective – the widening of the grounds allowing abortion to the pregnant woman's socio-economic background – represented a real ideological breakthrough. Although this clause was not officially kept, it has, however, been weighed in practitioners' decisions. It has moreover contributed to fostering discussions on women's right to choose. Together with the 1967 National Health Service (Family Planning) Act, this law was a springboard for British feminism and foreshadowed the struggles of the 1970s. As expressed by Roy Jenkins in 1997 for the thirtieth anniversary of the law, it also undermined the assumption according to which the state should seek to impose and enforce morality by law:

> I think broadly that people should as far as possible be free to make their own decisions about their lives, unless they are clearly offending the rights of others. I am often quoted as saying, in 1969, that the permissive society is the civilised society. What I actually said was that people talk about the permissive society and what I would prefer

to ask is whether the liberalising changes we made in the 1960s made Britain a more civilised society. And I would firmly answer, 'Yes'.

(Furedi and Hume, 2007, p. 56)

If we take the government's position and attitude towards the 1967 Abortion Act, it is important to place these considerations in the economic context of the period. The Wilson government inherited a record balance of payments deficit on coming to power and rightly or wrongly chose to give priority to dealing with this over other key policy priorities. A series of economic and financial crises led it to introduce a number of recessionary measures between 1964 and 1967. These were highly unpopular and affected the working classes in particular. We have seen several ministers say that even in normal circumstances a decision to undertake reform of such radically controversial issues as homosexuality and abortion would have been tantamount to committing political suicide. The Labour government was widely divided on both issues and might well have split had the government tried to force its MPs and Ministers in favour of Government Bills to reform them. Furthermore, despite the favourable polls on abortion that we discussed above, with backing particularly strong among middle-class voters, certain sections of public opinion appeared to oppose them, thus representing a risk in electoral terms. This was particularly true of Labour's traditional grass-roots working-class voters, traditionally conservative on social matters, and facing economic hardship, for whom legalizing abortion and homosexuality were either highly unpopular or were not considered important issues. It was therefore preferable to use the methods applied by Jenkins and Crossman to allow backbench MPs to have these measures passed in the form of Private Members' Bills. As a result, these controversial and, according to many, long overdue reforms became not only possible but legal reality, as Wilson's biographer Ben Pimlott puts it:

> For hundreds of thousands, if not millions, of people directly affected – and millions who benefitted later, without knowing when, or how, their liberation came about – these were the important changes of the Wilson administration. Wilson had strong egalitarian feelings, especially about race relations. The other issues did not interest him greatly ... However, he was happy to accept, and encourage a liberal reform programme that had the backing of the Labour Party intelligentsia.
>
> (1992, p. 487)

While the political commentators Chris Cook and Alan Sked have qualified the reforms as 'landmarks' in the history of British society, the social
historian Arthur Marwick described the year 1967 as 'something of an
annus mirabilis as far as liberal legislation in the sphere of sexual mores
was concerned'. In terms of the Abortion Act itself, the fact that thereafter all women could have greater control over their lives and decide
for themselves whether a pregnancy should be continued or not, and in
particular not have to put their health or lives at risk or suffer intense
pain as a result of a botched illegal termination, means that the Act was
indeed a fundamental reform. Justice Lane's conclusion on the benefits
of the Abortion Act, quoted above, sums up perfectly the impact of the
legislation passed by David Steel in 1967.

Notes

1. *Infant Life (Preservation) Act 1929, 1929 Chapter 34 19 and 20 Geo 5*, available at: www.legislation.gov.uk/ukpga/Geo5/19-20/34 (accessed 3 November
   2011).
2. The scandal had a tremendous impact on public views of birth control, family medicine and abortion. The sedative drug was given to thousands of
   pregnant women to calm the nausea they felt during the first term of their
   pregnancy. Many gave birth to children who had serious physical defects
   and the drug was banned in 1961.
3. As far as social reforms were concerned, the House of Lords had already
   voted on the law on decriminalizing homosexuality. The influence of the
   Life Peerage introduced by the 1958 *Peerage Act* could be felt and partly
   accounted for the emergence of more liberal views. Lord Silkin was one of
   the first Life Peers.
4. Beyond this favourable draw, he also benefited from a long parliamentary
   session which lasted from March 1966 to October 1967. He was also supported by key political figures like Kenneth Robinson, Minister of Health,
   Douglas Houghton and Roy Jenkins.
5. See Jenkins (1964).
6. For the 40th anniversary of the 1967 Act, David Steel declared: 'I inherited
   the Bill as it was in the House of Lords, it was Lord Silkin's Bill, not mine',
   cited in Furedi and Hume (2007), p. 51.
7. Norman St John-Stevas, HC Deb, 22 July 1966, vol. 732, cc1067–165, c1153.
   In her book on the Wilson years, Monica Charlot mentioned (1998, p. 61)
   that only 14 of the 32 Catholic MPs were present at the Second Reading of
   the Bill.
8. Jill Knight was MP for Birmingham and a SPUC member. Jill Knight, HC Deb,
   22 July 1966, vol. 732, cc1067–165, c1101.
9. The term 'whip' refers here to the party disciplinary process determining
   how MPs are required by the party leadership to vote in parliamentary
   divisions. A one-line whip simply indicates the party's stance on an issue.
   A two-line whip requires MPs to attend and vote along party lines, unless

an MP is unable to do so but – by an informal, mutual agreement – can arrange for his/her absence to be cancelled out by the absence of an MP from another party who cannot attend either. A three-line whip requires MPs to attend and vote respecting the party line, and failure can often lead to the MP losing his/her party whip, i.e. they are suspended from the party for a length of time determined by the leadership, although the MP continues to sit in the House.

10. Abortion Rights, available at: www.abortionrights.org.uk/content/view/119/92/ (accessed 3 February 2012).
11. These decisive societal changes were also taking place in the United States where the movement for abortion law reform proceeded at an even higher rate. The year 1967 marked a turning point when Colorado passed a reform Bill based on the 1962 American Law Institute (ALI) model penal code. This code suggested legalizing abortion for reasons including 'that continuation of pregnancy would greatly impair the physical or mental health of the mother, or that the child would be born with grave physical or mental defect, or that the pregnancy resulted from rape, incest or other felonious intercourse'. Between 1967 and 1971, 17 states liberalized or repealed their criminal abortion laws (Potts, Diggory and Peel, 1977, pp. 336–7). This reform movement culminated in the 1973 Roe v. Wade Supreme Court decision. This landmark ruling struck down restrictive state laws and prohibited states from proscribing abortion in the first two trimesters of pregnancy (McBride Stetson, 2001, p. 250).

Bibliography

Bartram, Peter (1981) *David Steel: His Life and Politics*, London: W. H. Allen.
BBC (2011) 'Daily Politics', BBC News. Series of interviews entitled 'Change Makers'. 'Lord Steel: Abortion Act a "fundamental change"', 4 February. Available at: http://www.bbc.co.uk/news/uk-politics-11913228.
Benn, Tony (1988) *Out of the Wilderness: Diaries, 1963–67*, London: Arrow Books.
Butler, David and Butler, Gareth (1994) *British Political Facts, 1900–1994*, London: Macmillan.
Charlot, Monica (1998) *The Wilson Years*, Paris: Didier-Erudition.
Crossman, Richard (1991) *The Crossman Diaries: Selections from the Diaries of a Cabinet Minister, 1964–1970*, London: Mandarin.
Family Planning Association (1966) *Conference on Abortion in Britain*, London: Pitman Medical.
Frison, Danièle *et al.* (1998) *Les Années Wilson 1964–1970*, Paris : Ellipses.
Furedi, Ann and Hume, Mick (2007) *Abortion Law Reformers: Pioneers of Change*, London: BPAS, originally published by Birth Control Trust, reissued by bpas.
HC Deb (1966–67) Vols 723–756.
Hindell, Keith and Simms, Madeleine (1971) *Abortion Law Reformed*, London: Peter Owen.
Jenkins, Alice (1964) *Law for the Rich: A Plea for the Reform of the Abortion Law*, 2nd edn, London: Charles Skilton Ltd.
Jenkins, Roy (1991) *A Life at the Centre*, London: Macmillan.
Lord Steel (2011) Interview carried out by the authors on 21 August 2011.

Marsh, David and Chambers, Joanna (1981), *Abortion Politics*, London: Junction Books.

Marwick, Arthur (1988) *British Society Since 1945*, 5th edn, The Pelican Social History of Britain, Harmondsworth: Pelican.

McBride Stetson, Dorothy E. (2001) *Abortion Politics, Women's Movements and the Democratic State: A Comparative Study of State Feminism*, Oxford: Oxford University Press.

Morgan, Austin (1992) *Harold Wilson*, London: Pluto Press.

Morgan, Kenneth O. (1992) *The People's Peace: British History Since 1945*, 2nd edn, Oxford: Oxford University Press.

O'Grady, Sean (2007) 'David Steel: Liberal conscience', *The Independent*, 27 October.

Owen, David (1991) *Time to Declare*, London: Michael Joseph.

Pimlott, Ben (1992) *Harold Wilson*, London: HarperCollins.

Ponting, Clive (1990) *Breach of Promise, Labour in Power 1964 to 1970*, Harmondsworth: Penguin.

Potts, Malcolm, Diggory, Peter and Peel, John (1977), *Abortion*, London: Cambridge University Press.

Rowbotham, Sheila (1999), *A Century of Women: The History of Women in Britain and the United States*, Harmondsworth: Penguin.

Sked, Alan and Cook, Chris (1990) *Post-War Britain: A Political History*, 3rd edn, Harmondsworth: Penguin.

Steel, David (1981) *Against Goliath, David Steel's Story*, London: Weidenfeld and Nicolson.

Steel, David (2004) 'We need to rethink my abortion law – but moves to limit late terminations will never satisfy the "pro-life lobby" ', *The Guardian*, 6 July.

Ward, Lucy (2007) 'The one that won't go away – David Steel changed history by steering through the landmark Abortion Act', *The Guardian*, 24 October.

4
Industrial relations in the 1960s
The end of voluntarism?

Alexis Chommeloux

At the beginning of the 1970s, the Industrial Relations Act was an unambiguous – if short-lived in its particular form – indication that the principles that had governed British industrial relations since the 1894 Royal Commission on Labour, distinguishing them in many significant ways from the American or European models, were no longer underpinned by the 70-year-old consensus that had become a central element of the broader post-war consensus. The 1971 legislation, seen by some as an attempt to Americanize industrial relations (Moran, 1977, p. 83), and by most as an unmitigated failure and the cause of Edward Heath's defeat in 1974, was a clear departure from the British model that had prevailed hitherto. That model was based on voluntary collective bargaining and limited intervention by the state which, while supportive and willing to create the right conditions for collective bargaining, was all the more loath to legislate since there was a consensus among employers and trade unionists that any 'legalization' should be resisted absolutely, not least the legal enforceability of collective agreements which characterized other systems. It was thus described, in prescriptive terms, as 'voluntary pluralism', 'voluntary collectivism', 'collective laissez-faire', or 'legal absenteeism', though there are authors who deplore the fact that the last expression is too dismissive of the role of the state, of 'its intervention in industrial disputes, with the goal of creating permanent bargaining institutions' and of its fostering of a 'climate of opinion in which collective bargaining with trade unions was presumed to be in the national interest' (Howell, 2005, p. 80). All agree, however, on the fact that 'by the Second World War, the central elements of what became known as collective *laissez-faire* were in place' (ibid., p. 79).

This chapter will therefore endeavour to ascertain when this particular consensus started to crumble and how the events and debates that shaped the 1960s led to a Conservative majority intent on passing the Industrial Relations Act, to the repeal of said Act, and in the longer run – despite pledges made by senior Tories in the late 1970s that 'when we return to office we shall not undertake sweeping changes in the law' (HC Deb, 27 January 1978, vol 942, c1847) – to a different, more determined and wide-ranging legislative onslaught on the trade unions in the 1980s. Whatever conclusions are drawn as to what could have been done differently by the protagonists and whether or not a different course could have been set, a vast array of elements in relation with the general consensus or collective bargaining as such made the 1960s a decade crucial to the shaping of future industrial relations in the UK. Among those elements were, *inter alia*, wage drift, strike levels, the economy generally, perceptions of the economy and industrial relations-related phenomena, changes in the level at which bargaining was conducted, ideological evolutions within the main parties, the role of judges, the use of legislation or threats thereof, and the more or less rational fears and preferences of the unions and employers.

Whether the more general 'post-war consensus' was in danger in the 1960s has been much debated and it seems over-simplistic to assert that it took the oil crises of the early 1970s, the Winter of Discontent or the determination of Margaret Thatcher to shake it to its foundations. If the Butskellism of the 1950s was a comforting exaggeration that happened to minimize the reality of disagreements on monetary policy or taxation, and if, as will be argued here, the industrial relations element of the consensus *had* begun to crumble in the 1960s, it may seem even more untenable to consider that the post-war consensus could have been unaffected. That said, the purpose and scope of this chapter are more modest as it will merely focus on the transformations undergone by industrial relations in the context of the economic, social, political and ideological changes of a tumultuous decade.

Voluntarism in doubt

There is still a great deal of disagreement as to when the traditional model of voluntarism ceased to offer a wholly realistic account of the realities of industrial relations. Unsurprisingly, the question often conjures up 1979, a year associated by many with the end – or the beginning of a process leading to the imminent end – of the more general economic and social consensus. Auerbach, in his book on the industrial relations policies of the 1980s, reminds us that, as late as 1990, the possible accommodation of that decade's legislation 'within this analytical framework' was still 'a matter for debate'. However, he goes on to add:

> notwithstanding the continuity of form of the structural legal framework through (the early 1960s), the continued tenability of voluntarism as the sole basis for Government policy was already a pressing issue on the agenda by the time of the return of a Labour Government in 1964.

Quoting one of the main proponents and contemporary architects of collective voluntarism, he also evokes Kahn-Freund's awareness, in 1967, at a time when the Donovan Commission (*Royal Commission on Trade Unions and Employers' Associations, 1965–1968*)[1] was still at work 'of the magnitude of the threat ... to the old traditions' (Auerbach, 1990, pp. 14–15). The Royal Commission's terms of reference were indeed 'to consider relations between managements and employees and the role of trade union and employers' associations ... with particular references to the law'.

In any case, between the time when Heath, as Minister of Labour in 1960, provided the Joint Consultative Committee of the National Joint Advisory Council (NJAC)[2] with a programme of discussion instructing them to improve industrial relations while remaining an 'abstentionist' (Moran, 1977, p. 19) and the introduction in 1970 of the interventionist Industrial Relations Bill under his premiership, the changes that occurred are multifaceted and the web of elements that explain why – temporarily or durably – the model was radically challenged is a complex one. What seems defendable, however, is that the early 1960s marked a change, with the increasing concern about the number of strikes, and particularly of unofficial strikes, which caused many politicians to gradually lose patience with the consensus that had more or less been the hallmark of the 1950s and had been symbolized by the longevity as Minister of Labour of non-partisan, voluntarist Monckton. No-one could possibly argue convincingly that the Conservative Party and indeed Conservative ministers were completely of one mind throughout the 1950s. Collective *laissez-faire* in a context of full employment resulted in a great deal of ambiguity: how indeed could the government abstain, or claim to abstain, when their economic policy objectives caused an imbalance in collective bargaining and led to wage claims that constituted a long-term risk for the economy? This inherent indecision was manifest in 1957, for example, when, as the government was facing the worst industrial unrest since 1926,

Macmillan and Macleod, the then Minister of Labour 'initially encouraged the engineering employers to resist a large wage claim, but having urged resistance when it came to the critical point, exercised pressure on the employers to reach a settlement' (ibid., p. 17). In such a context of chronic indecision and vacillation as regards wage negotiations,[3] there were naturally those in Tory circles whose impatience with the status quo manifested itself, though ministers and whips were quick to reprimand those who called for a Royal Commission on trade union activity and legislation to follow. *A Giant's Strength*, published in 1958 by Conservative lawyers, advocated legal restrictions on various types of industrial action. It called for secondary action and strikes aimed at enforcing the closed shop to be made illegal, for the introduction of an American-style cooling-off period and for the organization of a ballot where industrial action could have serious economic effects.

By the early 1960s, a time when the schizophrenia of Tory ministers on wage claims was as blatant as ever, the relationship between the unions and the Conservatives had evolved in a way that was described as follows:

> a lingering suspicion which was a legacy of the events before 1939; the relatively amicable relationship painstakingly established in the late forties and fifties; and, by the early 1960s the growing impatience with what seemed – in the eyes of Conservative ministers of Labour – to be a failure of union leaders to control their members in the national interest.
>
> (Moran, 1977, p. 20)

To make matters worse, the UK economy, while still producing full employment and unprecedented riches, was lagging behind other comparable economies, and a general perception of decline and even decadence was beginning to pervade society. As strikes were widely considered to account for the loss of productivity, the unions were cast as ideal villains, particularly in the press. Unreasonable wage demands along with unconstitutional, wildcat strikes and a more general 'strike-proneness'[4] were deemed responsible for Britain's status as the new Sick Man of Europe.

A doctrine with a history

The distinctive nature of national industrial relations made things that much easier for the unions' critics. While the British system was conspicuous – until the 1960s as we shall see – for the quasi-absence of legislation protecting individual employment rights, the collective system had developed in reaction to the hostility of judges and was thus founded on a limited number of 'abstentionist statutes' which had established a loose, voluntary system where trade unions were granted immunities rather than rights, as was the case overseas. The 1875 Conspiracy and Protection of Property Act is a perfect example of the logic behind the system that emerged. The 1871 Trade Union Act had aimed, *inter alia*, at protecting unions against prosecution in the event of strikes. In 1872, a judicial decision interpreted the law as to allow a return to a situation where criminal conspiracy could be used against organizers of industrial action. In the famous words of Kahn-Freund, the 1875 Act that followed ensured that

> two or more persons (could not) be indicted for conspiracy if the act they agreed or combined to do or to procure would not in itself have been a crime... provided it was to be done in contemplation or furtherance of a trade dispute.
>
> (Kahn-Freund, 1972, p. 229)

This logic was reiterated in 1906 when the Trade Disputes Act came to the rescue after the judicial hostility of the 1890s flourished as the century turned. With the notorious Taff Vale (Taff Vale Railway Co v. Amalgamated Society of Railway Servants, 1901, UKHL 1) ruling, where civil law was used to formidable effect where criminal law no longer could, crippling damages became as significant a threat as fines and imprisonment had been before 1875. Since the Tories were reluctant to take civil law out of industrial relations as they had criminal law, the Liberals did so in 1906 and the Trade Disputes Act granted the unions extensive immunities for almost any action that was in furtherance of a trade dispute.

This reliance on immunities rather than positive rights was never seriously called into question by trade unionists, and though it was legislation that had protected them, they did not call for more and remained, to the bitter end, favourable to a 'voluntary system' which limited the role and scope of the law. The logic of the fundamental statutes, along with an understandable distrust of judicial – and by extension legal – solutions meant that, notwithstanding the specificities of wartime and the necessities of the immediate post-war period,[5] collective *laissez-faire* was never challenged except by small minorities (for example, corporatist elements in the Conservative Party in the 1930s).

Consequently, the unions entered the 1960s, a decade obsessed with the idea of decline, as the beneficiaries of immunities and privileges, i.e., to sections of society that called for legislation to control industrial action, unions appeared as beneficiaries of special, undue favours and prerogatives. As Howell points out, after arguing that there is a strong point to be made that the unions were the *victims* of decline rather than its *cause*, from the end of the 1950s, 'regardless of the reality of trade union power, it became a central cultural trope, reappearing every time the level of industrial conflict became elevated or concern about economic decline heightened' (Howell, 2005, p. 4). Howell also reminds us that *I'm All Right Jack*, the 1959 film starring Peter Sellers as a Leninist shop steward was hugely popular and obtained several British Film Awards.[6] So, beyond the clichés conveyed by the press, the cinema and cabbies, and beyond the ideological interpretations of the dyed-in-the-wool voluntarists, corporatists and legal interventionists, what matters is to attempt to determine what was really happening in the 1960s that may have damaged collective *laissez-faire* and brought about a change in the organization of industrial relations, and whether or not it had a radical impact on the British model.

Borrowing the notions from Friedman (Friedman, 1951, Chapters X and XI) and adapting them, Auerbach, while acknowledging the reality of Kahn-Freund's claim that all major political parties in the 1950s agreed about the social value of collective bargaining and the right to strike, evokes the 'frictional', the 'structural' and the eventual 'political' effects of industrial conflict, in general terms and in the more specific terms of the context of the following decade's demands. Regarding the frictional aspects of industrial strife, the 'small-scale, unofficial, "wild-cat" disruptions' characteristic of the 1960s – as opposed to the 'large-scale, official, frequently public-sector' action of the following decade – did not necessarily worry the voluntarists who felt the framework of collective bargaining could be reviewed without endangering the voluntarist edifice. The structural effects on incomes and inflation and other macro-economic indicators, and the subsequent political effects, they may or may not have perceived as threatening the 'doctrine'. Auerbach asks whether these effects were ignored by the voluntarists and whether this apparent ignorance or this tendency, specific to the post-war consensus, to 'take such matters outside the range of political controversy and debate' constituted a flaw in the doctrine. His answer is that the structural and political effects of collective bargaining were in fact central to it, but that the persistence of the cross-party consensus on so many economic and social issues reassured them that the doctrine was not flawed. He also believed that this, along with 'the continuing commitment of Labour governments both in the 1960s and 1970s to the maintenance of a voluntarist framework', masked a growing questioning of a 1950s' model 'in the changed circumstances of the succeeding decades' (Auerbach, 1990, p. 14). Other historians and industrial relations specialists place greater emphasis on the questioning of the model rather than on the commitment to it or the masking of the mounting doubts. Marsh insists that the Labour governments over the two decades 'turned to a supply-side management and a neo-corporatist solution' that indicated that 'the pillars of voluntarism began to crumble in the 1960s' (1992, p. 5).

The pillars begin to crumble

Many agree that the balance between the analytical models, the 'traditions', changed most visibly under the Labour administration elected in 1964, but that these changes only confirmed a tendency that had become apparent, at least in the area of industrial relations, when their Tory predecessors were in office. The Conservative attitude that had been dominant since 1951, in apparent compliance with the broader consensus, increasingly came to be seen as ambiguous and even schizophrenic. Examples abound of tensions, inconsistencies and indecision, and nowhere as evidently as in the area of wage claims. The reconciliation of traditional collective *laissez-faire* and the role of government in maintaining a high level of employment became less and less convincing:

> Successive Conservative Chancellors urged the unions to restrain their wage demands – in other words to subdue the function which they had been assigned by the party before the 1951 election – while Conservative Cabinets, and the minister of Labour as their agent, conceded the unions' case in most instances.
>
> (Moran, 1977, p. 17)

Particularly in engineering where the problem worsened throughout the 1960s (Wigham, 1973, Chapters 8 and 9). Though the discourse remained officially abstentionist and voluntarist, and though those Tories who called for a Royal Commission to look into trade unions were asked to toe the line, the legal incursions started before the return to office of Labour. Dealing with the tensions meant legal absenteeism could not remain wholly unadulterated, if it had ever been that. Worried with 'the faltering consensus and...the wastefulness of a "Stop-Go" economic policy that appeared pitifully amateurish', the state also looked abroad and 'for the first time outside the demands of world war, the state embarked on a series of social partnership strategies that aimed not only to reverse Britain's relative economic decline but also to provide the remedy for social unrest' (Williams, 2002, p. 57). In other words, 'talk of imaginative planning experiments abroad was on every up-to-date politician's lips' (Pimlott, 1992, p. 276). The project was taken up enthusiastically by Wilson's incoming government with the setting up of the National Plan, that was to plan economic growth over five years, and the National Board for Prices and Incomes (NBPI), that was to control wages, but the enthusiasm was short-lived: 'For many people it was a great moment. But it was only a moment. Indeed one could date the life-cycle of the Plan as "conceived October 1964, born September 1965, died (possibly murdered) July 1966"' (Opie, 1972, p. 170). Though it was not successful in the long run and never became a permanent feature of British industrial relations, the experiment with planning nonetheless accompanied the emergence of what is still described as neo-corporatism – tripartite institutions survived the National Plan and did find a role – the decline of voluntarism and increased government intervention via legislation. As early as 1963 with the Contracts of Employment Act, legislation was used by the Conservatives which was followed by more and more Labour legislation from 1964 onwards – mainly in the area of workers' individual rights to start with and then, as economic and industrial conditions seemed to dictate, in the sacrosanct area of collective bargaining.

In that context, the report most frequently associated with in-depth reflection into the possible future – or futures – of industrial relations in the second half of the decade, the Donovan Report, was bound to be a complex beast to consider. On the one hand, its conclusions, with very few exceptions, reaffirmed the dogma, not least because of the role played by Kahn-Freund, Flanders or Clegg in the Commission's work. On the other hand, perhaps more significantly, as it returned to office in 1964, Labour was unconvinced about the tenability of relying solely on voluntarism and was hoping for the backing of a respectable, independent Royal Commission in order to introduce legislation. As the frictional effects came to bear and became perceived as more structural, the resulting political effects took the form of the setting-up of the Royal Commission, in 1965, in the hope that it would add gravitas and coherence to a change of course. They later gave rise to *In Place of Strife*, a White Paper that made no secret of the fact that voluntarism was no longer the preferred formula and whose main proposals concerned the registration of unions, the possibility of making collective agreements legally binding, a discretionary power which would have allowed the Secretary of State to impose an American-style cooling-off period or require a ballot before industrial action, and the setting-up of an industrial board able to fine unions for breach of the Secretary of State's orders. The said board was also supposed to hear complaints made by individual members against their union, and individuals were to be protected against unfair dismissal and granted the right to belong to a union (*In Place of Strife: A Policy for Industrial Relations*). What Donovan achieved, or failed to achieve, with its endorsement of voluntary collective bargaining and its emphasis on the employers' failure to formalize plant- and company-wide bargaining procedures – which had become increasingly decentralized – cannot mask the fact that the period almost brought about a change of software that government and, at times, its industrial partners were endorsing, beginning to endorse or on the verge of endorsing. That period marked, as Moran put it, a 'dialogue' between two traditions of collectivism: the voluntarist which excludes legal intervention and the corporatist which, while not necessarily involving any great measure of legal intervention, considered legislation as a very useful tool on that particular occasion.

The corporatist elements were clearly visible, from the start of the decade, in the economic strategy that developed in the 1960s and 1970s. The National Economic Development Council or 'NEDC' was conceived in 1961, set up the following year and epitomized that tripartite, corporatist solution that went out of fashion in the 1980s.[7] The NEDC's aim was to set production targets and issue guidelines with regard to pay awards, little 'Neddies' were set up in specific industries and 'Nicky' (the National Incomes Commission) was created in 1962 to arbitrate wage disputes. Neo-corporatism affected related areas such as vocational training, for instance, where the 'voluntarist tradition' had previously reigned unchallenged. Breaking with that tradition, policy-makers keen to improve labour efficiency were forced by Britain's loss of competitiveness, its employers' failure to coordinate vocational training and the need to reform apprenticeship, to find a 'new consensus on the role of the state in training' (Keep and Mayhew, 1994, p. 309). What ensued was a Conservative White Paper leading to Labour's Industrial Training Act of 1964, 'a watershed in peacetime state intervention in British training' which enabled ministers 'to establish Industrial Training Boards [and] set up a Central Training Council (CTC) to advise the government on training matters' (Buxton *et al.*, 1994, p. 310). A later statute, in the

early 1970s, consecrated corporatism with the replacement of the CTC
with the Manpower Services Commission, a tripartite body involving
the government, the CBI and the TUC.[8]

Collective *laissez-faire* vs the law

Whether, despite the emergence of such neo-corporatist features via legislation, there was a return to the 'old traditions' following the demise
of the National Plan, the voluntarist recommendations of Donovan,
the rejection of *In Place of Strife* and the subsequent failure – by the
Conservatives – to make the Industrial Relations Act work, or whether
the 1960s witnessed or set in motion a revolution in industrial relations depends to some extent on the analysis of the circumstances
in which the recommendations were made and reforms rejected. The
answer to that question also relies on potentially differing definitions of
voluntarism and labour law, and on the relative importance accorded to
changes affecting the voluntary consensus.

First, regarding the circumstances in which Donovan failed to draw
a line under voluntarism and in which some protagonists proved less
desirous of experimenting with the law than they might have been,
Moran's analysis is enlightening, particularly concerning the Labour
Movement and the Royal Commission's internal power relationships. In
the early 1960s, the unions had been concerned mainly with the restoration of the authority of the national leadership and such concerns were
reflected in their evidence before the Commission, but the question of
the role of the state in industrial relations also surfaced, as did divisions on the subject. The TUC 'put forward a purist case for keeping
the state in its place' opposing the legal enforcement of union recognition (Moran, 1977, p. 40), but individual unions were more hesitant:
the General and Municipal Workers Unions (GMWU) had a 'selective
and functional' approach to state intervention and did not necessarily
oppose a cooling-off period. Given certain guarantees, notably on the
closed shop, the Amalgamated Engineering Union (AEU) 'might be willing to "outlaw" unofficial strikes' (*Royal Commission on Trade Unions and
Employers' Associations*, 1965–1968, p. 974). On incomes, Moran shows
that a majority could be found on the General Council in favour of legislation in 1966,[9] not only out of a desire to reaffirm central control
but also, for some like the AEU's Bill Carron, because wages could not
sustainably exceed output. As politicians and employers were becoming more and more disillusioned with voluntarism in the second half of
the decade, the unions' temptation to give the law a chance, however,

proved short-lived. The need to accommodate shop stewards and the replacement of Carron at the AEU by Scanlon, a staunch voluntarist, meant that 'after a brief flirtation with compulsory collectivism, by the close of the decade voluntary collectivism had been strongly reasserted' (Moran, 1977, p. 42). This and similar movements within the Parliamentary Labour Party sealed the fate of *In Place of Strife*. Within the Donovan Commission, a group of dedicated individuals, who, according to Moran, illustrated J.S. Mill's dictum that 'One person with a belief is a social power equal to ninety-nine who have only interests' (Moran, 1977, p. 50) were just as effective in damping the government's legal enthusiasm.

Second, as regards the reality of a revolutionary legalization of industrial relations, definitions tend to differ. The 1960s saw various attempts by government to control wage drift through incomes policies. Though the state had of course taken an interest in wages for a long time, notably with the statutory establishment of the Wages Councils,[10] which by the 1960s had lost the confidence of the unions (Collins, 2010, p. 83), such direct intervention to limit pay increases went beyond supporting collective bargaining and, in itself, may be seen as having been fatal to the traditional model. That definitely seems to have been the view of the TUC which, having refused to allow the NEDC to discuss incomes, boycotted the National Incomes Commission, claiming that its intervention would undermine free collective bargaining. For Gospel and Palmer, 'Such policies have difficulty coexisting with voluntarism and, once state institutions are concerned to regulate wage increases, a voluntary system of free collective bargaining becomes untenable' (1993, p. 167). MacIlroy concurs, challenging those tempted to deny the 'limitations of voluntarism' by relying on an excessively narrow definition of labour law: referring to the incomes policy of the 1964–68 period, he contends that 'this legislation... went to the root of collective bargaining and can only be ignored at the expense of a most restrictive definition of labour law' (MacIlroy, 1995, p. 235). According to Wrigley, Wilson's government, when it set up the National Board for Prices and Incomes, intended 'to give the voluntary method every chance to prove that it can be made to work', but adds that 'in so doing [it] explicitly stated it relied on "persuasion and the pressure of public opinion",' before concluding that 1966 saw the 'collapse' of the voluntary approach (Wrigley, 2002, pp. 59–60) with the Prices and Incomes Act.

The 1960s, we mentioned, saw a deluge of legislation but its nature needs to be analyzed in greater detail before it can be assumed that a legalization of industrial relations was at work: some of the legislation constituted the traditional, voluntarist response by government and Parliament to judicial activity. Such statutes, in that they sought to re-establish immunities whittled down by increasingly hostile judges, can be seen as an endorsement of the voluntary model. In 1965, the Trade Disputes Act, like its 1906 namesake, was a swift reaction to the ruling in *Rookes v. Barnard*[11] where the union had been found liable for 'intimidation' for threatening to strike and where the Law Lords had awarded the plaintiff exemplary – i.e. punitive – damages. Another way of looking at it is that the climate was changing and that judges who had for decades seemed to respect the voluntarist consensus – though admittedly they *had* become more and more interested in union rule books in the late 1950s and early 1960s – reconnected with a tradition of activism, particularly at the very end of the decade. In 1969, for example, a new tort – interference with contract – and the use of injunctions against individual union members – and leaders – where the union itself was protected by the 1906 Act weakened the statutory protections,[12] demonstrating the judges' determination and creativity. Moran believes the political implications of this renewal in judicial activism were three-fold: *Rookes v. Barnard*, he claims, emboldened those in the Tory Party who craved radical change, increased union hostility towards the courts, and indirectly caused the setting up of the Donovan Commission with the stimulating debate it entailed (Moran, 1977, p. 35). 1965 was indeed the year of the setting up of the Royal Commission, whose *raison d'être* and purpose are widely believed to have been very different from those of the 1965 Trade Disputes Act.

Other elements in this 'legal deluge' clearly depart from the tradition. Beside the above-mentioned intervention into pay and prices – importantly from an industrial relations point of view – statutes fall into two main categories: those affecting individual rights and those pertaining to collective rights. Some consider that only the latter are truly symptomatic of a challenge to voluntarism, thus casting doubts on the notion that real change intervened before the neo-liberal legislation of the 1980s. And yet for the architects of the doctrine themselves, the voluntary approach 'extended to individual employment matters where, with a few exceptions, it also felt best to keep the law out' (Gospel and Palmer, 1993, p. 159). For Flanders, the system was voluntary not least because individual terms and conditions of employment relied on collective bargaining rather than the law. And even for those whose definition of voluntary collective bargaining underestimates the individual rights element, Gospel adds that legislation regarding individual rights also had a more indirect impact on the fate of the system, since the increased employee power in companies meant 'some employers began to see the solution in . . . political and legal change that would reshape industrial relations in Britain' (ibid., p. 167).

As was mentioned above, Marsh, for one, claims that the Labour governments of the 1960s and 1970s had a consistent neo-corporatist strategy. The success of that strategy depended on 'a developed framework of both individual and collective labour law' (Marsh, 1992, p. 5), and therefore on a series of employment law legislation which from 1967 to 1976 extended workers' rights, focusing on redundancy payments, health and safety, equal pay, race relations, etc. All this, along with the development of new industrial tribunals, indicated a desire to extend the individual rights of workers while in the area of collective rights legal intervention was hoped for with the setting up of a Royal Commission supposed to deliver recommendations that would facilitate industrial relations legislation and with *In Place of Strife*, a White Paper, whose aims were unambiguous, and which, according to Marsh, was 'a nail in the coffin of voluntarism' (ibid., p. 7), even though it never became law.

The gradual breakdown of the voluntary paradigm, whether it be erratic and uneven with one big trough in the early 1970s, or more consistent and planned, as Marsh argues, indicates that the broad consensus was being gnawed at by doubt in both major political parties. Moments of reforming courage, fuelled by a weariness with the economic situation, caused both sides to toy with the idea of trying something comprehensively different, to test radical policies and sometimes withdraw them. These withdrawals sometimes caused a return to the old formula; but each time, the old formula came out weaker, with elements of another formula gradually taking hold. This may have given a sense of continuity to what happened in the 1960s and the 1970s, thus minimizing the importance of the 1960s and conveying the notion that only Thatcher's neo-liberal conservative revolution, when it replaced collective *laissez-faire* with a very different, statute-based, economic *laissez-faire*, put a stop to voluntary collective bargaining. Much academic research has indeed 'tended to prefer the "sharp break" analysis', acknowledging the discontinuity of the early 1970s yet contending that the traditional approach returned unaffected, strengthened even, after this 'exceptional and aberrational episode, of limited lasting import' (Auerbach, 1990, p. 202). But beyond partisan rhetoric at election time, if not a consensus on a new consensus, at least a broad agreement on the need for industrial relations to change began to prevail in the 1960s. A gradual conversion to legalism, numerous parallels in the choices made by successive ministers and a growing incursion of neo-corporatist devices are clearly observable. What it eventually led to was not necessarily inevitable and depended on oil crises, the Winter of Discontent, the balance of forces within parties, unions or Cabinets. From the point of view of the great losers, the unions, it is difficult to say whether a more positive attitude to the law would have been more judicious and more favourable to their cause in the long run and whether it could have led to a rights-based system along the lines of what emerged after 1997, without the statutory bludgeoning of the Thatcher era.

Conclusion

What is argued here is that the old quasi-consensus on industrial relations mutated into another quasi-consensus imposed by circumstances. On the essential subject of the unions, 'in the early 1960s there was tacit agreement between the political parties that, the trade unions having shown themselves unable to set their own house in order, Parliament must impose order by legislation' (Phelps-Brown, 1983, p. 184). On incomes, in the 1960s and 1970s, there was 'no doubt that the government was interventionist for almost the entire period' (Marsh, 1992, p. 9). No fundamental ideological differences existed between the successive governments, or if they existed within sections of their majority they were not acted upon. The conversion to legalism was shared, as was most of the 'neo-corporatist experiment', as was also the awareness that elements of voluntarism would have to be retained to please elements of their respective constituencies – notably the TUC and the CBI. Governments introduced legislation on the basis of the previous majority's bills and shared their bitter experience of electoral defeat for having made similar attempts at changing the system: just as the Industrial Relations Act is believed to have caused the Tories to lose the 1974 general elections, so *In Place of Strife* is thought to have made a Labour victory impossible four years earlier. The brand of neo-corporatism that developed, mixed with traditional voluntary elements, was too weak to withstand the radical, neo-liberal Thatcherite agenda (McIlroy, 1995, pp. 418–19), and Auerbach considers that this tension between macro-economic strategies and the retention of voluntarism constitutes a persistent failure that led to 1979 and what came after (1990, pp. 15–16). The Social Contract in particular pushed some Conservatives away from the consensus on the relations with the unions while simultaneously radicalizing activists of the left against its policies.

A new consensus, less openly assumed and less sure of its doctrinal underpinnings, had come about, emerging from the ashes of the braver attempts of the late 1960s and their early-1970s avatar, the 'legal code of 1971' (Phelps-Brown, 1983, Chapter XI), whose failure is deplored by Phelps-Brown while Weekes *et al.* conclude that it was full of contradictions, 'judged on its utility and found wanting' (1975, p. 232). The Act was, at any rate, one of the most visible symptoms of the new quasi-consensus between successive governments, if not their followers, and many observers having listed the measures contemplated in the late 1960s and their early 1970s equivalents, claim that *In Place of Strife* was nothing less than the blueprint for the 1971 statute, itself 'presented as a means of facilitating many of the reforms advocated by Donovan' (ibid., p. 3). It was a symptom of the new compromise and epitomized its weaknesses.

There was no revolution in the 1960s in the United Kingdom, no workers' revolt, not even a clear politicization of industrial action. Shop stewards were a force to be reckoned with but, even though they were associated with 'wildcat' strikes and portrayed as Leninist militants at the time, the part they played was less negative than was often believed and was a product of a shift in the level at which bargaining took place rather than irresponsible militantism. There was no French-style 'May 1968' involving the labour movement either. If the edges of the 1980s' 'conservative revolution' are unquestionably sharp and the reality of the input of the New Right in that revolution evident – notwithstanding recent reassessments of the strength of the 'wets', indicating that the victory of that ideology was by no means a foregone conclusion in the early stages of Margaret Thatcher's premiership[13] – the 1960s set the course for a dismantling of a British idiosyncrasy, with the Butskellism of the decade before being replaced with a circumstantial compromise that led to the destruction of the consensus, not just in industrial relations, and, 40 years on, to Blatcherism. As for what would have happened had the conjuncture of the late 1960s allowed a comprehensive statutory apparatus to successfully replace collective *laissez-faire*, that question remains unanswered.

Notes

1. Also referred to as The Donovan Report. The remit of the Commission and the significance of the report and its conclusions will be discussed in greater detail below.
2. Bevin made use of the National Joint Advisory Council (NJAC), created before the war to represent both sides of industry, to obtain cooperation

between employers and the unions, and particularly of the Joint Consultative Committee which he had asked the NJAC to set up. See Calder (1992), pp. 115–16.

3. For an analysis of the period from the point of view of disgruntled employers, see Wigham (1973), Chapters 8 and 9.

4. For analyses on the reality of the alleged 'strike-proneness', see Ingham (1974), Turner (1969), Brown (1981) and Coates and Topman (1996).

5. Wartime intervention was symbolized by Bevin's Order 1305 (Conditions of Employment and National Arbitration Order, 1940) which made strikes and lockouts illegal unless they had been reported to the Minister of Labour and National Service who had 21 days to refer the matter for settlement.

6. Other films can be mentioned, such as *The Angry Silence* (1960) or *Carry On Cabby* (1963), along with television programmes such as London Weekend Television's *The Rag Trade*.

7. The NEDC itself saw its role significantly downgraded under Margaret Thatcher and was eventually – and logically – abolished under John Major in 1992.

8. See the Employment and Training Act, 1973.

9. Prices and Incomes Act. 1966. See below.

10. The relevant statutes are: Trade Boards Act, 1909; Trade Boards Act, 1918; Wages Councils Act, 1945 and Wages Councils Act, 1959.

11. Rookes v. Barnard (1964) A.C. 1129.

12. Torquay Hotel Co. Ltd v. Cousins (1969) 2 Ch 106.

13. The National Archives papers reveal, 30 years on, the reality of the battle lines inside the Cabinet in the early 1980s.

Bibliography

Auerbach, Simon (1990) *Legislating for Conflict*. Oxford Monographs on Labour Law, Oxford: Clarendon Press.

Brown, William (1981) *The Changing Contours of British Industrial Relations*, Oxford: Blackwell.

Buxton T., Chapman, P. and Temple, P. (eds) (1994) *Britain's Economic Performance*, London: Routledge.

Calder, Angus (1992) *The People's War: Britain 1939–1945*, London: Pimlico.

Chommeloux, Alexis (2004) 'Américanisation des relations sociales dans la Grande-Bretagne d'après-guerre.' *Histoire & Sociétés: Revue Européenne d'Histoire Sociale*, 11(juillet): 82–96.

Coates, Ken and Topham, Tony (1996) *Trade Unions and Politics*, Oxford: Blackwell.

Collins, Hugh (2010) *Employment Law*, Oxford: Oxford University Press.

Friedman, Milton (1951) 'Some comments on the significance of labor unions for economic policy', in McCord Wright, David (ed.) (1966) *The Impact of the Union: Eight Economic Theorists Evaluate the Labor Union Movement*, New York: A. M. Kelley.

Gospel, Howard F. and Palmer, Gill (1993) *British Industrial Relations*, London: Routledge.

HC Deb, 27 January 1978, vol. 942, cc1818–917.

Howell, Chris (2005) *Trade Unions and the State: The Construction of Industrial Relations Institutions in Britain, 1890–2000*, Princeton, NJ: Princeton University Press.

Ingham, Geoffrey K. (1974) *Strikes and Industrial Conflict: Britain and Scandinavia*, London: Macmillan.

In Place of Strife: A Policy for Industrial Relations (1969) Cmnd 3888, London: HMSO.

Kahn-Freund, Otto (1972) *Labour and the Law*, London: Stevens.

Keep, E. and Mayhew, K. (1994) 'The changing structure of training provision', in Buxton T., Chapman, P. and Temple, P. (eds) *Britain's Economic Performance*, London: Routledge, pp. 308–41.

MacIlroy, John (1995) *Trade Unions in Britain Today*, Manchester: Manchester University Press.

Marsh, David (1992) *The New Politics of British Trade Unionism: Union Power and the Thatcher Legacy*, London: Macmillan.

Moran, Michael (1977) *The Politics of Industrial Relations*, London: Macmillan.

Opie, R.G. (1972) 'Economic planning and growth', in Beckerman, Wilfred (ed.) *The Labour Government's Economic Record, 1964–1970*, London: Duckworth.

Phelps-Brown, Henry (1983) *The Origins of Trade Union Power*, Oxford: Clarendon Press.

Pimlott, Ben (1992) *Harold Wilson*, London: HarperCollins.

Royal Commission on Labour, Fifth and Final Report (1894) Cmnd 7421, London: HMSO.

Royal Commission on Trade Unions and Employers' Associations (1965–1968) Donovan Report. Cmnd 3623, London: HMSO.

The Inns of Court Conservative and Unionist Society (1958) *A Giant's Strength*, London: The Inns of Court Conservative and Unionist Society.

Turner, H.A. (1969) *Is Britain Really Strike-prone?*, Cambridge: Cambridge University Press.

Weekes, Brian, Mellish, Michael, Dickens, Linda and Lloyd, John (1975) *Industrial Relations and the Limits of the Law: The Industrial Effects of the Industrial Relations Act, 1971*, Oxford: Basil Blackwell.

Wigham, Eric (1973) *The Power to Manage: A History of the Engineering Employers' Federation*, London: Macmillan.

Williams, Chris (2002) 'Britain in historical perspective: from war concertation to the destruction of the social contract', in Berger, Stefan and Compston, Hugh (eds) *Policy Concertation and Social Partnership in Western Europe*, New York: Berghahn Books.

Wrigley, Chris (2002) *British Trade Unions Since 1933*, Cambridge: Cambridge University Press.

5
The radical left and popular music in the 1960s

Jeremy Tranmer

The 1960s was 'an era of social and cultural change' (Sandbrook, 2010, p. 200), at the heart of which was popular music, performed by young people for young people. By the middle of the decade, popular music had developed into a major social and economic force and had gained a certain degree of legitimacy, as is evidenced by Harold Wilson's controversial decision to decorate the Beatles in 1965. However, wedded to notions of respectability, the Labour Party was unable to engage with a phenomenon which was increasingly associated with embarrassing activities such as drug-taking, and with outlandish appearances. Sensing a political opportunity in the changing mood of the country's youth, sections of the radical left attempted to reach out to popular musicians and their fans. This chapter will suggest that there were two basic attitudes exemplified by the clumsy efforts of the Young Communist League (YCL) and the more sustained activities of parts of the New Left, which courted Mick Jagger and developed, at least temporarily, a working relationship with John Lennon. It will be argued that this tentative encounter between musicians and left-wing activists was the result of the inability of Labour to appeal to musicians and was the product of the changing cultural and political context. Moreover, it influenced future initiatives such as Rock Against Racism (RAR) in the late 1970s. A brief examination of RAR will allow new light to be shed on developments in the late 1960s and bring out their specificities.

Politics and 'Beatlemania'

In the late 1950s and early 1960s, full employment and rising disposable incomes for the young and the importing of American rock and roll had led to the emergence of the 'teenager' as a distinct economic, social and cultural section of the population. This was the context in which Beatlemania appeared in 1963. The Beatles' song, 'Please, please me' was a huge commercial success, as were the singles 'From me to you' and 'She loves you', which were released the same year. The album 'Please, please me' was also a hit. The four Liverpudlians' concerts were sold out and they performed in front of scenes of mass hysteria, as young women screamed their adulation. The press latched onto the phenomenon and published numerous articles and photographs. Beatlemania reinforced the transformation of youth into 'an independent social agent' (Hobsbawm, 1997, p. 324), which defined itself in opposition to older generations. Music became an important aspect in the lives of millions of young people throughout the country, and a central element in their sense of identity. At the same time, more groups were formed, and an increasing number of records were sold. Consequently, the music industry became a significant component of the British economy. In November 1963, the Beatles were invited to play at the annual Royal Variety Performance in London, an event which was later watched on television by approximately half the country's population. Having thus gained the Establishment's seal of approval, the Beatles were courted by politicians anxious to be associated with the heroes of the nation's youth.

The Conservative Prime Minister Sir Alec Douglas-Home regularly stated that he liked the Beatles, even asking them jokingly to stand as candidates for the Conservative Party in the 1964 general election (Lemonnier, 1995, p. 133). He even told a gathering of Young Conservatives that the Beatles were the secret weapon in his relationship with the American government, as they contributed greatly to Britain's overseas trade (Frontani, 2007, p. 45). However, the Conservatives were at a disadvantage since they were closely linked to the music and art forms traditionally appreciated by the middle and upper classes (classical music, ballet, etc.). While still leader of the Opposition, Labour's Harold Wilson was pleased to have his photograph taken with the Beatles, and he had the perfect excuse since his constituency was in Liverpool, their home town. In 1964, he presented them with a Variety Club award for being chosen as the show business personalities of the year (Denselowe, 1989, p. 92). Competition between the two parties to gain the support of the Beatles was so fierce that Labour and the Conservatives came to a tacit agreement during the 1964 election campaign, according to which neither party would to try to make excessive use of the group (Lemonnier, 1995, p. 134). In the face of open hostility from sections of the Establishment, Harold Wilson, the leader of the new Labour government, decided to make the Beatles Members of the British Empire (MBE). To a certain extent, he was responding to the social and cultural revolution that was under way, and being a Liverpool MP, he 'felt it like an avalanche and allowed himself to be swept along. Fashion in music, dress and art was beyond his understanding. Yet he sensed... that the tide could be harnessed to his advantage' (Pimlott, 1992, p. 268). Clearly, Wilson hoped that, by associating himself with youth culture, he would strengthen his image as a modern leader who was in touch with the young generation. This opportunism was not lost on his colleagues, such as Tony Benn, who wrote in his diaries: 'No doubt Harold did this to be popular and I expect it was popular' (Benn, 1988, p. 272).

However, there were limits to how close the relationship between Labour and popular music could be. The historian Willie Thompson has shown that the British labour movement was committed to pursuing limited objectives within the existing social, economic and political structures, an approach which he and others have termed Labourism (Thompson, 1993, p. 7). It shied away from open class conflict and sought to present itself as a decent, sensible and reliable force. It was, consequently, attached to notions of respectability and conformed to the dominant norms and conventions of British society. According to Thompson, it 'embrace[d] the bourgeois ethos in public affairs and lifestyle... parading its respectability and ethical tone" (ibid., p. 10). To begin with, the Beatles had a relatively respectable image – they were presented by their manager, their record company and the press as good-mannered, fun-loving, cheeky young men. Their hair was, admittedly, longer than the norm, but their dapper suits, shirts and ties shocked few. However, this image began to change from 1965/1966 onwards (Sandbrook, 2010, p. 412). Their music grew more sophisticated and innovative, which reflected the musical evolution of the group as well as its members' consumption of illegal substances such as marijuana and LSD. Their appearance also changed considerably. In line with drug-influenced psychedelia, their clothes became more outlandish and garish. This tendency was reinforced by the growing influence in Britain of the American hippie movement. As the Beatles moved increasingly in this direction, they were less respectable, according to the criteria of the Labour Party. It is symptomatic that in the 1966 general election campaign, Harold Wilson made no attempt to use the Beatles.

The relationship between Labour and popular music was also limited as Wilson had aroused little interest from musicians. According to one commentator, 'politics was no fun, and rarely idealistic' under Wilson, and 'he had managed to drain any youthful enthusiasm for democratic socialism out of the new musical rebels' (Denselowe, 1989, p. 92). Wilson was mentioned in one of the Beatles' songs, 'Taxman', but only to be criticized for the levels of taxation that high-earners such as the Liverpudlians were expected to pay. There was relatively little direct social comment in the lyrics of pop songs, with just a few exceptions, such as the Kinks' 'Dead End Street' which deals with poverty and deprivation. Songs by The Who, for instance, 'My Generation' and 'I Can't Explain', conveyed the pent-up frustration and aimless anger of the young. Yet most songs dealt with traditional themes such as love and boy–girl relationships, albeit in a more explicit way than before (for example, the Rolling Stones' 'Satisfaction' or 'Let's Spend the Night Together'). The absence of songs with an overtly political or social input can be explained partly by the fact that the American protest song trend of the early- to mid-1960s did not really catch on in Great Britain and did not spawn a British equivalent of Bob Dylan or Joan Baez (although some British artists such as Donovan attempted unsuccessfully to imitate them). Moreover, there was no unifying struggle in Britain capable of playing the same role as the civil rights movement, or later opposition to the war in Vietnam, in the United States. It must also be borne in mind that popular music was an example of young people expressing their youthful identity. If young musicians had been associated too closely to the adult world of governments, elections and parliamentary politics in general, they could have alienated sections of their audience who were more interested in the usual concerns of the young and in asserting themselves in opposition to older people. Finally, musicians had relatively little power in the 1960s and were under pressure from record companies and their managers not to say or do anything that could have an adverse impact on their image and record sales. The Beatles, for example, were prevented by their manager Brian Epstein from giving publicly their opinion on the Vietnam War (Doggett, 2008, p. 16). It was only in 1966 that they dared express their opposition to it at a press conference, and even then they remained quite vague.

The early 1960s thus saw attempts by politicians in general, and the Labour Party in particular, to benefit from the popularity of the Beatles. However, by 1966, Labour was no longer able to appeal to the Beatles if it were to retain its respectable image. As a result of Labour's growing inability to come to terms with youth culture and its representatives, and because of the Party's limited achievements in its first two years in office, an opportunity existed for the radical left to reach out to the country's most famous musicians.

The radical left and popular culture

The term 'radical left' will be used to refer to parties and groupings to the left of the Labour Party. The main force to Labour's left was the Communist Party of Great Britain (CP). Founded in 1920, following the Russian Revolution, the CP was a small organization, but it had a significant presence in the trade union movement and some intellectual influence over the non-Communist Left. The CP's attitude to popular culture was somewhat ambiguous. It had previously championed traditional folk music as the authentic music of revolt (Porter, 1998, pp. 171–91), though some members such as the historian Eric Hobsbawm had a keen interest in jazz (Morgan, 1998, pp. 123–41). However, in the context of the Cold War, it was openly hostile to American-influenced mass popular culture. In the early 1960s, the YCL welcomed the breakthrough of young working-class bands. In the words of the leading YCL activist Mike Power, 'Because the YCL was made up of young people, we were naturally more influenced by what was going on around us' (Cohen, 1997, p. 174). It deliberately, albeit, clumsily attempted to use contemporary youth culture to reach out to young people. For example, it included a picture of the Beatles on the front cover of its magazine *Challenge*, while in 1967, it published a leaflet entitled *The Trend is Communism*. The latter was printed in psychedelic colours, but contained, rather oddly, a photograph of an ageing trumpet player. The YCL also invited the Kinks to perform at its 1967 Congress in Skegness (Andrews, 2004, pp. 34–6). It was, however, uncomfortable with some of the cultural developments of the times. According to Mike Power again, 'We were hostile to the hippy movement in many ways. We were hostile to drug-taking and we didn't like flower power and meditation' (Cohen, 1997, p. 175).

Young Communists' limited engagement with youth culture met with open hostility from older Party members. The former YCL activist Nina Temple, who went on to lead the Party, has recalled growing up in a Communist family and has mentioned constant conflicts between herself and her brother, on the one hand, and their father, on the other, over fashion and music (Cohen, 1997, p. 94). Older Communists were extremely suspicious of the new musical trends, partly because they associated them with the United States, partly because they were afraid that any involvement with music might somehow dilute the YCL's politics. More fundamentally, the CP shared some of the baggage of Labourism, craving respectability, and expected members to dress and behave according to the norms and conventions of the skilled working class, where it was traditionally strongest (Thompson, 1992, p. 18). Furthermore, as well as being part of the British labour movement, the CP was also a section of the world Communist movement and viewed itself as being the sole legitimate representative of the Soviet Union in Britain. Communists were therefore encouraged to act in ways that would not be an embarrassment to the USSR and would correspond to the expectations of Soviet Communists. In other words, the social conservatism of Labourism was reinforced by that of world Communism. As a result, the CP's overall approach to the burgeoning youth culture was inevitably characterized by hesitancy and suspicion. It was therefore not particularly attractive to young musicians. The only well-known figure to have been closely linked to the party was Pete Townsend of The Who, who was a member of the YCL, though he did not publicize the fact.

The New Left took a closer interest in youth culture. The New Left was composed of small groups and parties that had emerged outside and in opposition to Labour and the CP. Their ideological references varied significantly, ranging from various forms of Trotskyism to Maoism, as well as libertarian socialism. These organizations had gained support since the crisis of Communism following the events of 1956 and occupied part of the space created by the Campaign for Nuclear Disarmament from the late 1950s onwards. The two most significant groupings were the International Marxist Group (IMG) and the International Socialists (which later, in a more Leninist guise, became the Socialist Workers Party (SWP)), both of which had a predominantly student base (Callaghan, 1987, p. 123). The IMG had a smaller membership but was 'the best-known faction' (Green, 1994, p. 242), as the leader of the Vietnam Solidarity Campaign, Tariq Ali, joined it in 1968, as well as having a disproportionately large political and cultural influence. The IMG saw youth as being in the vanguard of world revolution and hoped that British young people could spark off a similar chain of events to that which had led to millions of students and workers uniting in May 1968 in France.

The New Left could not be accused of lacking ambition or of hiding its light under a bushel, courting such high-profile figures as Mick Jagger of the Rolling Stones and John Lennon of the Beatles. Contributors to the unaligned New Left publication *Black Dwarf* debated the value to revolutionary politics of the Rolling Stones and the Beatles (Muldoon, 1968a, p. 1), as well as the merits of the former's song 'Street-Fighting Man' and the latter's 'Revolution' (Muldoon, 1968b). The newspaper even published Mick Jagger's hand-written lyrics to 'Street-Fighting Man', which were seen as an example of the progressive politics of the group

(Burley, 2008). Criticism of the Beatles' song 'Revolution' (Hoyland, 1968) led to the publication of an angry reply by its author John Lennon (Lennon, 1969). Lennon began having regular phone conversations with Tariq Ali, and they eventually met. The resulting interview was published in *Red Mole*, the IMG's newspaper. It is quite clear that elements of the New Left, particularly *Black Mole* and the IMG, took popular music seriously and attempted to engage with it. It would therefore seem a little harsh to suggest that 'the rigorously Marxist character of both the IMG's analysis and its organization left little opportunity for music to play anything other than a peripheral role' (Street, 1986, p. 75).

There was clearly an element of opportunism involved in the relationship between sections of the revolutionary Left and some leading artists. The New Left wanted to tap into and harness youth culture in order to further its own interests, showing that it was in touch with young people and hoping to attract them as new recruits. It must also be remembered that the membership of the New Left was predominantly young (its best-known figure, Tariq Ali, was only 25 in 1968), and that organizations like the International Socialists and the International Marxist Group succeeded in attracting quite a significant number of politicized students in the late 1960s, as well as cultural radicals (Rowbotham, 1999, p. 192). The young age and social background of members and sympathizers of the New Left encouraged it to continue this approach while further strengthening it. The New Left was also composed of relatively new groupings that were not constrained by fixed ideologies and traditions and had a less well-defined political culture than Labour or the CP. This gave it a certain degree of flexibility, allowing its members to reach out to contemporary youth culture. Some activists even straddled the two milieux, this being the case of David Widgery, who will be discussed in greater detail below.

By flirting with the revolutionary Left, Mick Jagger strengthened his and the Rolling Stones' image as rebellious outsiders. At a rather superficial level, the anti-Establishment stance of Jagger, whether it be his brushes with the law over drugs, his defence of young people against politicians or his opposition to the war in Vietnam which led him to participate in the largest British demonstration against the war (Doggett, 2008, pp. 67, 168), chimed in with the general approach of the radical left, which was based on the rejection of conventional, parliamentary politics. Ironically, the New Left, in its haste to latch on to youth culture, was attracted by the Rolling Stones' rebellious image, which had, to a large extent, been fabricated by the capitalist music industry to differentiate the Rolling Stones from the Beatles. It also had to deal with the group's political ambiguity symbolized by 'Street-Fighting Man' (ibid., pp. 197–8).

The lyrics have given rise to numerous interpretations and to endless debates about the intentions of the group. Clearly, the Rolling Stones were responding to the changing context of the late 1960s, in which the peaceful optimism of the 'Summer of Love' of 1967 gave way to the harsher realities of 1968 ('Ev'rywhere I hear the sound of marching feet, boy'), with the escalating opposition in the United States to the war in Vietnam, the events of May in France, the assassination of Bobby Kennedy, the Black Power salutes at the Summer Olympics, the violence outside the Democratic Convention in Chicago, the end of socialism with a human face in Czechoslovakia, etc. Even in the Rolling Stones' 'sleepy London Town', things were stirring. Protests broke out against the Labour government's refusal to condemn the Vietnam War, occupations were staged at the London School of Economics, and more generally the period saw 'a challenge to many established institutions – business, the State, the Church and the university' (Briggs, 1987, p. 359). Some musicians were aware of the new *Zeitgeist* but rather confused by it. The ambient confusion was described by Keith Richards, the guitarist of the Stones, in his recent autobiography:

> A different kind of fog descended and much energy was around and nobody quite knew what to do with it. Of course, being stoned all the time and experimenting, everybody, including me, had these vague half-baked ideas. You know, 'Things are changing.' 'Yeah, but for what? For where?' It was getting political in 1968, no way to avoid that.
>
> (Richards, 2010, p. 250)

He also admitted that without the war in Vietnam, 'Street Fighting Man' would never have been written. The members of the group were thus reacting to events around them. They vaguely sensed that a general atmosphere of conflict had appeared and wanted to be associated with it. This is not to suggest that they were not genuinely appalled by events in Vietnam, but they did not seriously commit themselves to a political cause and made no other political statements (Napier-Bell, 2002, p. 151). Jagger admitted several months later that he had little real interest in politics and continued to lead a hedonistic lifestyle, in which sex, alcohol and drugs were the prominent features. Interestingly, irrespective of the precise intentions of Jagger in writing the songs and of the political opinions of the group, Tariq Ali was able to use the song by interpreting it as suggesting that something had to be done to wake up people in London (Burley, 2008). Moreover, the music industry, fans and opponents all shared the interpretation of the New Left. For instance, Decca, the group's record company, refused to release the song as a single, deeming it to be too subversive (Doggett, 2008, p. 195), and many radio stations in the United Kingdom and the United States refused to play it. This would appear to confirm the general point that a 'song's meaning and politics lie beyond the control of its author' (Street, 1986, p. 131) and are created to a large extent by those who listen to it.

The case of John Lennon is in some ways, slightly different. He already had some interest in political matters, but by 1967 he had adopted a rather naïve vision of the world influenced by hippie ideals, Indian religions and drugs, which he never completely abandoned. However, his political opinions did not prevent him from going along with the Beatles' purchase of a Greek island in 1967 despite the military take-over in the country (Doggett, 2008, pp. 96–8). In 1968, he felt obliged to engage with the radical left and its ideas, which reveals his growing interest in political affairs as well as the extent of the influence of the New Left at the time. His ambiguities are best exemplified by his 1968 song 'Revolution' which was recorded by the Beatles.

In the best-known version of the song, he was scathingly critical of the radical left ('But if you go carrying pictures of Chairman Mao / You ain't going to make it with anyone anyhow') and declared himself to be opposed to violent revolution ('But when you talk about destruction / Don't you know that you can count me out'), while in another version he sat on the fence. The individualistic, peace and love ethos of the hippies was clearly present in the exhortation 'You'd better free your mind instead' and in the very un-political conclusion 'Don't you know it's gonna be alright.' His prevarication resulted in his being criticized in *Black Dwarf* (Hoyland, 1969). The elitist, idiosyncratic forms of protest that he pioneered in the latter part of the decade, such as 'bed-ins' in Amsterdam and Montreal (when he and Yoko Ono stayed in bed and invited journalists to visit them) and the use of billboards in major cities throughout the world to demand an end to war, were also ridiculed by left-wing activists, although his sending back of his MBE to protest against, among other things, the war in Vietnam created a stir, and his song 'Give Peace a Chance' was adopted by anti-war campaigners in the United States. By the early 1970s, he openly identified with the revolutionary Left, demonstrating in London against British policy in Northern Ireland, declaring his support for the Irish Republican Army, and composing songs such as 'Power to the People', a rather vague but fashionable slogan of the time, and 'Imagine', his utopian vision of a Communist society. Yet, his support for the numerous causes that he espoused was fleeting rather than sustained. For many on the Left, he was 'a great embarrassment, leaping from cause to cause, and revelling in the extravagant publicity that accompanied his solo political gestures' (Denselowe, 1989, p. 102). Lennon himself later admitted that he wanted above all to be liked by Tariq Ali and his comrades, and not to be accused of betraying the working class (Doggett, 2008, p. 403).

Attempts were thus made to bring together some musicians and political activists, producing mixed results. It is perhaps surprising that there was any cooperation at all, given the fact that the two sides were moving in very different circles. The lives of most left-wing activists were far removed from those of musicians, some of whom jetted around the world, making the most of the perks of their jobs, such as alcohol, drugs and sex. Their conception of political commitment activism was markedly different too. There was, after all, a huge difference between demonstrating against the Vietnam War on the streets of London and being threatened by policemen on horseback, on the one hand, and staying in bed in a luxury hotel to talk to journalists. Nevertheless, a precedent was created which influenced activists and musicians in the 1970s.

Creating a precedent

In fact, the short-term impact of the relationship between the New Left and musicians was somewhat limited, and neither side benefited a great deal from it. The New Left disintegrated quite rapidly, as the traditional fractiousness of the radical left reasserted itself. The main symbol of unity among its ranks, *Black Dwarf*, was weakened when a split occurred in its editorial board. This resulted in the departure of Tariq Ali and other supporters of the IMG, who went on to create the less successful *Red Mole* (Ali, 2005, pp. 329–30). As mentioned above, the Rolling Stones were quick to distance themselves from radical politics and were happy to continue with their hedonistic lifestyles, becoming tax exiles in the South of France in 1971. John Lennon's political phase continued after his move to the United States in September of the same year and culminated in the recording of *Some Time in New York City*, which was released in 1972. The album, containing only political songs, was panned by critics and snubbed by fans, reaching only number 12 in the UK album charts. It was generally felt that the lyrics were simplistic and the music uninspired (Street, 1986, pp. 163–5). The same year he withdrew from political activity, aware that the FBI had a hefty file on him and that he could eventually be deported as his chances of being granted a green card had been jeopardized. British musicians did not retreat completely into a world of their own. George Harrison organized two concerts for Bangladesh in 1971, which attracted the participation of Ringo Starr and Eric Clapton among others. Yet the concerts had no overtly political content and were intended simply to raise money and awareness. The early 1970s also saw a shift in the nature of the political conflicts taking place in the United Kingdom. The general contestation of the dominant norms and values of British society, in which young people had played a central role, gave way to more specifically economic struggles involving the trade union movement. The only song of any note to deal with these conflicts was 'Part of the Union' by the Strawbs, which was intended as a parody of trade union discourse (though it was taken up by demonstrators). There was, however, no serious interaction between musicians and activists in the first half of the decade.

It was not until 1976 that musicians and activists came together again, this time in a context of widespread racism, violent attacks on members of ethnic minorities and growing support for the neo-fascist National Front (Copsey, 2000, p. 123). That year, RAR was created by a group of left-wing activists who were passionate about music. Their aim was twofold. First, they hoped to fight against racism in the music industry: Eric Clapton had recently declared his support for the racist politics of Enoch Powell; David Bowie had given a Nazi salute in public and claimed that Britain was in need of a fascist dictator; and the swastika was being used as a symbol of revolt by some young people in the nascent punk movement. Second, they intended to promote unity between white and black young people and limit the attraction of the National Front. In order to fulfil these objectives, RAR organized local and national concerts, usually referred to as 'carnivals', bringing together punk and reggae artists in particular (Renton, 2006, pp. 115–35). The two national 'Carnivals against the Nazis', held in 1978, were huge successes. The Clash, the Buzzcocks, Steel Pulse, and X-Ray Spex played at the first, attracting over 80,000 fans, while Elvis Costello, Aswad and Stiff Little Fingers performed at the second, in front of 100,000 people. It is generally accepted that RAR contributed to limiting the National Front's appeal to the young, though the actual extent of its impact is open to debate among historians (Goodyer, 2009, pp. 22–43), and its success even led the National Front to attempt to replicate it by creating Rock Against Communism. RAR also helped the punk movement to spread throughout the country as a result of the number of local concerts that it organized involving punk bands. Moreover, the first national carnival was a launching pad for the Clash and its singer Joe Strummer, reinforcing their status as the premier punk band following the demise of the Sex Pistols. RAR was thus beneficial both for the anti-fascist cause, as support spread beyond its usual confines, and for musicians.

The concerts were the result of cooperation between activists, musicians and music lovers in general. The activists concerned were not members of the Labour Party, but were often members or sympathizers of the SWP. This is significant since the CP had a long tradition of popular anti-fascist and anti-racist activity, yet this initiative came from the smaller SWP, which gave RAR a considerable amount of organizational, financial and political support. One reason for this is the direct link that existed between RAR and the politico-musical milieu of the late 1960s, in the form of people such as Red Saunders, Roger Huddle and David Widgery. In the 1960s, all were young left-wing activists who were involved in the music scene of the time. Saunders and Huddle had been mods (Widgery, 1989, p. 119), while the former was also a member of the alternative theatre group Cartoon Archetypal Slogan Theatre (CAST). CAST had been created by Roland Muldoon who also contributed articles to *Black Dwarf*. Widgery is a particularly interesting example to discuss. A 'never terribly orthodox' member of the International Socialists (ibid., p. xiii), he championed rock music as a contributor to the counter-cultural paper *Oz* (which he even edited for a short time). He also spoke to local International Socialist groups about rock (Rowbotham, 1999, p. 216), wrote in a special issue of *Black Dwarf* about young people (ibid., p. 235), and tried to bring together Marxism and popular culture (Renton, n.d.). A decade later he was actively involved in RAR and even wrote the first book-length account of the organization, *Beating Time: Riot 'n' Race 'n' Rock 'n' Roll* (Widgery, 1986). He embodied attempts to create a close, positive relationship between the radical left and the world of popular music and to develop a new kind of politics and was an element of continuity between the late 1960s and the mid-1970s. To that extent, RAR was 'shaped' by the 1960s (Goodyer, 2009, p. 33).

It is interesting to briefly compare RAR with the interactions between activists and musicians in the late 1960s, since it helps to see more clearly why the impact of the latter was limited. Four elements will be examined. First, RAR was based on a single, well-defined cause (the struggle against the National Front) rather than the vague issue of support for the revolution and political violence. As a result, RAR was able to fix clear objectives and channel the energy of its members and sympathizers in a constructive way. Second, RAR was a movement, which gave it structure and a certain degree of coherence, allowing it to put down roots locally and become a dynamic bottom-up organization, whereas in the 1960s a top-down, elitist approach was adopted by the New Left, which sought to reach out mainly to the biggest names of the day. This would appear to be somewhat ironic for the Trotskyists, who tend to emphasize the importance of rank and file activity. However, some sections of the New Left were deliberately elitist. The abstract theoretical approach of the *New Left Review* is a good example of this. Third, through the Anti-Nazi League, with which it worked very closely, RAR was linked to the Labour movement and had financial and political support from trade unions and left-wing Labour MPs. Consequently, RAR was in touch with a large part of the population, unlike the New Left, which concentrated its efforts on students, whom it believed to be in the revolutionary vanguard, and was cut off from other sections of society. Finally, punk musicians were not super-stars like Lennon, who earned huge sums and lived in a mansion. They were, for the most part, ordinary young people who rejected the values of 'hippies', that is orthodox rock stars whose lives were very different from those of their fans (Longhurst, 2007, p. 106). Punks believed in breaking down the traditional barriers between performers and their audience, which gave them a certain credibility and legitimacy in the eyes of their followers. Furthermore, the DIY ethic of punk, which encouraged the young to take control of their own lives, could be articulated relatively easily with the active anti-fascism of RAR, based on young people organizing and publicizing concerts. The strengths of RAR thus allow us to see more clearly some of the weaknesses present in the late 1960s. RAR was clearly influenced by events and trends of the late 1960s, but it also came to define itself in opposition to them.

The 1960s saw various attempts to bring together the Left and musicians, from Harold Wilson's harnessing of the popularity of the Beatles to the New Left's courting of Mick Jagger and John Lennon. They are interesting in themselves as they reveal a great deal about the position that popular music had gained in British society in the 1960s. Sections of the Left clearly hoped that by being associated with well-known stars, they would gain credibility in the eyes of young people. However, during the latter part of the decade, the radicalization of young people extended to musicians, leading to a certain degree of mutual fascination. Furthermore, consorting with the revolutionary Left enabled musicians to strengthen their image as rebels or outsiders opposed to the Establishment. Although the peculiar political and cultural situation that had produced this limited interaction quickly passed, it created a precedent that was both a source of inspiration and revulsion for the activists and musicians that created RAR in the late 1970s. Events of the 1960s thus continued to have an impact positively and negatively ten years later.

Bibliography

Ali, Tariq (2005) *Street Fighting Years: An Autobiography of the Sixties*, London: Verso.

Andrews, Geoff (2004) *Endgames and New Times: The Final Years of British Communism, 1964–1991*, London: Lawrence and Wishart.

Benn, Tony (1988) *Out of the Wilderness: Diaries, 1963–1967*, London: Hutchinson.

Briggs, Asa (1987) *A Social History of England*, London: Penguin.

Burley, Leo (2008) 'Jagger vs Lennon: London's riots of 1968 provided the backdrop to a rock'n'roll battle royale', *Independent on Sunday*, 9 March. Available at: http://www.independent.co.uk/arts-entertainment/music/features/jagger-vs-lennon-londons-riots-of-1968-provided-the-backdrop-to-a-rocknroll-battle-royale-792450.html.

Callaghan, John (1987) *The Far Left in British Politics*, Oxford: Basil Blackwell.

Cohen, Phil (1997) *Children of the Revolution: Communist Childhood in Cold War Britain*, London: Lawrence and Wishart.

Copsey, Nigel (2000) *Anti-Fascism in Britain*, Basingstoke: Palgrave.

Denselowe, Robin (1989) *When the Music's Over: The Story of Political Pop*, London: Faber and Faber.

Doggett, Peter (2008) *There's a Riot Going On: Revolutionaries, Rock Stars and the Rise and Fall of '60s Counter-Culture*, Edinburgh: Canongate.

Frontani, Michael R. (2007) *The Beatles: Image and the Media* Jackson: University Press of Mississipi.

Goodyer, Ian (2009), *Crisis music: the cultural politics of rock against racism*, Manchester: Manchester University Press.

Green, Jonathon (1994) *All Dressed Up: The Sixties and the Counterculture*, London: Pimlico.

Hobsbawm, Eric (1997) *Age of Extremes: The Short Twentieth Century, 1914–1991*, London: Abacus.

Hoyland, John (1968) 'An open letter to John Lennon', *Black Dwarf*, 27 October, n.p.

Hoyland, John (1969) 'John Hoyland replies', *Black Dwarf*, 10 January, n.p.

Lemonnier, Bertrand (1995) *L'Angleterre des Beatles: Une histoire culturelle des années soixante*, Paris: Editions Kimé.

Lennon, John (1969) 'A very open letter to John Hoyland from John Lennon', *Black Dwarf*, 10 January.

Longhurst, Brian (2007) *Popular Music and Society*, Cambridge: Polity Press.

Morgan, Kevin (1998) 'King Street Blues: Jazz and the Left in Britain in the 1930s–1940s', in Croft, Andy (ed.) *A Weapon in the Struggle: The Cultural History of the Communist Party in Britain*, London: Pluto Press, pp. 123–41.

Muldoon, Roland (1968a) 'Marx/Engels/Mick Jagger', *Black Dwarf*, 27 October, p. 1.

Muldoon, Roland (1968b) 'Subculture: the street-fighting pop group', *Black Dwarf*, 15 October.

Napier-Bell, Simon (2002) *Black Vinyl, White Powder*, London: Ebury Press.

Porter, Gerald (1998) ' "The world's ill-divided": the Communist Party and progressive song', in Croft, Andy (ed.) *A Weapon in the Struggle: The Cultural History of the Communist Party in Britain*, London: Pluto Press, pp. 171–89.

Renton, Dave (2006) *When We Touched the Sky: The Anti-Nazi League, 1977–1981*, Cheltenham: New Clarion Press.

Renton, Dave (n.d.) 'The poetics of propaganda: David Widgery'. Available at: http://www.dkrenton.co.uk/anl/widgery.html (accessed 10 March 2012).

Richards, Keith (2010) *Life*, London: Weidenfeld and Nicolson.

Rowbotham, Sheila (1999), *A Century of Women: The History of Women in Britain and the United States*, Harmondsworth: Penguin.

Sandbrook, Dominic (2005) *Never Had It So Good: A History of Britain from Suez to the Beatles*, London: Little and Brown.

Sandbrook, Dominic (2010) *White Heat: A History of Britain in the Swinging Sixties*, London: Abacus.

Street, John (1986), *Rebel Rock: The Politics of Popular Music*, Oxford: Blackwell.

Thompson, Willie (1992) *The Good Old Cause: British Communism, 1920–1991*, London: Pluto Press.

Thompson, Willie (1993) *The Long Death of British Labourism*, London: Pluto Press.

Widgery, David (1986) *Beating Time: Riot 'n' Race 'n' Rock 'n' Roll*, London: Chatto and Windus.

Widgery, David (1989) *Preserving Disorder*, London: Pluto Press.

Part II
Culture

6
Civil Rights in Northern Ireland and Friel's *The Freedom of the City*

Martine Pelletier

The 1960s saw Ireland, North and South, facing new challenges and major evolutions. The Republic emerged from a long phase of economic protectionism ready to embrace an altogether different agenda through Whitaker's 1958 landmark Programme for Economic Expansion, paving the way for the influx of foreign, mostly American, capital and companies in the following decade. Social evolutions were slower and emigration remained massive, with the population hitting an all-time low of 2.8 million. That the Republic functioned like a Catholic state could be felt when it came to looking at issues of personal morality, which were still dictated by a strict Catholic ethos with a powerful and largely conservative Church whose position had been strengthened by de Valera's 1937 Constitution. The political system, in which the two main parties, Fianna Fail and Fine Gael, were separated less by ideological issues – as both leaned to the right of the political spectrum – than by the stance their founding figures had taken during the civil war on constitutional issues, remained anachronistic, favouring cronyism and provincialism. President Kennedy's visit to Ireland in 1963 was a major event and a cause for celebration. Preparations to join the EEC were underway, in a move that would alter Ireland's relationship to Great Britain through joint membership of this union and prove how open to the world Ireland now was, at least economically. It must be admitted that the re-unification of the island did not rank very high among the preoccupations of the time, though lip service was regularly paid to the ideal of a 32-county Republic. Two successive *Taoiseachs* in the 1960s accepted and returned invitations by Northern Premier Terence O'Neill, an unprecedented move on both sides, even if no official recognition of Northern Ireland was forthcoming from Dublin.

Across the border, Northern Ireland had settled, since its creation in 1922, into a Protestant state for a Protestant people, in keeping it seemed with the wishes of the majority of its population and of their leaders. The regional parliament, known as Stormont, was dominated by the Unionist Party without any challenge from the Nationalist Party, which pursued an abstentionist policy, refusing to recognize the legitimacy of the Northern state and the partition of the island. Thus the Catholic/Nationalist minority was deprived of any political agency. In the United Kingdom, it was understood that Northern Ireland's affairs were dealt with in Stormont, not in Westminster, which allowed Stormont to discard, or delay implementing elements of UK legislation which would have threatened the status quo and the sectarian Unionist domination. Thus Stormont made use of the Special Powers Act and the Flags and Emblems Act, trusted the exclusively Protestant RUC and the even more loyalist B-Specials to maintain law and order. Northern Ireland may not have been Southern Rhodesia, but discrimination against the minority by the majority was the norm in all aspects of life, as was regularly pointed out at the time. However, as the election of Terence O'Neill as the new Prime Minister of Northern Ireland in 1963 was soon followed by the election of a Labour government in Westminster, and in view of the demographic and social evolutions in Northern Ireland itself, changes were about to take place, indicating that the traditional quiescence of the Catholic/Nationalist minority could no longer be taken for granted.

There are numerous memoirs written by participants in the events of those heady and ultimately tragic days of the 1960s: Bernadette Devlin, Eamonn McCann, Raymond McClean, Terence O'Neill, John Hume, to name but a few leading figures, have all committed their versions of the momentous months and years of the civil rights movement to writing, so that some light could be shed on both what happened, but also on the part they played, their motivations, aspirations, achievements and regrets. Commentaries and analyses, journalistic and academic, have also proliferated testifying to the importance of those years between 1965 and 1970 for any understanding of the situation in Northern Ireland. Various novels, plays and poems also provide imaginative accounts, written either at the time or with the benefit of hindsight, and among these, Brian Friel's ([1974] 1992) play, *The Freedom of the City*, stands out and deserves a fuller analysis, navigating as it does between fact and fiction, and offering valuable insights into the rise of the civil rights movement and the ensuing escalation of sectarian violence in Northern Ireland.

Born in Omagh in 1929, Brian Friel moved to Derry in 1939 and thus grew up in what had only very recently become Northern Ireland in what he called 'a very traditional, Catholic nationalist home' (Boland, 1970, p. 12). As a child, he spent many holidays in Donegal, where his mother's family came from, thus developing a strong sense of the artificiality and porosity of the border. Friel came to fame with *Philadelphia, Here I Come!* first produced at the 1964 Dublin Theatre Festival, and soon a success across the Atlantic. He subsequently wrote a quartet of plays that addressed the contemporary situation in Ireland, North and South: *The Mundy Scheme* (written in 1968 and produced in 1969) is a savage, Swiftian satire of Ireland's embrace of American-style materialism and an early critique of globalization Irish style. *The Gentle Island* (produced in 1971), also set in the Republic on one of the deserted western isles is a daring work, introducing homosexual characters at a time when homosexuality was criminalized and rarely mentioned in public, let alone on stage. Revisiting the myth of the rural west, Friel shows an Ireland in the throes of intense frustration and yielding to violence as a result of an inability to adjust to change. *The Freedom of the City* (written in 1972 and produced in February 1973) is set in Derry in 1970 and deals with the onset of the troubles in Northern Ireland, creating a fictional dramatic situation in which the hopes and promises of emancipation contained in the civil rights movement, the violence of Bloody Sunday and the outrage provoked by the Widgery Report, are amalgamated and condensed. Finally, *Volunteers* (produced in 1975 and dedicated to fellow northerner, Seamus Heaney), returns to a Dublin setting and deals with Republican prisoners and southern attitudes to the violence in the North. All four plays thus share a contemporary setting, a desire to anatomize without concession the condition of Ireland, on both sides of the border. They are also characterized by a violence and a bleakness thankfully relieved by a wry sense of humour, moments of manic theatrical energy and a large measure of compassion. Formally daring, intellectually challenging and emotionally disturbing, this quartet of plays established Brian Friel as a major, though not necessarily popular, dramatist. In 1970, Friel recalled:

In those days one's whole nationalism and religion were constantly interwoven and inextricable. As a young boy in Derry there were certain areas one didn't go into. I remember bringing shoes to the shoemaker's shop at the end of the street. This was a terrifying experience because if the Protestant boys caught you in this kind of no-man's-land, they'd kill you... If you were caught, you were finished. It was absolutely terrifying. That sort of thing leaves scars for the rest of one's life.

(Linehan, 1970, p. 26)

In spite of its Catholic majority, through gerrymandering, Derry, the Maiden City, was controlled by the Unionists, fuelling resentment and frustration, as Friel remembered:

There were two aspects to Derry: one was of a gentle and, in those days, sleepy town; the other was of a frustrating and frustrated town in which the majority of people were disinherited. From the first point of view it was an easygoing town in which to grow up, but from a spiritual point of view, it wasn't a good town. Although the Civil Rights fires had been kindled in many places throughout the North, they burst into flames in Derry, because it was there the suppression was greatest.

(Hickey and Smith, 1972, p. 221)

Brian Friel went to Saint Columb's secondary school (like Seamus Heaney, Seamus Deane, Eamon McCann or John Hume), and then on to Maynooth, close to Dublin to train for the priesthood. Having lost his vocation, he returned to Northern Ireland to train as a primary-school teacher, taking up a post in Derry, as his father had done before him. He started writing stories and then plays, first for radio, then for the stage. He also joined the Nationalist Party, again like his father:

I was a member of the Nationalist Party for several years. I don't remember how long. Those were very dreary days because the Nationalist Party... was a very despised enterprise by everybody. We used to meet once a month wherever it was in a grotty wee room and there'd be four or five old men who'd sit there and mull over things. It was really hopeless.

(O'Toole, 1982, pp. 110–11)

In 1968, Friel left Derry and Northern Ireland to settle in the Republic, in County Donegal, a move he explained bluntly in 1970:

The Border has never been relevant to me. It has been an irritation, but I've never intellectually or emotionally accepted it... I would much prefer to be under the jurisdiction of the Dublin Government. Stormont is either absurd or iniquitous, probably both.

(Rushe, 1970, p. 28)

The sense of Stormont being 'either absurd or iniquitous, probably both' must have been shared by many in the Nationalist community at the time. On 1 February 1967, Belfast saw the formation of NICRA – the Northern Ireland Civil Rights Association – calling for a universal franchise ('one man one vote') for local government elections instead of one based on rate-payers and the ending of the company vote; the redrawing of electoral boundaries to end gerrymandering; the introduction of laws to end discrimination in local government employment; a compulsory points system for public housing to ensure fair allocation; the repeal of the Special Powers Act; and the disbanding of the wholly Protestant police reserve force, the Ulster Special Constabulary. The meeting leading to the creation of NICRA took place at the Blue Bar of the International Hotel in Belfast. Only a few months earlier in June 1966, Peter Ward, a Catholic barman of that same hotel had been shot by the revived UVF (Ulster Volunteer Force, a loyalist paramilitary organization), a tragic event that writer Glenn Patterson has since used as the starting point of his 1999 novel, *The International*.

NICRA did not emerge in a vacuum and several factors leading to the organization of a civil rights movement in Northern Ireland can be, and have been, duly identified: education and the effect of the 1944 Butler Act which enabled a generation of Catholics to have access to secondary school education, and later to university, thus contributing to the development of a Catholic middle class that would look for job opportunities in a society where they were still barred from occupying many posts in the civil service and police force. Prime Minister O'Neill had a more open, less sectarian attitude towards the Catholic community, the Catholic Church and the Republic of Ireland. Much to the dismay and later outrage of right-wing Unionists, fuelling the rise of Paisleyism and of the DUP, O'Neill invited the Irish *Taoiseach* Jack Lynch to Stormont in January 1965 and paid him a return visit in Dublin. This in turn led to the Nationalist Party agreeing to become the official opposition at Stormont, a role that had hitherto been devolved to the small Northern Ireland Labour Party. It was nonetheless too late to save the Nationalist Party from irrelevance as time would soon show. O'Neill repeated the opening (or the offence) with Lynch's successor, Sean Lemass, in December 1967, again raising hopes among the Catholic community and further alienating hard-line Unionists within his own party who worried that Harold Wilson, in office in London at the head of a Labour government since 1964, was known to have spoken semi-officially in favour of a United Ireland. Thus, Campaign for Democracy in Ulster (CDU) was created in June 1965, a cross-party group of fifty to a hundred MPs with a Labour majority led by Manchester MP, Paul

Rose. The CDU demanded a full and impartial enquiry into the administration of government in Northern Ireland and into allegations of discrimination against Catholics. As Jonathan Moore puts it: 'The call was for "British standards" for British people' (1991, p. 76) and they thought their cause was so obviously just that the Labour government would act. This proved not really to be the case, though in the late Sixties Wilson and later Callaghan would indeed put some pressure on Stormont to grant reforms, but only after violence had erupted and divisions had hardened. Wilson is reported to have evinced characteristic caution in 1964 saying that, 'Any politician who wants to become involved in Ulster ought to have his head examined' (ibid., p. 77).[1] If the Labour Party was hesitant when it came to reopening the Irish question, it must also be admitted that the issue of discrimination was rarely addressed by Nationalists who tended to blame all problems on the border so that there was little or no direct campaigning to highlight and seek to end discrimination. Other institutions and media also played down this unpalatable reality. John Boyd, a Belfast radio producer for the BBC in Belfast and a Labour man, acknowledged that

> The BBC failed to reflect the objective social conditions that prevailed in Northern Ireland, and its timidity was inexcusable...Problems like unemployment, housing and religious discrimination were of course mentioned *en passant* in certain programmes, but never given adequate treatment.
>
> (1990, p. 204)

Mary Beckett, in her novel *Give Them Stones*, has Martha, her protagonist comment somewhat cynically:

> I had heard on the radio about Catholics beginning to look for civil rights – houses that they were entitled to and local government votes for all. I didn't pay a lot of heed to it. I heard about the Protestant girl in Co. Tyrone being given a house for herself instead of a Catholic family but it was no great wonder. It was the way of life we were used to. In June 1968 when Austin Currie protested and was carried out by the police, I thought, 'He's young. He'll learn.'
>
> (1987, p. 117)

At the grassroots though, something had changed; in the summer of 1963 the 'Homeless Citizens' League' was founded; by January 1964, the 'Campaign for Social Justice' was set up. Meanwhile in Derry, a campaign had been organized to have the new university located in the city. John Hume, a young local teacher, proved particularly active in the campaign – which was lost, as the University of Ulster set up home in the impeccably Unionist Coleraine, thus ensuring Derry lost confidence in O'Neill's promises. John Hume, among others, was well aware of the American civil rights movement in the South of the United States and, as it developed and grew in international appeal, parallels between the fight against segregation in America and discrimination in Northern Ireland also grew in popularity. John Hume has repeatedly claimed its influence on him personally:

> I read a huge amount of the writings of Martin Luther King in those days. I am certain that it was no accident that the civil rights movement began here in the Sixties, directly inspired, I believe, by the American movement. Six months after the death of Martin Luther King, we in Northern Ireland became involved in our own civil rights struggle against discrimination.
>
> (1996, p. 30)

Hume concludes:

> The American civil rights movement in the 1960s gave birth to ours. Their successes were for us a cause of hope. The songs of their movement were also ours. We also believe that 'we shall overcome'; that rallying song is sung every year at my party conference.
>
> (ibid., p. 45)

Another important political figure of the time, Bernadette Devlin, recalls a similar political – and musical – influence in her memoir, *The Price of my Soul*:

> There was more real politics in the Folk Music Society than in any of the parties. They sang black civil rights songs in the folk music society before anybody else in Queen's was interested in the race problem, and they were singing songs about unemployment in Belfast long before the civil rights movement took it up. It was a good society. It had a strong American influence in it, but because of this, there was another section which was determined to keep the Irish influence, so you had the best of both American protest song and traditional Irish folk music.
>
> (1969, p. 76)

The political scientist, Richard Rose, gave his interpretation of the rise of the civil rights movement, also drawing on the US parallel:

> Inspired in part by the civil rights movement in America, Catholic activists took to the streets in massive protest marches...The constitution of the Northern Ireland Civil Rights Association gave most prominence to political rights. The civil rights campaign was also novel in that its leaders offered an alternative to two traditional forms of Ulster Catholic political activity, losing elections and losing IRA gun battles with security forces. Civil rights groups organized massive street marches to demonstrate their opposition to the status quo in Ulster, and the marches were held whether the Stormont government granted permits or declared them illegal. The violence of Protestant counter-demonstrators and, upon occasion, of the RUC generated international publicity and considerable sympathy in Britain and America for the civil rights campaigners...The civil rights campaign was also distinctive in its leadership. In place of veteran Nationalist or republican politicians, many of its leaders were younger Catholics who were less concerned with traditions than with the present problems of Ulster.
>
> (1976, p. 22, p. 52)

Poet and academic Seamus Deane, also from Derry, underlined the parallels between the two situations in an article entitled 'Why Bogside?' which is of particular interest since Brian Friel and Deane would work together through the 1980s with Field Day, the Derry-based theatre company Friel co-founded with Belfast actor Stephen Rea – who had played the part of Skinner in the London production of *The Freedom of the City*. In his provocative article, Deane declares:

> The resemblances between the North and the southern states of the USA stem from the fact that in each area a single institution – slavery, sectarianism – became the basis of social privilege for a few, economic security for many, and a sense of superiority for all not condemned by it. This gave the opponents of this system a ready-made moral base for political attacks be they on State Rights or on Partition. Moreover, just as most Northern Protestants have no direct profit from sectarianism, few Southerners ever profited directly from slavery...
>
> If civil war ever does break out in the North, it too will be like the American 'a rich man's war and a poor man's fight'. The landowners

have until recently had no fear of the Catholic niggers; they have always feared the illumination of their own poor whites.

(1992, pp. 397–8)

The protest method favoured by NICRA, as it was by the US civil rights movement, was marching. But in Northern Ireland marches were not a new phenomenon and they carried overt, territorial connotations. Prime Minister Terence O'Neill suggests somewhat mischievously that the Civil Rights Association may well have taken their lead from the loyalist marches:

I don't think anyone then realized that the Protestant marches of 1966 would be copied by the Civil Rights marches of 1968. I am not suggesting for a moment that the Civil Rights movement would not have got under way in any case and presumably the example of Martin Luther King was in the forefront of their minds when they started in October 1968. Nevertheless when they saw the notoriety which Paisley achieved for himself in 1966, they must have realized that only in such a manner could they achieve fame and TV coverage in 1968.

(1972, p. 80)

Having left Derry precisely at the time when the civil rights movement was shaping up and gathering momentum, Brian Friel nonetheless supported the movement and took part in some of the marches in the late 1960s, at a time when peaceful protest often degenerated into violent confrontation with the authorities, or loyalist counter-marches:

I think it was in '68 (that we moved) and the trouble began in '69 and we might have been better to be in there. Just to be part of the experience. Instead of driving into a civil rights march, coming out your front door and joining it might have been more real. It would have been less deliberate and less conscious than doing it from here.

(O'Toole, 1982, p. 22)

For Friel, the Derry march on 5 October 1968 proved a turning point:

Until 5 October 1968, which was a red-letter day, I thought that society was absolutely dead. Then suddenly five young men, who had nothing to gain in temporal terms, organized a very shabby rally. The parallel is not accurate, but suddenly the whole thing was dignified, as in 1916. The police beat hell out of these fellows. And suddenly the conscience of Derry was aroused.

(Rushe, 1970, p. 28)

In contrast, Derrywoman Frances Molloy's 1985 novel, *No Mate for the Magpie*, provides a humorous version of this newly found awareness:

Well, when this news broke, a lot of ordinary people were surprised te learn that they had been citizens all their lives, an' not only citizens, but second-class citizens too at that. My god, they were sayin' te wan another, te think that all this time we have been only wan step down from the tap an' didn't know it. They were delighted so they took te the streets in their droves, an' a want way them.

(1985, p. 127)

Eamonn McCann commented wryly on the retrospective success of the same march:

Had all those who now claim to have marched that day actually done so, the carriageway would have collapsed. It was a small demonstration, perhaps four hundred strong – a hundred of these were students from Belfast... The march had been organized by a loose group of radicals who had been trying for months, with some success, to create general political mayhem in the city.

(1974, p. 27)

Paul Bew concurs as to the importance of this march, writing that 'it could be argued that the march marks the pivotal point at which the Troubles changed from being primarily about civil rights to the more ancient disputes concerning religious and national identities' (Bew and Gillespie, 1993, p. 12). Brian Friel supported the CRA, but he was also conscious that the struggle to obtain civil rights was obliterating or superseding the nationalist ideal of a 32-county republic, which to him remained sacred: 'What people are looking for is human rights at a very basic level, and I think they will possibly achieve these. But the danger is that they are losing something very important – their orientation towards an Irish Republic' (Rushe, 1970, p. 28). Bernadette Devlin explains why she moved away from republicanism to embrace socialism which in turn led to her involvement in People's Democracy, the militant student association that was born in Queen's shortly after the first Derry march:

> I began moving away from traditional Republicanism to being generally opposed to the system…The problem in Northern Ireland, I decided, was not partition. If we took away partition, what did we join? If we had a truly free Ireland on the other side, we would have something to join, but what was the point of ending partition merely to alter the borders of injustice…Let's go and ask for British democracy. If they're going to make us British by law, we must be British by standard of living as well.
>
> (Devlin, 1969, pp. 89–90)

The reform package granted by O'Neill in November 1968 did not end the marches as by then elements within and outside the CRA had radicalized. People's Democracy, a student organization based in Queen's University, organized a march from Belfast to Derry, modelled on the 1965 Selma–Montgomery US march. It was brutally attacked. Devlin, McCann and Frances Molloy all offer versions of this march with the infamous Burntollet Bridge ambush by loyalists who pelted the marchers with rocks and attacked them with all weapons at their disposal while the RUC looked on. Frances Molloy's protagonist remembers the Civil Rights anthem 'We're on our way to Derry' becoming 'We're on our way to heaven' as the marchers fear they are about to die. Bernadette Devlin for her part recalls:

> There we were trudging up the road, battered and bruised, singing, 'we shall overcome – some day.' But that song was too resigned so we resorted to the *Internationale*, and it was never sung with more fervour than coming away from Burntollet Bridge.
>
> (Devlin, 1969, p. 142)

From then on, rioting and sectarian violence would escalate, leading to the deployment of British troops on the streets of Northern Ireland in 1969 and paving the way for further deadly clashes between marchers, the re-born IRA and British forces.

Asked in 1970 why he was not writing a play about the current situation in Ulster, Friel explained:

> People ask why I have not written a play about the Civil Rights movement. One answer is that I have no objectivity in this situation.

I am much too involved emotionally to view it with any calm. Again I don't think there is the stuff of drama in the situation. To have a conflict in drama, you must have a conflict of equals, or at least near equals. There is no drama in Rhodesia or South Africa, and similarly there is no drama in the North of Ireland.

(Smith and Hickey, 1972, p. 222)

However, early in February 1973, his own *The Freedom of the City* opened at the Abbey Theatre and transferred to the Royal Court in London. What had happened in between was Bloody Sunday, when on 30 January 1972, British paratroopers had killed 13 civil rights marchers on the streets of Derry and, thanks to the subsequent Widgery Report, had been able to literally and officially get away with murder. At the time, Friel offered none too credible a disclaimer seeking to establish some distance between the all too recognizable tragedy and the location and time frame of his own play:

It's not about Bloody Sunday. In fact the play began long before Bloody Sunday happened. I was working on this theme for about ten months before Bloody Sunday. And then Bloody Sunday happened and the play I was writing, and wasn't succeeding with, suddenly found a focus. I was stuck until this point and this was a kind of clarification. The play in fact is the story of three people who are on a Civil Rights march in Derry City in 1970. The march finishes in the Guildhall square. There's a public meeting. Then the British Army moves in, breaks up the meeting and these three people find refuge in the Guildhall and find themselves in the Mayor's Parlour.

(Boland, 1970, p. 12)

To try and keep the real events of Bloody Sunday at some critical and creative distance, *The Freedom of the City* breaks away from linear representation and uses an open, some would say Brechtian, form with episodes rather than acts and scenes. As the curtain rises, three bodies are lying on stage and the play moves back in time to recount in fragmented fashion the events which led to the deaths of the three. Blinded by tear gas, they unwittingly enter the Guildhall, that bastion of Unionist supremacy, causing everyone outside to think this is an insurrection of some kind, with tragic consequences for all. Lily Doherty, Michael Hegarty and Adrian Casimir Fitzgerald, nicknamed Skinner, can be seen as embodying different trends within the civil rights movement and as the play progresses, the audience will learn about what motivated them to take part in the march. Michael stands for the 'dignified John Hume/Citizens' Action Committee' tendency within the movement: 'It was a good, disciplined, responsible march. And that's what we must show them – that we're responsible and respectable; and they'll come to respect what we're campaigning for' (*Freedom*, 1972, p. 35). Coming from the working class, struggling to keep a job, engaged to be married, he attends night-classes and the values he adheres to are definitely middle-class and socially conservative:

> What I want, Skinner, what the vast majority of the people out there want is something that a bum like you wouldn't understand: a decent job, a decent place to live, a decent town to bring up our children in – that's what we want.
>
> (*Freedom*, 1974, p. 70)

He is a great believer in peaceful protests, echoing Hume again:

> The civil rights movement's strategy of non-violence was greatly influenced by Martin Luther King's philosophy. Don't retaliate, let the world see who the real aggressor is – that was our fundamental message to our fellow marchers when we were attacked by baton-wielding police.
>
> (*Freedom*, 1974, p. 32)

Michael, who has been, he claims, on every single march since 5 October, welcomes the violent repression of the forces of law and order as it means more and more people are now marching in protest; warming to his theme, he condemns what he calls 'the hooligan element', 'the strange characters [who] knuckled in on the act that didn't give a shite about real civil rights' (*Freedom*, 1974, p. 33).

Michael is opposed and contradicted by Skinner, or Adrian Casimir, whose wry humour, lack of respect for authority and flippancy horrify the law-abiding Gandhi supporter. Skinner is an orphan with no fixed address, used to living on his wits; as he puts it: 'If I'm sick, the entire wisdom of the health service is at my service. And should I die, the welfare people would bury me in style. It's only when I'm alive and well, that I'm a problem' (*Freedom*, 1974, p. 61). Skinner has little patience with Michael's admiration for the dignified silent marches and makes fun of his dedication to non-violence: 'Mr Hegarty is of the belief that if five thousand of us are demonstrating peacefully and they come along and shoot us down, then automatically we ... we ... *(To Michael)* Sorry, what's the theory again?' (*Freedom*, 1974, p. 48). It is Skinner who will stick a sword through the portrait of a 'forgotten civic dignitary', who makes free with the drinks and cigars in the Mayor's parlour or plays at holding a corporation meeting. Skinner is more keenly aware than the others of what awaits them outside, of the price that will be exacted for their trespassing on the seat of Unionist power: 'Because you presumed, boy. Because this is theirs, boy, and your very presence here is a sacrilege' (*Freedom*, 1974, p. 47). Thus, Michael and Skinner enact on stage the debates between the moderates and the radicals, the John Hume/CAC vs Eamonn McCann/PD opposition described in McCann's own words:

> The unemployed youth of areas like the Bogside had, at the outset of the civil rights campaign, been regarded as marching fodder. Energetic and instinctively aggressive, they could be counted on to turn out for sit-downs, marches, pickets or any other protest activity which was organized ... It was their impatience which had then impelled the CAC into more activity, and more militant activity, than its leading members would have wished. It was their energy and aggression which had powered the civil rights campaign through its first frenetic months. It the end it was they, not the RUC, who frightened organizations like the CAC off the streets. The CAC died in Derry after the riots of 19 April. It was difficult after that to organize a demonstration which did not end in riot, and the CAC was not about to assume such responsibility. But by ending demonstrations the moderates took away from the youth any channel for expression *other* than riot. The rage and frustration which lay just beneath the surface of life in the Bogside could no longer be contained within the thin shell of the CAC's timid respectability. The 'hooligans' had taken over, and the stage was set for a decisive clash between them and the forces of the state.
>
> (McCann, 1985, pp. 57–8)

In a stylized speech the playwright grants his three characters before their execution, he has Skinner express his regret at having underestimated the situation:

> And as we stood on the Guildhall steps, two thoughts raced through my mind: how seriously they took us and how unpardonably casual we were about them; and that to match their seriousness would demand a total dedication, a solemnity as formal as theirs.
>
> (*Freedom*, p. 58)

It would take an army to match another army so that Skinner as proto-IRA volunteer comes to mind when reading McCann again:

> The provisional IRA is entitled to see itself, and to demand to be regarded by others, as the legitimate inheritor of the struggle for civil rights launched in the North in 1968. This is not a view which commends itself to many who, retrospectively at least, declare their support for the civil rights movement...Wherein, they ask, lies the similarity between those whose harmonic choral renditions of 'We Shall Overcome' so stirred the soul of the world in 1968 and the cold-eyed killers who, in 1979, bark out a harsh belief in the bullet and the bomb?...The men and women of the Provisional IRA today are the rioting children of a decade ago. To my knowledge there is no member of the command staff of the Provos in Derry whose first conscious political experience was other than attendance at a civil rights march or rally and, probably, whatever bout of stone throwing ensued. At that time they were praised, patronized and patted on the head by the civil rights leaders, urged to stay on the streets unless and until 'our demands' were met. And they took us at our word, even when real weapons replaced words as the tools of the struggle.
>
> (1974, pp. 129–30)

Counterpointing the two male characters, Lily Doherty embodies a less openly militant strand. Prematurely aged by 11 pregnancies and hard work as a charwoman to feed her family while the father, unemployed, sits at home and lords it over the household, Lily shares Skinner's sense of fun and admires Michael's responsibility, though she can poke fun at his lack of humour. Generous and motherly, she has no political awareness though she has been marching regularly. Skinner challenges her:

> I'll tell you why you march...Because you live with eleven kids and a sick husband in two rooms that aren't fit for animals. Because you exist on a state subsistence that's about enough to keep you alive but too small to fire your guts...Because for the first time in your life you grumbled and someone else grumbled and someone else, and you heard each other, and became aware that there were hundreds, thousands, millions of us all over the world, and in vague groping way you were outraged. That's what it's all about, Lily. And it has nothing to do with doctors and accountants and teachers and dignity

and boy-scout honour. It's about us – the poor – the majority – stirring in our sleep. And if that's not what it's all about, then it has nothing to do with us.

Freedom, 1974, p. 63)

But for all his assurance, Skinner may not have guessed at the whole truth, as Lily later admits:

I told you a lie about our Declan. That's what our Declan is. He's not just shy, our Declan. He's a mongol...And it's for him I go on all the civil rights marches. Isn't that stupid? You and him (*Michael*) and everybody else marching and protesting about sensible things like politics and stuff and me in the middle of you all marching for Declan. Isn't that the stupidest thing you ever heard? Sure I could march and protest from here to Dublin and sure what good would it do to Declan? Stupid and all as I am, I know that much. But I still march – every Saturday.

(*Freedom*, 1974, p. 64)

Grief and grievance, a sense of being listened to, of finally mattering: Lily reminds us all that the civil rights marches became mass movements because through marching and protesting the voices of an underclass, a long-suffering and much-neglected community could finally be heard. And among that community, women often bore the brunt of the violence, victims of male brutality, self-hatred and despair: 'That's what the Chairman said when I – you know – when I tried to tell him what I was thinking...he said "You're a bone stupid bitch. No wonder the kid's bone stupid too." The Chairman, that's what he said' (*Freedom*, 1974, p. 64).

The voices of those three individuals who come to represent various aspects within the civil rights, are soon to be drowned or silenced as other authoritative voices take over: the tribunal of enquiry, strongly reminiscent of Widgery, the Church, the media and, somewhat unexpectedly, an American academic. For the judge: 'It is essentially a fact-finding exercise; and our concern, and our only concern is with that period of time when these three people came together, seized possession of a civic building, and openly defied the security forces' (*Freedom*, 1974, p. 13). Case opened and closed, the premise is, as the audience knows, entirely counter-factual, but cannot be challenged. It would take three decades for the Saville Enquiry to prove Widgery was a whitewash. In the play, the Catholic Church hardly fares better than the British judicial system; two sermons are given in remembrance of the victims; in the first, Michael, Lily and Skinner are turned into martyrs, their 'dream' an echo of another American dreamer:

> They died for their beliefs. They died for their fellow citizens. They died because they could endure no longer the injuries and injustices and indignities that have been their lot for so many years... May we be worthy of that dream, of their trust. May we have the courage to implement their noble hopes. May we have God's strength to carry on where they left off.
>
> (*Freedom*, 1974, p. 31)

Later in the play, seemingly the same priest returns to deliver an altogether different sermon warning against 'the dark dungeons of Godless communism', as a revolutionary conspiracy is corrupting the once peaceful and dignified movement: 'certain evil elements attached themselves to it and contaminated it and ultimately poisoned it, with the result that it has long ago become an instrument for corruption' (*Freedom*, 1974, p. 65). Socialist ideas had indeed gained some ground, in particular with People's Democracy as Bernadette Devlin recalls:

> Second in command of the Belfast left (behind Michael Farrell) was Cyril Toman. Cyril was a theoretician: he preached the gospel according to St Marx. He would take it out of his pocket at meetings and quote it in great big theoretical chunks of socialist jargon. He started every speech with 'This reminds me of the Sorbonne...', and we got bored with this grand drawing of comparisons and roared back, 'Never mind the Sorbonne! We're interested in the slums of Belfast.'
>
> (1969, p. 118)

Faced with the threat of St Marx, the Church could only revert to a very conservative stance that young articulate and radical Bogsiders like McCann or Deane would attack mercilessly. The media also feature, none too gloriously, in the play; a photographer hovers, vulture-like, over the corpses in the first scene while the RTE presenter reports from the funeral, resorting to all the traditional, lachrymose clichés, the intended pathos ironically undercut by his inability to remember the names of the three victims. Here again, Friel shows a keen awareness of the role played by the media in alerting public opinion nationally and internationally, though the media people themselves may have had little understanding of the local situation as McCann's account of the behaviour of journalists after the October march testifies:

> The Bogside was deluged with journalists. Some spent their time try-ing to identify a local Danny the Red. (The May events in France were fresh in the memory.) Others wandered into the area and asked to be introduced to someone who had been discriminated against.
>
> (McCann, 1974, p. 43)

A final and only partly successful addition to the range of commenta-tors in the play is Dr Dodds, clearly a remnant from the poverty play Friel thought he could write, rather than a fully developed character in this Bloody Sunday play. The American sociologist strolls onstage and addresses the audience as though he were in a university giving a lecture on what he calls 'the subculture of poverty'. The term is bor-rowed from Oscar Lewis, an American sociologist whose 1966 book, *La Vida*, is a study of the living conditions of a Puerto-Rican family in New York. Friel either borrows from or sometimes quotes verbatim from Lewis, the better to emphasize how certain general observations or concepts may transfer from their American original to a Belfast environment:

> And the first thing to be said about this culture or way of life is that it has two aspects: it is the way the poor adapt to their marginal position in a society which is capitalistic, stratified into classes, and highly individuated; and it is also their method of reacting against that society. In other words it is the method they have devised to cope with the hopelessness and despair they experience because they know they'll never be successful in terms of the values and goals of the dominant society.
>
> (*Freedom*, 1974, p. 14)

> People with a culture of poverty are provincial and locally oriented and have very little sense of history. They only know their own trou-bles, their own neighbourhood, their own local conditions, their own way of life.
>
> (Lewis, 1966, p. xlviii; *Freedom*, 1974, p. 15)

The Freedom of the City received very mixed reactions, with unfair accusa-tions of being a bad piece of Republican propaganda being matched by a worrying level of unquestioning support from Nationalist dignitaries in the North and Irish politicians south of the border. The ambiguity of the play fell victim to the political climate of 1974 as the IRA campaign in Ulster and on the mainland claimed more lives. Friel confessed some years later that the writing of *The Freedom of the City* had been thera-peutic: 'some kind of emotional inflammation, the way you get a sore throat as protection against a more serious infection'. Though he won-dered too: 'Was it an abdication of real, more humane things, under the pressure and hysteria of the moment?' (Radin, 1981, p. 34). Critic Fintan O'Toole has rightly suggested that 'it is a play about the impossibility of writing a play about Bloody Sunday' (O'Toole, 1992, p. 206) and Friel has commented in retrospect that the events of 30 January 1972 which he had witnessed at first hand had been too raw, too real for him at the time to allow for a successful transfer to the realm of fiction:

> I think one of the problems with that play was that the experience of Bloody Sunday wasn't adequately distilled in me. I wrote it out of some kind of heat and some kind of immediate passion that I would want to have quieted a bit before I did it. It was really – do you remember that time? – it was a very emotive time. It was really a shat-tering experience that the British Army, this disciplined instrument, would go in as they did that time and shoot thirteen people. To be there on that occasion and – I didn't actually see people get shot – but I mean, to have to throw yourself on the ground because people are firing at you is a very terrifying experience. Then the whole cover-up afterwards was shattering too. We still have some kind of belief that the law is above reproach.
>
> (O'Toole, 1982, p. 110)

The Freedom of the City thus comes to read like a palimpsest or a series of strata helping us chart our way through the complex issues opened up by the civil rights movement in Northern Ireland, its brutal repres-sion and the explosion of violence it led to, even before the 1960s ended. Divisive when it was first produced, the play would still prove controversial in 1992 when Field Day planned a revival in their new location of choice, the Derry Guildhall, and the event was cancelled by the local authorities. *The Freedom of the City* was not revived until 1999 when it was finally performed at the Abbey and directed by Friel's own nephew, Conall Morrison, as part of the celebrations of the Friel Festival, marking Friel's 70th birthday. Shortly before, the UK govern-ment had agreed to set up the Saville Inquiry, as part of the ongoing peace process following in the wake of the signing of the Good Friday Peace Agreement. The cover of the Abbey programme used the famous picture of British soldiers in front of Free Derry corner and the programme included a piece written by Michael Farrell which ended thus: 'In preparation for their inquiry which is due to open in the autumn, Lord Saville and his team could do worse than visit this production.' Twenty-five years after it was produced and 27 years after the events that set its writing in motion, no one doubted that *The Freedom of the City* could offer an unparalleled and challenging insight into Bloody Sunday and its consequences.

Note

1. Sunday Times Insight Team, *Ulster* (Harmondsworth: Penguin, 1972)), p. 80: quoted in Moore (1991).

Bibliography

Beckett, Mary (1987) *Give Them Stones*, London: Bloomsbury.

Bew, Paul and Gillespie, Gordon (1993) *Northern Ireland: A Chronology of the Troubles, 1968–1993*, Dublin: Gill and Macmillan.

Boland, Eavan (1970) 'The Northern writer's crisis of conscience', *The Irish Times*, 12 August, p. 12.

Boyd, John (1990) *The Middle of My Journey*, Belfast: Blackstaff.

Deane, Seamus (1992) 'Why Bogside?' [(1971) *Honest Ulsterman*, January–March], in Craig, Patricia (ed.) *The Rattle of the North*, Belfast: Blackstaff, pp. 397–8.

Devlin, Bernadette (1969) *The Price of My Soul*, London: Pan.

Friel, Brian [1974] (1992) *The Freedom of the City*, Oldcastle: Gallery Press.

Hickey, Des and Smith, Gus (1972) *A Paler Shade of Green*, London: Leslie Frewin.

Hume, John (1996) *A New Ireland*, Boulder, CO: Roberts Rinehart Publishers.

Lewis, Oscar (1966) *La Vida*, New York: Random House.

Linehan, Brian (1970) 'The future of Irish drama', *The Irish Times*, 12 February, p. 12.

McCann, Eamonn (1974) *War and an Irish Town*, Harmondsworth: Penguin.

Molloy, Frances (1985) *No Mate for the Magpie*, London: Virago.

Moore, Jonathan (1991) 'The Labour Party and Northern Ireland in the 1960s', in Hughes, E. (ed.) *Culture and Politics in NI, 1960–90*, Buckingham: Open University Press.

Murray, Christopher (1999) *Brian Friel: Essays, Diaries, Interviews, 1964–1999*, London: Faber.

O'Neill, Terence (1972) *The Autobiography of Terence O'Neill, Prime Minister of Northern Ireland, 1963–1969*, London: Granada Publishing.

O'Toole, Fintan (1982) 'The man from God knows where', in Murray, Christopher (1999) *Brian Friel: Essays, Diaries, Interviews, 1964–1999*, London: Faber, pp. 105–15.

O'Toole, Fintan (1992) 'Marking time' in Peacock, Alan (ed.) *The Achievement of Brian Friel*, Gerrards Cross: Colin Smythe, pp. 202–14.

Radin, Victoria (1981) 'Voice from Ireland', *The Observer*, 1 March, p. 34.

Rose, Richard (1976) *Northern Ireland: A Time of Choice*, London: Macmillan.

Rushe, Desmond (1970) 'Kathleen Mavourneen, here comes Brian Friel', in Murray, Christopher (1999) *Brian Friel: Essays, Diaries, Interviews: 1964–1999*, London: Faber, pp. 25–34.

7
Pulp diction
Stereotypes in 1960s British literature
Peter Vernon

This chapter will first consider the terms 'Freedom' and 'Oppression' and see that, though they might be applied to any era, the terms have particular application to the Sixties. We will then compare and contrast the literary scene in London and the Provinces, and see that the stereotypes of fiction (not only in popular fiction) are much older than the decade and are often still with us today. Finally, we will argue that these stereotypes are part of a general commodification of society, which began to break down working-class solidarity in the Sixties: a process which continued in the Eighties, under the Thatcher governments, the results of which we can see today in the devastation of manufacturing industry and concomitant fragmentation of society. In fiction, the stereotypes themselves may be seen to oppress by luring the reader into a closed system, in which freedom of interpretation is severely limited; thus the closure has a further, political dimension in that it tends to reinforce the status quo.

We begin with two initial points about the terms: 'freedom' and 'oppression'. The first point is obvious: the terms could take us back as far as the ethical dilemma expressed in the story of Antigone and Creon, for there have always been oppressors and oppressed; those who are free to oppress, and those who lack that freedom. The second is that one might productively recuperate these concepts in terms of a debate going back to the Reformation: oppression through the clerical authority of Catholicism opposed to freedom of faith under Protestantism. However, concerning 1960s Britain, a more fertile debate might be found within Protestantism itself: liberty-loving Protestantism may be seen in opposition to neo-Israelite, fundamentalist, authoritarian Protestantism (closely allied to the Zionist faction in Israel). The latter are 'The People of the Book', with the authority of Old Testament Commandments behind them, and they are in a dialectic with those who want the freedom to read and interpret the Book for themselves. It is perhaps not coincidental that the 1611 King James Version of the Bible became obsolete in regular Anglican services towards the end of the 1960s.

Oppression and tyranny inevitably create and co-exist with their dual opposites: irony and paranoia. Irony, and indeed satire, may be seen as a necessary reaction to oppression, while paranoia generates conspiracy theories in attempting to make sense and understand oppression. Certain events are immediately perceived as belonging to history: they are significant rather than banal. Schopenhauer famously opposes history and boredom:

> History shows us the life of nations and can find nothing to relate except wars and insurrections; the years of peace appear here and there only as short pauses, as intervals between the acts. And in the same way, the life of the individual is a perpetual struggle, not merely metaphorically with want and boredom but actually with others.
>
> (Schopenhauer, 2010, p. 2)

Looking back to the Sixties, after the passage of 50 years, we can perceive that memorable events in the West from that period – for example, the Cuban missile crisis, the assassination of President Kennedy, followed with horrifying rapidity by the assassination of Martin Luther King and Bobby Kennedy – created feelings of paranoia in the contemporary observer but simultaneously stimulated an awareness that he was witnessing history in the making.

The terms 'freedom' and 'oppression' have particular application to the Sixties, a decade that witnessed post-war austerity giving way to Macmillan's 'You've never had it so good' and Wilson's 'white heat of technology'. Although, we will argue, having it good and enjoying hot technology was for the few, not the many. In the 1960s, there was a general feeling that the powers of Establishment authority needed to be dismantled, for example, the subservient attitude shown by the media to political authority. This argument has been heard before: England was engaged in the same debate exactly one hundred years earlier. In the 1860s, the argument about freedom and oppression was given memorable form in Matthew Arnold's chapter 'Doing as One Likes', from *Culture and Anarchy* (1869); the piece was written in the context of the Hyde Park riots of 1866, which led to the Second Reform Bill of 1867: 'Freedom, [Arnold] said, was one of the things we thus worshipped in itself, without enough regarding the ends for which freedom is to be desired' (Arnold, [1869] 1966, p. 74). None of the classes in society, whom Arnold caricatures as 'Barbarians', 'Philistines' and 'Populace', is capable of governing, for they have no light to see that 'the central idea of English life and politics is *the assertion of personal liberty*' (Arnold's emphasis, ibid., p. 74). For Arnold, this assertion is a worship of machinery, which needs to be transcended unless anarchy is to reign. Arnold's appeal is to 'right reason' which, through culture, will inevitably lead one to transcend class in an idea of the *State*, which we will come to through our 'best self'. His final, very conservative, argument is to 'uphold the occupants of the executive power, whoever they may be' in order to avoid anarchy (ibid., p. 97).

The 1960s is brilliantly summarized in Larkin's lines: 'Sexual intercourse began/ In nineteen-sixty-three/ (Which was rather late for me) —'. They are taken from his poem 'Annus Mirabilis' (dated 16 June 1967), and come from his collection *High Windows* (1974). The poem ends:

> So life was never better than
> In nineteen sixty-three
> (Though just too late for me) –
> Between the end of the *Chatterley* ban
> And the Beatle's first LP.

> (Larkin, 1988, p. 167)

These lines are a paradigm of the debate expressed in the terms 'freedom' and 'oppression' in 1960s Britain: that is to say a general feeling that the decade could be perceived as a period of euphoria, coexisting with individual feelings of somehow having missed out on the euphoria. In 1960s Britain, freedom co-existed with oppression. Looking back 50 years, it is possible to see Britain in the 1960s as a place of liberation and freedom, but many, perhaps most, individuals were leading lives of quiet desperation. Today's vision of the 1960s is marked by retro-chic manifested in clothes and hair fashions (mini-skirts and bouffant) and the style of reproduced articles such as kitchen gear or Roberts Transistor Radios or new versions of the iconic Mini Cooper. Looking back from the twenty-first century to the 1960s, the media present a view of the decade as an Austin Powers-like Technicolour, LSD-drenched, groovy, metropolitan world, centred on Piccadilly and Carnaby Street, London. It is a view exemplified by some of the hit shows of the decade, such as *Joseph's Technicolour Dreamcoat*, and *Jesus Christ Superstar*. Some 1960s entertainments were notorious for nudity such as *O Calcutta!* and *Hair*, while the members of the Danish and Dutch Ballet Companies divested themselves of tutus and tights, and could be found bouncing all over the London Coliseum stage. In contrast, the individual experience in the 1960s was frequently one of austerity, dreadful bread, flat warm beer, and racism. In London, in the early 1960s, the packed wooden carriages of the 'Tube' permitted smoking everywhere, coal fires and other pollutions caused the great smog of 1963; the sign 'No Blacks No Irish' was openly displayed on rooms for rent in London (though dogs were often welcome). In the provinces in the early Sixties one paid one shilling extra to sit in the bucket seats in the back of the cinema, and the first expresso-bars became popular. Very few, if any, women were to be found in public bars, though some were permitted in lounge bars; while in North Wales it was rare to see women in pubs at all. In the metropolis there was freedom for the few, but for many in Britain there was only drab, economic oppression.

Larkin's lines wonderfully encapsulate for us the myth of freedom in the Sixties; a myth which Larkin clearly recognizes as a false nostalgia which he combines with the regret of somehow having missed the dream of liberation. Obviously at some level there was a freedom of expression allied to sexual liberation (the contraceptive pill was generally available on the National Health in 1961). Larkin's idea may also be seen as a reworking of Romantic exultation at political revolution in the Europe of 1790s: 'Bliss was it in that dawn to be alive, / But to be young was very Heaven', Wordsworth wrote, both of the French Revolution and his own sexual awakening with Annette Vallon in Blois.[1] Larkin expresses the idea in more demotic phraseology: 'the end of the *Chatterley* ban', combined with musical and media liberation in his reference to The Beatles' music. In contrast to the loss of the myth of freedom, another of Larkin's poems, 'Toads', underlines the oppression of the daily grind:

> Ah, were I courageous enough
> To shout *stuff your pension!*
> But I know, all too well, that's the stuff
> That dreams are made on.

> (Larkin, 1988, p. 89)

The poet, and we, are oppressed by the necessary tyranny of having to earn a living, and insure ourselves against the discomforts and vicissitudes of old age with a comfortable pension; but, simultaneously, the reader is given the freedom to recuperate the intertextual reference to Prospero's late speech, which Larkin achieves, quite brilliantly, with a polysemic play on the word 'stuff': '*stuff your pension!*' giving way to 'the stuff/ That dreams are made on'. However, in so accessing *The Tempest* (Shakespeare, 1984, IV. 1. 156–8) we are forced to remember that the subject of 'the stuff/ That dreams are made on' is not Larkin's 'that' but Prospero's 'We': 'We are such stuff/ As dreams are made on; and our little life/ Is rounded with a sleep.' We are not free, Larkin tells us: 'To shout *stuff your pension!*', and even if we were, it would not make any difference for we are but destined to die, and our lives are merely the stuff on which dreams may be created.

There is nothing new under the sun, and there's certainly nothing new about the British class system, and the minute differentiations that may be found within those classes. As we have noted, the same dialectic between freedom and oppression was current in the 1860s. Indeed, one could take the argument back to the sumptuary laws of Tudor England, or to the long reign of Queen Victoria (1837–1901), where behaviour and rules of society became ever more ossified, even to the extent of how much black crepe you should put on your undergarments when you were in mourning. The complex rules and dress codes for mourning were laid out in journals such as *The Queen* or *Cassell's*, while Jay's of Regent Street operated as a kind of warehouse for mourners.[2] Britain was then, and still is, split into North and South, rich and poor, as manifest in Disraeli's 'Two Nations', which is the subtitle to his novel *Sybil* (1845), and further manifest by 'The Condition of England Question' posed by Carlyle in 1843 (Carlyle, 1843, p. 7). Thus by the beginning of the First World War, the class structure was thought of as being virtually impermeable upwards, although it was relatively easy to lose caste (a major preoccupation in the novels of Dickens).

Popular fiction, the pulp fiction from the 1920s through the 1960s and beyond – Dornford Yates, E. Phillips Oppenheim, Edgar Wallace, Sapper, Sax Rohmer, Buchan, Charteris (who gave us The Saint) and hundreds more – all reflect a vision of England that is moribund and class-ridden.[3] It is a world of gentry who, in the case of Dornford Yates, drive around in Rolls Royces, rescue damsels in distress, and right wrongs. The protagonists are anti-intellectual; they seem to find unnecessary a university education, for these are men of action, who frequently work beyond the law, although subservient, forelock-tugging policemen sometimes aid them. They are vigilantes and mavericks, who are seldom interested in the subtleties of life, and have a very ambivalent attitude to women who sometimes have androgynous names like Steve or Pat and are portrayed as immature men, rather than women. In John

Buchan's novels, for example, Hannay's wife-to-be, Mary Lamington, moves 'with the free grace of an athletic boy', and frequently laughs by flinging 'back her head like a gallant boy' (Buchan, 1992, pp. 357, 499). These stereotypes are an oppression which is still very much with us: in August and September 2011, the BBC Radio 4 feature drama slot at 12.30 was devoted to a rebroadcast of a Paul Temple series which fulfils every conceivable stereotype.[4] Temple's wife, Steve, takes hours to dress, listens at the door, and the poor little woman never understands what is happening, which of course gives Paul Temple the opportunity to explain to her, and the inattentive listener, what is going on. The Chief Commissioner of Scotland Yard, Sir Graham Forbes, addresses him as an equal 'Temple' but Police Superintendents and lower ranks address Temple as 'Sir'. Temple also has friends in the underworld who respect and admire him and seem to know their place in the social hierarchy; they speak a sort of cod-cockney: 'Cor lumme, O cor, bless my soul, if it isn't Mr. Temple. How are you, sir?' The stereotypes of class are also preserved in the BBC serial 'The Archers' which began in the 1950s, and is still very popular. The programme presents us with a time-warp village, which certainly incorporates contemporary agricultural themes, but simultaneously reinforces the idea of an ossified class system in unchanging stereotypes of character.

The paranoia expressed in popular fiction, fear of the underclass, and foreigners, lies very close to the surface. It might be thought that class barriers broke down after the First World War, and perhaps even more after the Second World War, when the 1945 Labour government implemented the Beveridge Report and launched the Welfare State in July 1948. However, advances in science and technology, gained in the first part of the twentieth century, served only to increase the power of the few. Aldous Huxley makes the point well in his brief essay *Science, Liberty and Peace* which opens with a quotation from Tolstoy:

> If the arrangement of society is bad (as ours is), and a small number of people have power over the majority and oppress it, every victory over Nature will inevitably serve only to increase that power and that oppression. This is what is actually happening.
>
> (Huxley, [1947], 1950, p. 5)

It is evident that the structures and voices of entrenched class distinction carried on into the Sixties, and beyond. Very simply put, the voices express the class divide found in public schools and the services – officer class or squaddies, director's boardroom or factory floor – the stereotyped voices of Pulp Diction. The British class system is a matter of infinite gradation, with someone always looking upwards or looking downwards to somebody else (exceptions being the reigning monarch, looking down; and Joe, the Crossing sweeper, looking up). The idea is given classic form in the 1966 John Cleese, Ronnie Barker, and Ronnie Corbett sketch of upper, middle and lower classes, signalled for us by the actors' relative height, accents and hats.[5] The sketch brilliantly encapsulates entrenched class distinctions, with all of them 'knowing their place'. Simultaneously it explodes the notion of class, when it asks which one profits from it: Cleese, as upper class, gets a feeling of superiority as he looks down on both; Barker, as middle class, gets a feeling of inferiority, looking up to Cleese, but a feeling of superiority while looking down on Corbett; while Corbett's 'All I get is a pain in the back of my neck', undercuts the whole stereotyped structure. The class system, as with any such caste distinctions, works by inclusion and more importantly exclusion, and one of its most obvious signs is language.

Freedom and oppression, we have argued, co-exist in the 1960s, and probably in every decade one cares to look at. In our period, freedom is, by and large, reflected in the literature and art of the metropolis, while oppressions of various sorts can be seen more readily in regional literature. I re-emphasize that these are generalizations and there are certainly exceptions to them – it is finally, perhaps, merely a question of nuance. For example, if we look back at London in the 1960s what strikes one is the flowering of satire and sophistication in the theatre that emerged from university drama groups, particularly the Cambridge Footlights. While, on television, David Frost, Millicent Martin, Bernard Levin, and Roy Kinnear on *TW3*[6] overtly mocked politics and pomposity. Although *TW3* was in some ways daring for its time, London was not yet free to have a resident black comedian in the cast; indeed, the regular item of a topical calypso was sung by a white man (Lance Percival). However, the American version of *TW3* (again compered by Frost) had the black actor, Bill Cosby, as resident comedian from 1964–65 and his contribution was certainly significant in raising awareness, and confronting racism in the USA. *TW3*, imported into America, clearly inspired Rowan and Martin's *Laugh In*, which started in 1968, from 'Beautiful Downtown, Burbank', the programme featured the black comedian, Flip Wilson. The satiric journal *Private Eye* (amazingly still with us, although in a slightly less samizdat form) was born in 1961 with an essentially public school humour which mocks the political, social, economic and artistic orthodoxies, but mocks them from the inside, which is why, in a sense, it is all very comfortable – there is nothing really at stake. The writers and cartoonists of *Private Eye* such as Richard Ingrams, Willy Rushton, Auberon Waugh, and Peter Cook, made a fine job of mocking the Establishment from within it. However, it should be noted that *Private Eye* is also capable of good muckraking, investigative journalism particularly on economic, political and media subjects. Meanwhile, Peter Cook, together with Dudley Moore, Alan Bennett and Jonathan Miller created the most emblematic of Satirical Reviews of the Sixties: *Beyond the Fringe* (1961), which had quite wonderful spoofs of emblematic authority figures and subjects such as Harold Macmillan, Dame Myra Hess, Shakespeare, the War...

If we think, then, of the 1960s in London as freedom being reflected in art, we can also say that freedom co-existed with existential oppression in productions at the Royal Court Theatre of Samuel Beckett, and also John Osborne's 'Look Back in Anger' and other 'kitchen sink' drama, together with political and social engagement at Joan Littlewood's Theatre Workshop, Stratford East, with the ground-breaking production of 'O, What a Lovely War' (1963). The voices of provincial England also came to London in the engaged theatre of David Storey, Lindsey Anderson, among others, at the Court. The medium of television, a growing influence in the 1960s, brought us *Z Cars* (located in a fictionalized Liverpool) with strong regional accents, seamy low-life violence, grimy provincial city locations, and a very catchy tune. *Z Cars* moves on a leap from *Dixon of Dock Green's* homely London copper, with his catchphrase: 'Evening all!' Since television in the Sixties was truly a national phenomenon, the medium enabled a mass audience from the provinces and metropolis to observe each other more readily, and perhaps an argument could be made for television being a cohesive force in England at that time.

From this necessarily sketchy overview of the literary and artistic scene in the 1960s, we will now consider in more detail the contrast between certain regional and metropolitan novels of the period.

In what follows, the choice of works is inevitably personal, but I trust that the regional and metropolitan novels chosen are representative, rather than random. If one were to increase the selection a hundredfold, it might nuance the conclusions concerning stereotypes, but would not alter them in essentials. Though the number of examples cited is too small for us to be able to generalize about the syntax of 1960s novels, it is worth noting that the prose of regional novels under discussion is often paratactic, there is little subordinated syntax, and there is frequent use of dialect to give an impression of authenticity and verisimilitude. In contrast, a representative novel from the Sixties, located in the metropolis, shows a more hypotactic, internalized narrative that verges on the dramatic monologue. Our example of a metropolitan novel, Iris Murdoch's *A Severed Head* (1961), presents us with Martin Lynch-Gibbons, married to rich and well-connected Antonia, but having an affair with Georgie Hand, a 26-year-old lecturer at the LSE, who has just had an abortion. Martin is feeling very pleased with himself and with life in general; he muses:

> I was lying on the big sofa at Hereford Square reading Napier's *History of the Peninsular War* and wondering whether Georgie's incense was going to give me asthma. A bright fire of coal and wood was glowing and murmuring in the grate, and intermittent lamps lit with a soft gold the long room which, even in winter, by some magic of Antonia's, contrived to smell of roses.
>
> ([1961] 1965, p. 21)

His self-complacency is about to be shattered when Antonia arrives to say she has been having an affair with her psychiatrist. How coded this writing is: a house in Hereford Square, in the heart of South Kensington, would cost several millions today; the 'big sofa' for there are obviously many sofas in the large house; the value expressed by the images of 'soft gold' light in 'the long room', as opposed to the numerous less long rooms, the magic of roses in winter, all bespeak not simply comfort, but Establishment riches. This locus is the dream that many regional protagonists wish to see fulfilled. However, Murdoch points to the artificiality in images of decadence seen in incense, and images of disease in Martin's latent asthma. If this is the stuff that dreams are made on, the dream might very well turn out to be empty, and lacking in significance.

One of the most representative novels of the 1960s is John Fowles' *The French Lieutenant's Woman* (1969). Purporting to be a recreation of a classic Victorian novel, it everywhere breaks the narrative contract with atemporal references: to Henry Moore on the second page of the first chapter; to a modern existentialist on the last page, with aeroplanes, jet engines, television and radar also appearing (ibid., pp. 10, 445, 17). There is also a knowing wilfulness in the narrative voice, that lets the reader into the narrative manipulations used;

> But what you must not think is that this is a less plausible ending to their story.
>
> For I have returned, albeit deviously, to my original principle: that there is no intervening god beyond whatever can be seen, in that

way, in the first epigraph to this chapter; thus only life as we have, within our hazard-given abilities, made it ourselves.

(ibid., p. 445)[7]

Above all, Fowles plays with narrative time and emphasizes that play in a post-modern manner:

> The supposed great misery of our century is the lack of time; our sense of that, *not* a disinterested love of science, and certainly not wisdom, is why we devote such a huge proportion of the ingenuity and income of our societies to finding faster ways of doing things – as if the final aim of mankind was to grow closer not to a perfect human-ity, but to a perfect lightning-flash. But for Charles, and for almost all his contemporaries and social peers, the time-signature over existence was firmly *adagio*.
>
> (ibid., pp. 17–18)

In contrast to Murdoch and Fowles, the regional literature of the 1960s expresses a more obvious feeling of social and economic oppression. Here one could draw a line back to *Middlemarch* not forgetting its sub-title, 'A Study in Provincial Life', and continue through Thomas Hardy and D.H. Lawrence. Although the provincial novels of the 1960s have not worn very well, some of the film adaptations are still worth watch-ing.[8] Let us briefly consider a few regional novels of the period, some of them published just before the Sixties, but very much forming part of the Sixties experience. *Room at the Top*, by John Braine, is narrated, in the first person, by the protagonist, Joe Lampton; he speaks in Standard English but is very aware of the subtleties of English accent. Here he comments on his landlady's voice:

> We live at the top. It's always T'Top in Warley, though, with a capital T...She spoke very well, I noticed; she had a low but clear voice, with no hint either of the over-buxom vowels of Yorkshire or the plum-in-the-mouth of the Home Counties.
>
> ([1957] 1989, pp. 9–10)

In the sequel, *Life at the Top*, published five years later, Joe has moved to London. Walking out from the Savoy Hotel,

> [He] stopped at the British and Colonial showrooms to look at a pink Thunderbird...It wasn't as simple as all that; in the first place, I didn't want the Thunderbird...I had stopped wanting things.

I wanted power, power to put through my own ideas; I wanted to be taken seriously, I wanted to be something more than the boss's son-in-law.

([1962] 1987, p. 52)

The dream of emigration South, from the Provinces, has been achieved, and the move has brought with it material success, but the dream is seen to be empty. Emblematically he leaves one of the most expensive hotels in London, the Savoy, to gaze at the ultimate consumer item of the 1960s, a pink Ford Thunderbird.[9] (The 1960s version was the sleekest ever produced, and figured prominently in John F. Kennedy's inaugural campaign.) However, this symbolic car is rejected for a more existential ambition, left deliberately vague, to his becoming 'something more'.

Keith Waterhouse's *Billy Liar* presents us with the first person narrative of a Yorkshire Walter Mitty, called Billy Fisher; he too speaks Standard English but is surrounded by regional voices:

I slipped back a couple of notches into the family dialect and said: 'Look, do you wanna know or don't you? Cos if you do ah'll tell you, and if you don't ah won't...'. 'You just eat your breakfast, and don't have so much off,' my mother said. 'Else get your mucky self washed. And stop always yawning at meal-times...'. 'And get to bloody work,' the old man said.

([1959] 1974, p. 14)

Billy works at a funeral parlour at Stradhoughton, but spends his days dreaming of crossing the class divide and moving to the South. Waterhouse generates considerable irony by privileging the reader, in giving references beyond the world of his characters. Billy works for the wonderfully named 'Shadrack and Duxbury's' Funeral Parlour: 'Our task was to...greet prospective customers with a suitably gloomy expression before shuffling them off to Shadrack' (ibid., p. 27). The *Hamlet* reference: 'shuffled off this mortal coil' (III, 1, 67), amuses the reader in the rupture of tone and the bathos created, from the high rhetoric of Hamlet's most famous speech, to the lugubrious absurdity of 'Shadrack and Duxbury'. In Billy's dreamworld he has moved to London where he is encouraged to smoke and drink by his upper-middle-class parents, in the first of three levels of fantasy existence: 'My No. 1 father – the old man disguised as a company director – clapped me on the back and said: "*And* about time, you old loafer. Simone and I were thinking of kicking you out of the old nest any day now. Better come into the library and talk about the money end" ' (ibid., p. 16).

The same dream, expressed in Braine's novels, is found here in Billy's fantasy of riches and independence, signified in the move South to London. The shallowness and emptiness of the dream are underlined by the stereotypes of colloquial upper-middle-class language: 'old loafer', 'kicking you out', 'old nest',[10] but at the same time the dream is touchingly naïve and innocent. Billy expresses a mechanical view of language, seen in terms of a cog-railway, or cog-wheel system: talking to his real family he 'slipped back a couple of notches into the family dialect', while in the upper-class dialect, cited above, he has clearly climbed a couple of notches. In the last tragi-comic scene of the novel, the dream of the move to London is not fulfilled in reality: Billy turns his back on the train, and the girl turns her back on him. Billy once more takes refuge in fantasy and, in the end, begins the long, slow, walk home in the dark. His narrative, being interspersed with quotations from Psalm 23, highlights the bathos of the melancholy scene:

> I could not summon up my No. 1 mother, only my real one, with her pressed, depressed mouth and her pretty frown...He restoreth my soul, he leadeth me in the paths of righteousness for his name's sake. I saw Liz in the Chelsea attic, and Rita whoring it in the streets outside. I tried hard to shut it down and find myself, myself, but not knowing what to do for characteristics. Yea, though I walk through the valley of the shadow of death, I will fear no evil.
>
> (ibid., p. 186)[11]

Stan Barstow's *The Watchers on the Shore* (the title comes from Stevie Smith's 'Not Waving but Drowning') continues the story of Vic Brown trapped in a loveless marriage to Ingrid, who first appeared in *A Kind of Loving* (1960). The dream of escape to the South is this time augmented with classical music as a medium of enlightenment and liberation – but Vic is unable to transmit this passion to Ingrid. In his first move South, for a job interview, he is pleasantly surprised to find that North and South are not so divided as he had thought: 'What did I expect? That people two hundred miles South of Cressley would have two heads or four eyes and talk a lingo I couldn't understand' ([1966] 1968, p. 39). At the end of the novel, in a narrative move very similar to that of Paul Morel in Lawrence's ([1913] 1963) *Sons and Lovers*, Vic leaves the security and comforts of what he knows and goes in search of something new: 'Going, forward...It's all you can do. Going in fear and trembling, maybe, but forward, knowing the best and hoping against hope that it'll come to you; and just refusing to notice, just simply trying not to acknowledge, how cold and dark it is outside' ([1966] 1968, p. 206). This is clearly a much more mature and realistic approach to existence than that expressed in Billy's fantasy world. Barlow expresses a positive desire to go forward, despite the awareness of isolation and danger; whereas Waterhouse's Billy retreats from the possibility of freedom, returns to the tedium of Stradhoughton and the unreality of his immature fantasies.

In *Saturday Night and Sunday Morning*, Alan Sillitoe wrote perhaps the most emblematic and engaged of the regional novels of the period. An external narrator presents us with the story in Standard English, while the protagonist, Arthur Seaton, speaks in Nottingham dialect. Like Lawrence before him, Sillitoe presents a man who, although oppressed in working-class poverty, can nevertheless be himself. 'So you earned your living in spite of the firm, the rate-checker, the foreman, and the tool-setters, who always seemed to be at each other's throats except when they ganged up to get at yours' ([1958] 1967, p. 31). Arthur's commitments are more anarchist than socialist, but his basic position is anti-Establishment:

> I ain't a communist, I tell you. I like 'em though, because they're different from these big fat Tory bastards in parliament. And them Labour bleeders too. They rob our wage packets every week with insurance and income tax and try to tell us it's all for our own good.
>
> (ibid., p. 34)

In a subsequent novel, *The Loneliness of the Long-Distance Runner*, anti-Establishment individualism is even more apparent. The protagonist, called Smith by the Borstal headmaster (he is otherwise anonymous), likens himself to an isolated, wild animal, estranged from society, on which he wreaks revenge through cunning:

> They're cunning, and I'm cunning. If only 'them' and 'us' had the same ideas we'd get on like a house on fire, but they don't see eye to eye with us and we don't see eye to eye with them, so that's how it stands... my own war's all that I'll ever be bothered about.
>
> ([1959] 1967, pp. 7–8, 17)

His is a willed life of criminality: 'for what I knew I had to do once free; and what I'll do again if netted by the poaching coppers' (ibid., p. 54). Whether through music, daydreaming, myth making, or a physical move South, escape is a strong theme in these novels, where marriage, family, work and the economic situation are all seen as an entrapment, which oppresses the individual, male protagonist.

In conclusion, we can see the oppression of the stereotypes based on class, the sterility of a dream of riches, independence and comfort in the South may be perceived as reflecting a general breakdown of society in the 1960s. In a prescient statement, Rilke rails against the sham that is engendered by mass-produced goods in America, which he feels is about to take over Europe (his ideas will later be refined by Walter Benjamin):

> Now, from America, empty indifferent things are pouring across, sham things, *dummy life*...Live things, things lived and conscient of us, are running out and can no longer be replaced. *We are perhaps the last still to have known such things.*
>
> (emphasis in original: quoted in Agamben, 1993, p. 36)

Rilke's fears have been more than fulfilled in the years following the Sixties: shopping malls, those temples to Mammon, fill the country with meaningless articles, whose value is only in exchange and not use, or function. Fictions are consumed like the stereotypes: books have become as disposable as nappies. A recent interview of Owen Jones' book *Chavs*, makes the point that loss of working-class solidarity will inevitably engender ethnic solidarity to replace it, with all the dangers of extremism which that entails (Gamble, 2011, p. 14). Lack of respect for law, order and any authority is the downside of the freedoms (sometimes illusory) created in the Sixties.

After the Sixties, Thatcher's England continued the decline of manufacturing and shipping which had the effect of further fragmenting society and continued to break down working-class solidarity. As we have seen, malaise in society is expressed in literature and other media of the Sixties, in the language and stereotypes of character and class that we have examined. But more profoundly and subtly, these stereotypes lure the reader into closed systems. The longevity of the stereotypes, inscribed in clichéd images, removes our freedom of interpretation and reinforces the socio-political status quo.

Notes

1. See *The Prelude* (1932), XI, lines 107–8.
2. See http://www.victoriana.com/VictorianPeriod/mourning.htm, and www.morbidoutlook.com/fashion/historical/2001_3_victorianmourning.html.

3. Loan stamps from Cheshire County Library Headquarters, in the early 1960s, show that books by these authors were almost continually on loan.
4. The Paul Temple series was broadcast on the BBC from 1938–1968.
5. First broadcast 7 April 1966, in *The Frost Report*, written by Marty Feldman and John Law.
6. *That Was The Week That Was* (1962–63) shown late on Saturday evening to an audience of over 12 million. It was produced and directed by Ned Sherrin.
7. The first epigraph to the final chapter, taken from Martin Gardner, *The Ambidextrous Universe* (1967) reads: 'Evolution is simply the process by which chance (the random mutations in the nucleic acid helix caused by natural radiation) co-operates with natural law to create living forms better and better adapted to survive.'
8. John Schlesinger's *A Kind of Loving*; Karel Reisz's *Saturday Night and Sunday Morning*, Jack Clayton's *Room at the Top*, Lindsey Anderson's *This Sporting Life*, and Tony Richardson's *The Loneliness of the Long Distance Runner* are particularly well-achieved adaptations.
9. Perhaps it is significant that Joe gazes at an American Ford Thunderbird, rather than the British dream car of the 1960s, the E-Type Jaguar, since it reinforces liberation and the post-war American Dream.
10. This upper-class register can be still heard, preserved by some commentators, on the BBC's 'Test Match Special' programme.
11. The final scene closes the narrative of the two girls in his life: Liz, whom he loves, but cannot commit to, and Rita who is with his drunken work-mate Stamp. The scene is reminiscent of the conclusion to *Jude the Obscure*, with Jude quoting from Job, 3: 'Let the day perish wherein I was born' intercalated with 'Hurrahs' from the crowds at the Remembrance games (Hardy, 1964, p. 411).

Bibliography

Agamben, Georgio (1993) *Stanzas: World and Phantasm in Western Culture*. Trans. Ronald L. Martinez. Theory and History of Literature, vol. 69, Minneapolis: University of Minnesota Press.

Arnold, Matthew ([1869] 1966) *Culture and Anarchy*, Cambridge: Cambridge University Press.

Barstow, Stan ([1966] 1968) *The Watchers on the Shore*, Harmondsworth: Penguin.

Braine, John ([1957] 1989) *Room at the Top*, London: Methuen.

Braine, John ([1962] 1987) *Life at the Top*, London: Methuen.

Buchan, John (1992) *The Complete Richard Hannay*, London: Penguin.

Carlyle, Thomas [1843] 'Midas', in Altick, Richard D. (ed.) (1965) *Past and Present*, Boston: Houghton Mifflin, Riverside Editions.

Disraeli, Benjamin ([1845] 2008) *Sybil, or the Two Nations*, ed. Sheila Smith, Oxford: Oxford University Press.

Fowles, John (1969) *The French Lieutenant's Woman*, London: Jonathan Cape.

Gamble, Andrew (2011) Review of Owen Jones (2011) *Chavs*, London: Verso. *TLS* 5655/5656 (19 and 26 August), p. 14.

Hardy, Thomas (1964) *Jude the Obscure*, New York: Dell Publishing.

Huxley, Aldous ([1947] 1950) *Science, Liberty and Peace*, London: Chatto and Windus.

Larkin, Philip (1988) *Collected Poems*. Ed. and Intr. Anthony Thwaite, London: Faber and Faber.

Lawrence, D. H. ([1913] 1963) *Sons and Lovers*, New York: Viking Press.

Murdoch, Iris ([1961] 1965) *A Severed Head*, Harmondsworth: Penguin.

Sillitoe, Alan ([1958] 1967) *Saturday Night and Sunday Morning*, London: W. H. Allen.

Sillitoe, Alan ([1959] 1967) *The Loneliness of the Long-Distance Runner*, London: W. H. Allen.

Schopenhauer, Arthur (2010) *The Essential Schopenhauer*. Ed. and Intr. Wolfgang Schirmacher, New York: Harper Perennial.

Shakespeare, William (1982) *Hamlet*. Ed. Harold Jenkins. The Arden Shakespeare, London: Methuen.

Shakespeare, William (1984) *The Tempest*. Ed. Frank Kermode. The Arden Shakespeare, London: Methuen

Waterhouse, Keith ([1959] 1974) *Billy Liar*, Harmondsworth: Penguin.

Wordsworth, William (1932) *The Complete Poetical Works*, Boston, MA: Houghton Mifflin Co., The Riverside Press.

8
Sketchy counter-culture

Judith Roof

And now for something completely different. A man with three buttocks.

The wish of *Monty Python* is the dream of any counter-culture conscious of itself as such. Something completely different: rearranging orders, evacuating belief systems, re-purposing disciplines, travestying the travesty of institutions, satirizing satires of stereotypes, all in the hope that these might, in the spirit of satire, correct the absurdities they elucidate. We can ask if any of this is really 'completely different', but we don't need to because we already know it isn't, and that is the point. 'Difference' isn't different at all, but the same all over. Three buttocks instead of two. So how can comedy, which is by nature not so very different, afford useful impetus for political change? And did it do so in Britain in the 1960s?

Any estimation of the political efficacy of comedy as a form of counter-culture depends upon concepts of the political, of counter-culture, and of comedy itself. One way to address questions about the political efficacy of comic counter-culture is to understand the political as sets of power relations that can be addressed at many sites and in many ways, one of them being the very forms of culture itself as both cultural forms and cultural receptions. Counter-culture is not sets of discourses that run counter to any culture (as we know opposites are two sides of the same thing), but consists instead of various deviations from recognizable norms and ideologies (for example, extended families instead of nuclear families). Comedy consists in the sudden collision of multiple cultural systems, discourses, and ideologies in such a way that for a moment the systems and their incompatibilities become visible. Comedy (especially parody and satire) is an art of deviation that plays upon the absurdities of such cultural incompatibilities by torquing conventions, expectations, and traditions, and making their inequities evident. Thus, comedy functions as politically 'counter,' even if this 'counter' is neither oppositional, nor quite different. But more than even producing an awareness of inequities, comedy enacts a counter-cultural impetus by producing an awareness of the forms of culture itself – of how norms and conventions are perpetuated by intrinsically absurd institutional discourses and media superficiality.

In 1960s Britain, some forms of comedy became a mainstream strategy for counter-cultural resistance in just this way. Then, as now, comedy's operations involve both subtle formal protest and overt critique, the latter possibly mitigated by television comedy's mainstream sponsorship. But still, perhaps the subtle, minutely structural tactics of the ever-sophisticating practices of comedy nudge revolution by inflecting ways of thinking, while its broader satire provides an outlet for more obvious critique. The Sixties revolution in comic forms in British popular culture enacted a comic countering that both paralleled and pushed reconsiderations of the state of affairs as an effect of comic practice, not so much in terms of content, but in the very forms of comedy itself.

Beyond the Fringe

Opening with a lampoon of nationalism, *Beyond the Fringe*'s satirical stage review took over the fast-talking, caricatured, situational method of *The Goon Show* radio show, which had been aired from 1951 to 1960.[1] *Beyond the Fringe*'s stage was minimalist; their comedy depended upon rapidly establishing a situation – a national anthem, a church, a movie casting – on a stage unadorned except for a platform, three steps and a piano. Four men – Dudley Moore, Alan Bennett, Jonathan Miller, and Peter Cook – appearing in dark suits and ties played all of the parts and contrived their positions by enacting stereotypical speech, phraseology, and especially hackneyed slogans typical of cultural positionings. Opening, for example, with Dudley Moore pounding *The Star Spangled Banner* out on the piano, the first sketch, 'Home Thoughts from Abroad', lampoons American nationalism from a British perspective. Commenting that one needs to be able to play *The Star Spangled Banner* in order to get a visa, the group assures that the United States needs 'these regulations or any old riff-raff could get in'. Noting that 'they have a lot of riff-raff already', the group moves on to observe that 'the first thing that will strike you about Americans is that they are not English'. At the same time, describing the Statue of Liberty, they note that the statue's invitation to 'the poor, the huddled masses', indeed resulted in a response: 'The huddled masses leapt at the opportunity.' Moving on to what they refer to as the 'colour problem', Alan Bennett observes, 'I gather the Negroes are sweeping the country', to which Jonathan Miller responds, 'Yes, they are. It's about the only job they can get.' Finally, in response to the question, 'Isn't there a lot of poverty over there?', Peter Cook responds, 'There is, but luckily it has all been concentrated in the slums. It's beautifully done. You barely notice it at all.'

This series of one-line set-ups aimed at America's obvious 1960s social problems is not, however, merely a transatlantic casting of gibes, nor a securing of nationhood or national stereotypes. The group's overt critique of America, especially their continued observation that 'Americans...are not English', draws attention to the fact that Americans and the English are more alike than they would like to think. Their persistent self-distancing from the United States functions as a clever displacement of a critique of Britain itself. Deploying stereotypical nationalist jokes, while funnelling direct critique in antanaclasis produces the slight wrinkle that reflects critique back on to those observing America's ills while simultaneously igniting sparks of national pride. Britons could in the 1960s make fun of America's racial ills, but aspersions were never too far from England's own growing issues with poverty and immigration. This becomes evident at the end of the sketch, when, after comparing the ideological irregularities of the 'two-party system', the group attempts to discern where the 'real America' is located. After eliminating the South, New York, Los Angeles, San Francisco, and the North, they settle on Massachusetts. Alan Bennett comments, 'That's just a little bit of England', to which they respond ensemble: 'That's America!' In a final connection, the group comments that Americans are 'naive about sex', suggesting that Americans only think about blond women with big breasts. When Peter Cook asks Dudley Moore if he ever thinks about sex, Moore responds that he doesn't because when he does, all he can think about are 'blond women with big...'.

Using irony gradually to compare the United States and the United Kingdom edges into the obvious, appearing to follow and reaffirm audience perceptions. The irony of similarity works mostly because the troop seems blind to it, their commentary on Britain occluded by their overt observations about the United States. Using another country as a way to point out problems in the UK is one strategy for torquing critique that invites viewers to make the comparison themselves. Asking audiences for active engagement is one way to suggest that the same kind of active engagement might be necessary to identify and solve their own social ills.

Another way *Beyond the Fringe* makes evident the obscuring mythologies of nationalist narratives is by means of parodies of specifically nationalist performances such as post-war documentaries. In 'Aftermyth of War', the group points to conventional war reminiscences of English citizens as well as the British take on the militarism of the Germans. Presented as a musical, the sketch deploys the parody of hackneyed reminiscence as a way to make class issues evident. Again using one target as the avenue to another, *Beyond the Fringe* makes class snobbery evident in its presentation of the war's apparent absence of such snobbery. Ironically pointing out the ease with which classes mix is the very moment classes no longer mix. This same tactic appears in the group's short sketch, 'Real Class', in which Miller and Cook smugly declare themselves upper class, while congratulating themselves for working with such working-class nobs as Alan Bennett and Dudley Moore. Bennett and Moore proudly own their working-class roots at the moment they comment on Jonathan Miller's Jewishness, saying that being working class may be better than being Jewish. Miller then declares that he is 'not a Jew', but just a little bit Jewish. Constantly shifting from one perspective to another offers the same torquing as presenting one issue through the lens of another. If war nostalgia reveals classism, then overt classism reveals anti-Semitism. With *Beyond the Fringe*, the issue is always the one to the side, the indirect target whose ironic connection invites the audience to see it.

One of the show's final sketches illustrates another way in which comedy might illuminate cultural assumptions as a way to make social issues evident. In a sketch about movie casting in which a one-legged Dudley Moore auditions for the part of Tarzan, movie producer Peter Cook points out, 'The leg division ... you are deficient in it to the tune of one.' The absurdity of auditioning with one leg is trumped by the literal response of the producer, whose careful treatment of the auditioner points to the hypocrisy of cultural over-sensitivity. The sketch is completely straightforward; its circumstance creates a situation in which the producer can either be kind or cruel even if the kind response in its offer of optimism might actually be cruel. Treating a limb as a slight problem – a mere deficiency – recasts the limb as merely one part among many, all removable, all simply parts. Adumbrating parts as if they are in fact removable, repeatable, and proliferable enacts a parody of over-compensatory cultural practices. Taking these practices literally as focused only on a single deficient part points to attempts to solve large problems by focusing only on excisable parts. Hyperbolizing and repeating the part (and literally a body part) as the premise for comedy enacts what is out of kilter in the *socius* while appearing to take cultural responses literally. Just as focusing on one element of a complex system distorts the system, so parody itself works through a similar species of hyperbolic distortion. In 1960s British parody and satire, the literalization of parts characterizes the way comedy deploys both synecdoche and *reductio ad absurdum* as indirect ways to parse, examine, and critique social and political issues. Treating the literal part not as a symptom, but as itself the point illustrates the way systems address only one issue at a time.

TW3

The 1960s model of British television satire was David Frost's *That Was the Week That Was* (*TW3*) aired by the BBC. *TW3* mixed satirical commentary with parody, addressing such topics as the inefficacy of British leaders, religion and corporatism, and American race non-relations (and those at the height of the American civil rights movement) through familiar forms of commercial television. *TW3*'s satire was more biting and direct than that of *Beyond the Fringe*, mostly because it deployed its own medium – television – as the register through which it approached most topics, reducing everything to the 30-second rhythm of commercials and the glitzy but cheap production values of broadcast variety shows. This mix of parody and satire was multi-directional, critiquing not only its political and social targets, but the televisual medium itself as a persistently superficial, already derivative means of delivering information and reconfirming cultural stereotypes. One episode from early 1963, for example, contained an extended satire of Harold Wilson, recently elected leader of the Labour Party, via an array of commercial jingles for toothpaste and other products. This was followed by an elaborate blackface musical revue starring Millicent Martin on the subject of American race relations, an educational television-style presentation of a Consumer's Guide to Religion offered by host David Frost, a short demonstration of the requirements for the Royal Academy Art Show, a song satirizing Italy by Millicent Martin, a 'Silent Salute to the Men of Westminster', hailing all MPs who hadn't spoken in Parliament for four years, and finally an extended lecture by Bernard Levin excoriating barristers. These sketches were separated by a repeated sketch in which Kenneth Cope sings the first few bars of 'Maria' from *West Side Story* to a repeatedly unexpected referent – an overweight woman, a man.

More focused on contemporaneous events that went right to the heart of a problem – American racism, the corporate character of religion – *TW3* used the very tropes by which both American racism and corporatism were dissembled and celebrated. The episode's musical presentation of American race relations followed the Great March on Washington that had taken place on 28 August 1963. In overt response to a murdered black freedom protestor in Alabama, singer Millicent Martin, costumed in Yankee Doodle top hat, red and white striped gauntlets, and leotard, performed the song 'I Want to Go Back to Mississippi.' The song's lyrics began in a bucolic vein, but shifted to descriptions of lynching. Two minutes into the song, Martin was joined by the George Mitchell Singers, dressed as minstrels, who took up the song in an elaborate production number. The song lyrics prominently featured the 'N' word, and continued to embrace such other southern tropes as religious intolerance and the Ku Klux Klan with a musical accompaniment that became increasingly jazzy.[2] In this elaborate number, *TW3* took a representative trope – in this case the minstrel number – and deployed that form parodically as a vehicle for a decoded commentary – in this case the overtly racist song lyrics minstrelsy both performs and obscures. The juxtaposition of the minstrel form with racist lyrics simultaneously undid minstrelsy's celebratory cover-up and commented on racism through a form mediated by tradition. This mode of parody/satire used existing forms as ways to reveal the problems with other existing forms by decoding what those forms were really saying – in a sense by aligning form with content. The political impetus of the commentary was complicated by the displacement of critique to the UK from the United States, which did not have immediate access to the show. So the political effect of a British satire show airing a critique of southern American racial relations was complicated, though the broader condemnation was certainly a part of the move towards palliative legislation in the United States.[3]

David Frost's 'Consumer's Guide to Religion' satirized both religion and consumerism via a parody of consumerist analyses. Following the protocols of consumers' publications, Frost rated the world's six great religions – Judaism, Roman Catholicism, Protestantism, Islam, Buddhism, and Communism – on the basis of three criteria: 'What you put into it', 'What you get out of it', and 'How much it cost.' Mixing the discourses of consumerism and religion not only exposed religion as a discourse of self-interest, it also revealed the religious fervour of consumerism. The inclusion of Communism as a religion and a consumer choice was an added Cold War commentary on political hypocrisies as well as the superficial character of a worn-out revolutionary impetus. Frost's analysis concluded with the overtly self-interested recommendation that the Church of England offers the best bargain as it requires little input, provides easy forgiveness, and is generally low cost.

TW3's format mixed short repeated sequences with extended sketches, producing a rhythm of shifting tropes and targets that produced a layering effect. Although the sketches were more elaborate, the mingling of political satire with often silly parody (such as the 'Maria' bits) produced a self-reflexive commentary that softened the satire while sharpening the silliness. The one blunted the other, the intermingling and comparison providing both alibi – this is all in fun – and the species of deflection required to sustain satire as such. When satire is too direct, as is Bernard Levin's extended panegyric of barristers, it ceases to be satire and becomes instead a scolding that loses its edge because it no longer appears to have any distance from its target. This could be Levin's method: that in imitating the superficial profundity of barristers it simultaneously critiques, it ironically satirizes them. But the more direct tone of his address loses satire's resonant array of other targets. So while Martin's minstrelsy sprays everything from musical tradition, American southern language, overt racism, and a British willingness to displace such racism onto Americans, and Frost's consumer analysis illuminates the corporatism of both institutions and believers, Levin's lecture on the evil of barristers delivered to a group of barristers only critiques the barristers, demonstrating how more direct critique loses its edge.

'And now a man with three buttocks': *Monty Python*

Both *Beyond the Fringe* and *TW3* served as models for *Monty Python's Flying Circus* (1969–1974), which followed another less trenchant sketch show, *At Last the 1948 Show* (1967). The rapid shift from sketch to sketch intermingled with short bits repeated with small differences organized the programmes whose satire, filtered through parody, scattered critique among a number of targets. All deployed a small troupe of performers who were capable of undertaking a number of different character types, rapidly switching one to the other. The shows, too, shared participants: John Cleese, featured in both *Python* and *At Last the 1948 Show*, was a writer for *TW3* as was *Beyond the Fringe*'s Peter Cook. David Frost's company produced *At Last the 1948 Show*, which continued the multiple sketch organization of the others, but focused more on absurd situation and character comedy (much like the work in the later *A Bit of Fry and Laurie*). *TW3* served as an inspiration for future members of *Python*. John Cleese comments:

It had a huge impact on me, but not the impact it had in London. Everyone in London shouted 'satire!' for people discovered satire...and that changed the society. I'm not exaggerating because the result of that show, *That Was the Week That Was*, the first really satirical and bitingly, rudely, savagely satirical show that ever had appeared on English television was suddenly there and that changed the society because it was the beginning of the end of...what's the word?...um...deference. When I saw it, I had a completely different take on it. It was just the funniest show I had ever seen in my life and that I could ever imagine having seen.

(The Pythons, 2005, *The Pythons: Autobiography*)

Monty Python's Flying Circus was even then already a legacy and a retrospective, a summary and comic processor that milled the counter into the mainstream and vice versa. Like *Beyond the Fringe* and *That Was the Week That Was*, *Monty Python* exponentialized comic techniques as themselves the stuff of critique, taking it all one step further, pushing what had already been pushed, reflecting on the modes of critique that had circulated since the early 1960s in British television. Like the others, *Monty Python* refracted its satire through forms of the absurd, but *Monty Python's* one step is one step beyond satire as such, insofar as satire counters by exaggerating selected elements to reveal their inherent ridiculousness, with, as formalists remind us, a 'corrective purpose'. Instead of perpetuating *TW3's* parodical/satirical mode, *Monty Python* appropriated its interruptive dynamic, shifting from sketch to sketch and bit to bit before any of them had actually concluded, in a way reminiscent of the way *TW3's* 'Mississippi' or 'Maria' sketches had shifted from one musical genre to another or simply interrupted themselves.

Python's programmes always began with the repeated dilemma of a ragged man (Michael Palin) struggling through a hostile environment, and intermingled Terry Gilliam's collage animations with running bits that interrupted one another as well as the show's more sustained sketches. For example, the third show, 'Owl-Stretching Time', featured sketches about two Cockney women at an art gallery with uncontrollable children eating the paintings. This sketch suddenly shifts to an art critic eating a painting, then to a sketch about a man trying to change into bathing attire at the beach whose efforts are consistently thwarted until he ends up as a burlesque dancer on a stage, then to a sketch about a military self-defence class protecting itself from fresh fruits, and finally to an extended spy spoof about espionage dentists. These sketches are interrupted by a running bit featuring an army general complaining about the commercialization of the military, stretches of Eric Idle as a lounge singer in Libya, appearances by a Viking (in response to the general), a comparison of newsreel sports with books, an interrupted feature on rural life, and the brief sketch of valets undressing an eighteenth-century aristocrat for the beach.

The apparent random ordering of this material produced a surface absurdity that belied the episode's more sustained critiques of the military and of males as sex objects (reluctant or not). On the way, the episode parodies James Bond films, German and British militarists, silent films, lounge lizards, and the asceticism of North Africa. The effect of this rapid shifting was a sketch collage (repeated in a different medium by Gilliam's animations) that repeated the same critique in multiple, serially interruptive registers, but that also shifted emphasis from a concluding punch line (or lesson) to the sketch's premise as itself the whole point. If there is a joke, it exists all at once, from the start, in the very set-up of the joke itself – self-defence against fresh fruit, for example, or the constant frustrations of a modest man, or the roarings of a general over the style of advertisements. Social critique is always already there: the military is overkill, fake modesty is hypocritical. Setting comic situations is a means of making such a critique appear in sharp relief so that it simultaneously surprises and reconfirms what audiences already expected. Self-defence, yes. Against fresh fruit? Using deadly force? The *Python*'s comic sketch is, hence, both a discovery and a version of cynicism, a before and after all wrapped into one exploding moment. This mode of discovering/rediscovering socio-cultural issues and inequities has a way of bringing the known back into view, or making it immediate and urgent, even as its televisual form keeps viewers at a certain remove.

'And now for something completely different'

A joke. 'The train to Milan will leave at 3:30, the train to Madrid will leave at 4:45, the train to Brussels will depart when the big hand gets to the 5 . . .' This is a joke, a bad one, perhaps, but also an example of that joke staple, the nationalistic joke, the almost-but-not-quite political joke, the joke by which regional and national anxieties are displaced onto some other, the joke that consolidates the community of 'us' and a minor drama of aggression versus 'them'. Such jokes, and there is a plethora of them, already enwrap culture and its counter in so far as they deploy cultural material as fodder for their twists. The joke is a structure that collides one set of discursive systems with another, thereby momentarily linking these systems in such a way as to illuminate suddenly their connections and commonality. Jokes are explosions, sudden openings out. The intersection of systems and/or discourses reveals a momentary affinity among systems and discourses that also exposes the stakes of both teller and recipient of the joke, both as intrinsic parts of the joke and insofar as the joke is re-conveyed – insofar as the joke persistently repeats the same teller/recipient relationship. These systems and discourses are also the cultural/political structures of the joke's environment, the larger systems whose interplay and cooperation jokes expose. A joke requires the simultaneous recognition of cultural forms and the vaguely transgressive effects of their torsion. This is why jokes tend to be local and cultural. And simple.

And so the train departure time joke, presumably shared among non-Belgians by people who might measure themselves against Belgians, collides the transportation system with discourses of national identity and reputation, using an indirect, performative statement to comment on Belgians' intelligence. Jokes about the character of the alien 'other' are jokes that collide a knowledge of national stereotype with the often technological mechanisms of its perpetual revelation. The only culture such jokes seem to counter is the culture of the other, whoever that might be. They also supply a remainder in the form of insight about the culture from whose perspective the joke is produced and especially what that culture might deem important – in this case intelligence. By playing on 'the remainder', the joke enacts a critique of its own culture's biases and weaknesses hidden by the attack on the other, but subtly effective at pointing out issues just the same.

Arranged among Terry Gilliam's famous collage sequences, sketches, and repeated one-line bits such as 'And now for something completely different', the joke sketch is the basic countering block that counters by countering itself, performing in both its structure and its topic (and in the interplay between the two) the relation between the counter and the mainstream while also countering the counter itself. Although neither parody nor satire actually needs a plot of its own, and sketches based on those dynamics parasite themselves on the forms they travesty, the joke sketch depends upon the structure of the joke, making this structure visible as such, and using the visibility of the joke structure both as the joke and as a mode of the political countering itself. The counter-cultural impetus of *Monty Python* is its consistent illustration of the ways cultural forms themselves constitute the basis of inequities. By focusing on conventions – jokes, sketch forms, odd combinations – *Monty Python* exposes both the absurdity of conventional political assumptions and modes of their dissemination as well as the necessary way these are inextricably linked.

Because these cultural jokes already refer to themselves, they can be turned on their heads, becoming jokes about the power of jokes, which become jokes about power; and jokes about power enact a counter-cultural impetus insofar as culture itself is perceived as the locus of power. A good example of this is *Monty Python*'s 'Lethal Joke' sketch, featured in the very first episode of the show in 1969. The premise of the sketch is a joke so funny that it kills the recipient, including its own author. A joke writer, Ernest Scribbler, writes the 'funniest joke in the world' that causes him to laugh so hard that he dies. 'It was obvious,' the voiceover comments, 'that this joke was lethal. No one could read it and live.' Scribbler's wife comes upon her dead husband, finds the joke, reads it, and expires laughing as well. The scene shifts to a contemporary news announcer outside the Scribbler's home talking about 'sudden, violent comedy' as Scotland Yard attempts to remove the joke, accompanied by the offsetting effects of sad music and the laments of a trio of police. The ploy fails, the Inspector dies laughing, and the sketch shifts to the army which has become interested in the military potential of the lethal joke. Having been transported to a meeting of Allied Commanders, the joke kills them all. Top Brass, impressed by the joke's power, test its effective range, which they determine to be 50 yards. The sketch abruptly shifts to an officer who takes over as announcer, describing the development of a German edition produced under 'joke-proof conditions', in which the lethal joke developers each worked on a single word to increase safety.

The German version of the joke, which the English could not understand, was deployed in the field in July in the Ardennes. Soldiers, pinned down by enemy fire, read the joke to their attackers with the effect that the Germans laughed themselves to death. The joke proved successful, 'over 60 thousand times more powerful than Britain's great pre-war joke'. Using clips from the war, the sketch moves to joke escalation with German attempts to produce their own lethal joke (including footage of Hitler), and continues with bits about allied soldiers using the joke to their advantage. This is interrupted by a scene of interrogation in which the Germans try to gain the joke, going to extent of torturing the captive soldier with a feather. He gives in and tells them the joke, which is again lethal. The sketch continues with more German efforts, as the Gestapo executes all of the failures. Nonetheless finally armed with their own joke, the Germans broadcast the joke via radio, which falls flat. The sketch then cuts to 1945, the outbreak of peace, as the joke is laid to rest, never to be told again … This is a joke, then, about jokes, and in this sketch a joke about the power of a joke that is never actually told in English, each bit leading to another, taking approximately ten minutes of air time. The joke of the joke is that there is no joke and that despite the sketch's ten-minute, elaborated tale of joke warfare with the Germans, the joke ends up in the 'Tomb of the Unknown Joke'.

The sketch's obvious counter-cultural commentary is a satire of weapons' escalation that replaces weapons with what is already a counter-cultural tool – the joke itself. Even though the sketch ultimately takes on the Germans as victims of nonsense (one of those national-istic jokes), its remainder enacts an extended critique of the military state. The joke weapon makes weapons jokes; the reversal of genre – such a thing as 'sudden violent comedy' – exposes the tragic violence of violence as well as the intrinsic violence of comedy itself. But that is obvious and not very subtle. What is subtle is the sketch's sophisticated comment on comedy itself as intrinsically counter-cultural.

The 'Lethal Joke' sketch occupies the last third of the very first episode of *Monty Python's Flying Circus*, offering the template for its counter-cultural comic method which is to produce comedy by not producing it – to produce comedy by pointing to the absurdity of the comic itself. Via the repeated use of the meta-joke, *Python* reflects not only on the joke as joke and the role of the joke, but also uses that joke as the pretext for parody and satire about cultural forms and their expectations which eventually – as jokes do – reveals, in its collision of systems, what is at stake in the comic itself: the absurdity of the cultural forms that bear it. This absurdity, already the stuff of satire, is not merely a commentary about the abuses of power, but is also about the intrinsic absurdity of the forms such power might take. But is this too subtle an approach? How insidious are the complexities of form?

The joke template also founds *Python*'s use of the progressive revela-tions of the meta-sketch – the sketch that comments on the sketch that comments on the sketch. The second episode begins with a regional joke about a farmer's observation of sheep who are attempting to fly. A farmer and a bowler-hatted City gent lean on a rural fence, facing the camera. Sounds of bleating sheep come from off-screen, and the gent asks the farmer why the sheep are in the trees. The farmer tells the gent that the sheep are nesting and that they 'are under the mis-apprehension that they are birds'. He points out that the sheep walk about on their hind legs, and in trying to fly from tree to tree, 'plum-met'. He comments finally that sheep are ill-adapted 'for aviation', though they are 'too dim' to realize it. When the gent asks why the sheep are trying to fly at all, the farmer points to 'Harold', a 'clever' sheep who is the 'ring-leader'. When the gent asks why the farmer simply doesn't get rid of Harold, the farmer responds: 'Because of the enormous commercial possibilities if he succeeds.' At this point the Farmer sketch is interrupted by a scene of two stereotypically dressed Frenchmen (striped shirts, berets) in lab coats in front of a diagram of a sheep. These two scientists explain the mechanisms of commercially flying sheep in a travestied version of stereotypical French manner-isms combined with the stereotypes of pseudo-science and infomercials. As the French scientists run around their lab bleating, the scene is inter-rupted by a sketch about four British housewives in a grocery store commenting on the literary and philosophical contributions of French culture. The sketches' commentary/meta-commentary stacks class-based and nationalistic jokes upon class-based and nationalistic jokes.

The rural joke (which is a class satire) turns into the nationalistic joke which is then turned on its head, in the end making fun of the British for being unable to grasp the possibilities envisioned by both the farmer and French science. At the same time, the sketch travesties the French scientists as silly opportunists, but also travesties the British stereotype of the French itself, as the sketch becomes a hyperbolic performance of stereotype. In the end, the stacking of the sketches produces a collision that reveals the intransigency of class and national attitudes, reversing the satire on the French to a satire about British stereotypes about the French which then turns out to reveal a mode of British ignorance – and all of this around the already allegorical character of sheep. This stack-ing, however, proceeds entirely from the sequence's original set-up – that British sheep ultimately fail at flying. It's not that they fly, or don't fly, but that they feel compelled to fly and fail. The French try mightily to transform the failed flying sheep into a commercial airliner, while the housewives comment on French intellectual tradition. This enacts finally a comment on catachresis, on the way signifiers shift from context to context, and on the inevitability of progressive misunder-standing, which ultimately produces an understanding about cultural misunderstanding itself.

Critique of the British class system is also an intrinsic part of the *Monty Python* joke, the most renowned of which is the series of layered sketches 'The 127th Upper Class Twit of the Year Show', which aired on the twelfth episode of the first series. This is an extended satire on upper-class 'twits', engaged in a contest that challenges their skill at walking straight lines, jumping three-inch hurdles, beating beggars, running over old ladies, waking neighbors, insulting waiters, killing rabbits, and finally shooting themselves in the head. Of course, no twit can actually negotiate these tasks easily, and hence, the class commentary (though the fact that the twits all appeared to have some form of palsy made the Finns pull the series from further broadcast). But as in the flying sheep sketch, this sketch, too, has several follow-up sketch commentaries, first a letter by an elderly twit, read in an exaggerated upper-class accent, that questions the class premise of the sketch: 'How splendid it is to see the flower of British manhood wiping itself out with such pluck and tenacity. Britain need have no fear with leaders of this calibre. If only a few of the so-called working classes would destroy themselves so sportingly.' This bit is followed by a collage of a soldier who can only fall to pieces.

Although this series of jokes on jokes seems to be more directly satirical, it also suggests the inevitable collapse of a class system as the classes themselves are *in se* inept at everything but self-destruction. This series continues in another sketch about a hyperbolically lower-class man who is courting the daughter of an upper-class squire, a sort of playing out of what happens when class attitudes no longer prevent class mixing. The portrait of 'Ken Swabby' is itself a satire, not so much of a lower class, but of upper-class stereotypes about the lower classes as well as the absurdity of a liberalism that accepts class difference without changing the system that produces the inequities in the first place.

Monty Python's constant shifting from sketch to sketch also re-calibrates audience distance by affording a constant process of rediscovery as well as a sustained meditation, not on any specific issue, but on its perpetual ramifications, presented from several perspectives. Just as satire is always to some extent a meta-commentary on both the form and the absurdity of what it travesties, so does the joke of the joke or the travesty of the travesty produce both joke and meta-commentary on its own form – a kind of inward spiral that also spirals outwardly. *Python* multiplies the 'jokeness' of its jokes through this meta-joke structure established in the very first episode and developed and repeated in the 'sketches' that comprise substantial portions of the series. This metastructure is always a commentary both on the joke form itself and on what the joke is joking about. This double consciousness constitutes *Python*'s 'revolutionary' one step further. Its version of the counter of the 'counter' is the 'meta'. If a *Python* sketch is counter-cultural, its self-reflexive – 'meta' – structure draws attention to the ways it enacts political critique. It is fairly easy to see how satire and parody can exist as self-reflexive – 'meta' – forms since they are by definition already self-reflexive – the forms that use the forms to make fun of the forms or the matter that uses the matter to make fun of the matter. It is also easy to see how sketches participate in this 'meta' economy by being parodical and/or satirical. And many sketches are. But the meta-form of the sketch *Monty Python* perfects is the sketch formed by the meta-joke.

And now for something completely different – a man with three buttocks. The counter-cultural tactics of *Monty Python*'s comic method function as counter precisely in so far as they make evident the joke of the joke as both structure and commentary, as revelation and insight, not so much about the state of affairs, but about the state of their apprehension via precisely the same media outlets as those deployed and parodied by *Python* itself. We never actually need to go beyond the set-up. There is no need to play out the ramifications of a man with three buttocks – and in fact we never see them. All that has to happen is the premise, then the commentary on the premise. Then the commentary on the commentary. Then we see how we see. And then. In the end, comedy's impetus towards change may aim at the ways we think as the root of the problem.[4]

Notes

1. *Beyond the Fringe*, exclusively a stage show, ran from 1960 until 1966 in both the UK and on Broadway. References here are from the DVD of a 1963 stage show. *The Goon Show* was a BBC radio programme that ran from 1951 to 1960.
2. Mitchell's minstrel troupe, *The Black and White Minstrel Show*, enjoyed a long success in the UK before critiques of its racism encouraged Mitchell to discontinue the blackface performances in the late 1960s. See www.telegraph.co.uk/news/obituaries/1405656/George-Mitchell.html (accessed 28 May 2013).
3. In 1964 the American Congress passed the Civil Rights Act of 1964 which extended broad civil rights protections to African-Americans and women.
4. Although cultural historians might want more 'quantitative proof' of *Python*'s political effect, estimations of audience reception, documentation of influence or other such 'measures' neither consider the complexity of what the group was doing nor the many ways such comic forays might change ways of thinking, influence a few key individuals, become a part of a cultural outlook, or continue to operate on both comic practice and cultural attitudes years into the future. If we understand the category of the 'political' as changes in ways of thinking, evidence of those changes exists in the ways other groups copied the Pythons. Broader influence is subtle, unlooked-for, and often indirect.

Bibliography

At Last the 1948 Show (1967) Associated-Rediffusion Television. John Cleese, Graham Chapman, and Marty Feldman.

Bennett, Alan, Peter Cook, Jonathan Miller, and Dudley Moore (2005) *Beyond the Fringe* (Acorn Media).

'George Mitchell,' Obituary. *The Daily Telegraph*, 29 August 2002. Available at: http://www.telegraph.co.uk/news/obituaries/1405656/George-Mitchell.html (accessed 1 March 2012).

Monty Python's Flying Circus (1969–1974) BBC. John Cleese, Eric Idle, Graham Chapman, Michael Palin, Terry Jones, and Terry Gilliam.

That Was the Week That Was (1962–1963) BBC. David Frost, Millicent Martin, Bernard Levin.

The Goon Show (1951–60) BBC Home Service.

The Pythons, Graham Chapman, *et al.* (2005) *The Pythons: Autobiography*, New York: St. Martin's Griffin. Audiobook.

9
Psychic liberation in *Sgt. Pepper's Lonely Hearts Club Band*

Ben Winsworth

When Beatlemania finally swept through England in 1963 with the speed of a forest fire, there can be little doubt that part of its appeal lay in the manner in which it burnt away the last vestiges of the dense, dark moral vegetation planted by the Victorians. The aftermath of the Second World War, while clearly a moment of great triumph, did little to remove the obfuscating greyness of the nineteenth century and in some senses validated the rigidity of class structures, the power of the Establishment, the terminally ill British Empire and the repressive moral codes that were propagated therein. In the 1964 Beatles film, *A Hard Day's Night*, there is a scene in which a bowler-hatted commuter on a train is teased playfully by the Beatles: 'I fought the war for your sort,' he pompously states, only for Ringo to reply, 'I bet you're sorry you won.' It is a humorous exchange, but one that reflects the generational conflict that characterized relations between those forever marked by Great Britain's 'finest hour' and those who believed that the best was yet to come. Rock and roll in America had reacted against the power of conservative ideology and authority in the 1950s, and while it had been embraced and adopted in the UK, it was not until its influence had been slowly digested that its full effects were felt in the following decade. England had produced Cliff Richard, and with it the first English rock and roll record – 'Move It' – in 1958, but Cliff was only ever the English Elvis, and a fairly pale imitation at that. Four years later, in the same year as the Beatles released their first single, Cliff found his true vocation while travelling down the 'middle of the road' in a double-decker bus in the film *Summer Holiday*.

The Beatles record, 'Love Me Do', released in October 1962, had little real impact, charting modestly in the top twenty as a result of the Liverpool faithful buying up the disc with a little help from Beatles manager and record shop owner, Brian Epstein.[1] However, by August 1963, in the same month as 'She Loves You' was released, the Beatles were taking the whole country – at least the vast majority of its teenage population – on a new, exciting journey that made Cliff Richard's 'Summer Holiday' look like a day trip for old age pensioners. The almost orgasmic excitement of the music – punctuated with escalating screams and encouraging 'yeahs' – together with their youthful good looks, cocky humour, thick accents, defiantly long hair and hip, original fashion sense, turned the Beatles into *agents provocateurs* for change, at the same time as they seemed to encapsulate the desires and wishes of their ever-growing fan-base. The screaming, fainting, and excitement generated and experienced at their concerts can be understood either as a rallying cry for the sexual revolution, or as an hysteric tidal wave of relief and release, that – if it did not signal anything more than desire and fantasy just yet – certainly expressed dissatisfaction with the repressive world outside the concert hall.[2] Defiantly working-class – Northern working-class at that – the Beatles also contributed to subtle shifts taking place within the system that defined them as such. Their appearance at the Royal Variety Show on 4 November 1963 is a case in point. According to Derek Taylor (Anthology, DVD 2), the press were out to get them, hoping to promote the idea that the Beatles had sold out, betrayed their young fans, in kowtowing to royalty, but Ringo's comment that he 'wanted to play me drums for the Queen Mum' defused such a media offensive with resolute Scouse charm. John Lennon's on-stage request, just before launching into a raucous version of 'Twist and Shout', had an even greater impact: 'will those of you in the cheaper seats clap your hands...the rest of you, if you'll just rattle your jewellery'. Footage of the performance shows the Queen Mum being suitably amused, and waving approval at the cheeky thumbs-upping Lennon who, more than simply getting away with it, had struck a significant blow against the Establishment and the social boundaries it tried to maintain.[3]

1964 and the conquering of America confirmed the Beatles as international stars and the centre point of the socio-cultural phenomenon later described by *Time* magazine in April 1966 as 'Swinging London'. While it is debatable whether the Beatles themselves opened the floodgates to a period of intense activity in the popular arts, they certainly gave them a big push, and helped to focus attention on a UK where talent mattered more than one's connections, and where it was hip to be working-class. World tours, phenomenal record sales, merchandise and other spin-offs, made the Beatles one of Britain's best exports, but the euphoria of *A Hard Day's Night* – on both film and LP – in the high summer of 1964 seemed to give way to a sense of disillusion by the end of the year. *Beatles for Sale*, released in time for Christmas, is a fairly shoddily compiled collection of rock and roll covers and dark originals that contrasts starkly with the energy and *joie de vivre* of their previous work. It is difficult not to take issue with Derek Taylor's sleeve notes that this 'isn't a potboiling quick-sale any-old-thing-will-do-for-Christmas mixture'. The title of the album itself is highly cynical, and can be read as a self-conscious acknowledgement that the Beatles knew full well that the weight of EMI's own demands were starting to oppress them. There was, perhaps for the first time, a sense that they were beginning to sell out. Even the photograph on the front of the lavish gatefold sleeve shows a decidedly morose and tired-looking group, anything but fab. This sense of fatigue and frustration rumbled on beneath the laminate surface into 1965, Lennon later confirming in post-Beatle interviews that *Help* (released in July) was indeed the cry for help of a man feeling himself drowning in a business where only one's superficial identity and plastic pop productivity seemed to matter.[4] Both the film, and the eponymous LP, while full of what can now be regarded as Beatles classics – some of which were more self-reflective and inward-looking than earlier material – still seems to fall collectively short. Songs like 'Yesterday', 'You've Got to Hide Your Love Away', 'Help' and 'Ticket to Ride' have their brilliance somehow diluted by the marketing demands of an industry that was still selling the Beatles as a product, as a brand, and that while it was all 'jolly good fun', both the Beatles and their fans were being exploited by forces much larger than either of them put together. The MBE awards – news of which reached the Beatles in the Summer of 1965 – also confirmed that they were in danger of becoming part of the Establishment themselves, that they were losing their position in the *avant-garde* of pop, and that – like Elvis before them – they were slipping into a hegemonic commercial wasteland.

However, unlike Elvis, the Beatles were starting to react against the safe neutrality of their position as 'lovable mop tops'. Striking even deeper than their disillusion, but clearly related to it, was their growing experimentation with drugs. Cannabis had long been enjoyed after a meeting with Bob Dylan on the first American tour, but the introduction of LSD 'some time' in 1965 had a much more profound effect, especially on John Lennon and George Harrison: Ringo, and then Paul were to indulge a little later on. More than simply recreational, LSD radically altered the way in which they saw themselves, thought about the world, and their position as members of a band. Both Harrison and Lennon describe their first trip – when acid was apparently slipped into their coffee by the legendary 'wicked dentist' – as being 'terrifying but... fantastic' (Lennon), as an experience in which, Harrison recalls, 'I felt in love, not with anything or anybody in particular, but with everything.' Beyond these common trippy feelings of universal love, subsequent experimentation opened up new perspectives and questions. To quote once more from George:

> And although it has a downside, I see my acid experience more as a blessing because it saved me many years of indifference. It was the awakening, and the realization that the important thing in life is to ask 'Who am I?', 'Where am I going?' and 'Where have I come from?' All the rest is, as John said, 'just a little rock and roll band'. It wasn't that important.
>
> (*Anthology*, 2000, pp. 177–9)

Such a shift in attitude was to have a major effect on the Beatles, and even before they had dropped out of the tour circuit in August 1966 and transformed themselves into a studio band, the liberating experiences offered by acid start to make an appearance on their records.

Rubber Soul, released in the same month as the Beatles collected their MBEs from the Queen, contains many clues as to the new direction that the band would take. Several songs, most notably 'Nowhere Man', and 'The Word', are new departures in trying to make an intellectual connection with the listener through the lyrics, even if they are – as James M. Decker has remarked – smuggled in via an LP package that contains enough conventional 'pop' not to cause any alarm (Womack, 2009, pp. 75–89). As this suggests, the Beatles were in their own subtle way starting to use an industry that had used them and – in the process – almost used them up. 'Nowhere Man' is a comment on indifference and lack of direction in contemporary life, about the need to open up and look around, to think for oneself and not take anything for granted, while 'The Word' is about love: not in the romantic 'love-me-do-she-loves-you' sense, but love as a universal force for good, able to liberate us all from being nowhere people. *Rubber Soul* was the first Beatles album not to have the band's name on the front cover photo. Rather than this being an egotistical statement about their fame, it is perhaps best to see it as a first step towards the band demythologizing themselves. At the very least, it signals that changes are taking place, that the Beatles are not indifferent to being labelled as a 'pop group' – and everything that this implies. The 'little rock and roll band' is starting to make important statements, helping pop to transcend its traditional (for the mid-1960s) boundaries. The slightly stretched faces on the front cover can also be read as a visual prediction not only of how the Beatles were attempting to transform themselves, but the ways in which they would stretch and expand the minds of their listeners over the next two years.

The flip-side of the Spring 1966 single 'Paperback Writer', a seemingly innocuous song entitled 'Rain', took things a step further with Lennon trying to persuade the listener that whether it rains or shines 'it's just a state of mind', and by implication that what is important is not the weather or external details, but that which lies within. 'I can show you, I can show you...Can you hear me, can you hear me?', Lennon drawls hypnotically in a song that contains the first backward recorded lyrics, a technique recreating through sound an aural taste of the acid trip: normal perception is disturbed, distorted, turned upside down, liberating the sleeping listener from a more conventional pop experience and so reality. Ian MacDonald observes that this was the first record to create a division between 'them and us' and that: 'Here, the post-war "generation gap" acquires a philosophical significance which would soon seize the imagination of Western Youth' (MacDonald, 2005, p. 197). 'Rain' was recorded in the middle of the *Revolver* sessions, an album eventually released in the same month as the Beatles stopped touring in August 1966. It carries on the transitional work of *Rubber Soul*, this time with a greater number of 'alternative' songs. Beyond the poetic artistry and sugary romance of Paul McCartney's 'Eleanor Rigby' and 'Here, There and Everywhere', there are explicit songs by Lennon about acid trips – 'She Said, She Said', 'Dr Robert'– and songs in which he attacks and resists the material world of objects and possessions – 'And Your Bird Can Sing' – encouraging the listener to do the same. George Harrison follows a similar path with 'Love You To' and 'I Want to Tell You', which testify to his growing interest in Indian music and religion, another significant influence feeding into the Beatles' change of direction and inner questing. Even Paul McCartney, in the penultimate song of the album – 'Got To Get You Into My Life' – hints at his own experience with acid, but it is the final track 'Tomorrow Never Knows' that takes *Revolver*, the Beatles and the listener through the looking glass and into a landscape far removed from the familiar, stable territory of Beatlemania:

> Turn off your mind, relax and float downstream...lay down all thoughts surrender to the void...that you may see the meaning of within...it is Being, it is Being...love is all and love is everyone...it is knowing...play the game existence to the end of the beginning, of the beginning...

Lyrics clearly influenced by Timothy Leary's *The Psychedelic Experience* and *The Tibetan Book of the Dead*, and sung mantra-like to a hypnotic C major chord overdubbed with backward tapes and strange mystical sounds. Russell Reising and Jim LeBlanc rightly point out, in a highly illuminating article on the Beatles and psychedelia, that they were not the first or only band to be influenced by acid and celebrate its effects (Womack, 2009, pp. 90–111). The Byrds, the Doors, and Jefferson Airplane, were all experimenting in their own ways as part of the burgeoning American counter-culture that clearly had a trans-Atlantic influence. Reising and LeBlanc interestingly note that Sam Andrew, guitarist with Big Brother and the Holding Company, realized that with *Revolver*, 'the Beatles had definitely come "on board"', but it was not until the release of their next album that they became fully paid-up members of the psychedelic club.

Finally liberated from an oppressive media circus that compromised their creative integrity, the Beatles set to work on an extended series of recording sessions from late November 1966 until the following Spring: sessions that resulted in *Sgt. Pepper's Lonely Hearts Club Band* being released on 1 June 1967. It was originally conceived as a concept album based on recollections of childhood in Liverpool, traces of which are seen on 'Penny Lane/Strawberry Fields Forever', extracted from the early sessions and released as a single to satisfy EMI and Brian Epstein: both worried that creative exclusion would result in a loss of popularity and – no doubt – profit. Such corporate greed dented the Proustian incentive. McCartney's idea of Sgt. Pepper's band representing the Beatles' alter egos and taking the album 'on tour' into the living rooms and bedrooms of their fans remained, but never really got past the album cover, the first two songs or the reprise of the title track. The original idea clearly fails, but there is a sense in which it works in conjunction with a much more powerful concept running through the album at a deeper level than the dressing up that sometimes appears as an almost naïve form of make-believe, even though McCartney has stated that the adoption of a different persona was fundamental in helping to free the band.[5] The opulent album cover – designed with the help of Peter Blake – already gives clues to the fact that *Sgt. Pepper* is both a major turning point and a self-conscious attempt to turn pop into art. Like the Pop artists finding serious themes in the everyday objects and experience(s) of popular/consumer culture and accommodating them in their paintings, so *Sgt. Pepper* shows how serious ideas and themes can be accommodated in a popular/pop genre that was generally regarded (at the time) as superficial, temporary, and without any real intellectual weight.[6]

Blake's collage of artists, writers, poets, philosophers, psychoanalysts, musicians, actors, all placed behind the Beatles at the focal point of the LP cover, is both an acknowledgement of influence and a statement about how the Beatles conceived of themselves as being equally deserving of critical attention. It's also a collage that breaks down barriers between high culture and popular culture, something – of course – that the album as a whole is attempting to do. Standing to the right of 'Sgt. Pepper's Band' we find waxwork models of the Beatles circa 1964/65. The visual contrast between the two groups is dramatic, and as if to underline the point that the fab four are dead, the name 'Beatles' that figures in the foreground is spelt out in the form of a funeral wreath complete with floral guitar tribute. Buddha-like figures, Indian statuettes, what looked temptingly like – but wasn't – a bed of cannabis plants, all helped to signify that the fully reincarnated Beatles were travelling to new places and that the listener of the album was free to follow them into an experience far more dynamic and challenging than anything that Beatlemania – for all its undeniable energy and breath-of-fresh-air freedoms – had served up. For the first time in the history of pop, the lyrics were printed on the fire engine red back cover of the gatefold sleeve: another indication that they had something important to say, that they were no longer a dance band, a beat group, and that while they may have played an important part in dragging Britain out of the black-and-white world of post-war austerity and repression, they now had a more revolutionary objective in mind.[7]

Sgt. Pepper's Lonely Hearts Club Band was influenced by, articulated, and fed energy back into the growing counter-cultural movement that had gradually become more manifest in America and parts of Europe from the mid-1960s, and which the Beatles – like many other bands – had already helped to propagate through being icons of teenage rebellion. The complex nature of the songs testifies to the fact that the Beatles – like many of their generation – were growing up, becoming more politically aware, and starting to find a more confident voice with which to define themselves.[8] While some of the tracks, like the controversially entitled 'Lucy in the Sky with Diamonds' are superficial examples of Sixties psychedelia, others are more engaged and look beyond the subjectivity of LSD as a purely aesthetic/sensory experience. Of course, many of the Beatles' early psychedelic songs followed this idea, but in *Sgt. Pepper* they found the space and freedom to be more explicit in communicating the Word.[9] Even some of the more whimsical songs speak of the importance of community and love: 'With a Little Help from My Friends', while others mark the changes and transitions that had been happening to the band and the individual members within it: 'Getting Better' celebrates personal growth and awareness, while 'Fixing a Hole' shows McCartney almost catching up with Lennon as he observes the 'silly people' running around pointlessly, unable to pass through the 'door' of perception that he himself has finally entered. It is, however, George Harrison's 'Within You, Without You' and – principally – John Lennon's 'A Day in the Life' that stand out.

'A Day in the Life', while the final track on *Sgt. Pepper*, was one of the first songs that the Beatles began working on for the new album. Clearly LSD-inspired – but not necessarily a call to try it out – Lennon, in the three principal verses, gives examples of the futility and pointless nature of existence and the superficial manner in which the vast majority perceive it, or are encouraged to perceive it by the media (see MacDonald, 2005, pp. 227–32; Moore, 2001, pp. 52–7). Life is short: the early death of Tara Browne (one of the heirs to the Guinness fortune) blowing 'his mind out in a car' is testament enough, while the crowd assembling around the smashed vehicle are blinded to this stark fact in their attempt to identify the celebrity victim. Similarly, that same crowd will turn away from anything too confrontational or challenging, rejecting the deeper questions posed, for example, by war films that Lennon – perhaps with a veiled, indirect reference to Vietnam – feels one needs to answer. The council workers in Blackburn counting holes in the road – clearly a metaphor for the inability to focus on anything but the physically concrete – and a tabloid press reporting such trivial 'news', adds to the bleak picture of a world where we are, to quote from George Harrison's final solo recording, 'brainwashed by the media, brainwashed by the press' into a state of passive indifference.[10] McCartney's contribution to 'A Day in the Life', while lifting the tempo musically speaking, adds to the gloominess with its overt 'cheery portrait' of a day in the life of most ordinary people getting up, going to work, getting bored, and escaping into fantasy and daydream.[11] The long drawn-out cry that follows almost seamlessly on from McCartney's vocal, sounds like a wailing scream of frustration and boredom, the inner voice of the true self trapped in a prison of quotidian concerns. 'I'd love to turn you on', a Leary-like lyric repeated at the end of the second and third verse, is clearly a wake-up call: not especially to take LSD, but to realize that there is so much more to life, that one can free oneself through a change of perspective. LSD can help – as earlier Beatles' lyrics clearly try to illustrate – but only in a catalytic sense if the dynamic vision one gains during the acid trip is to be critically applied. In this sense, the two dramatic/orgasmic orchestral crescendos that provide such an exciting musical feature on the track can be understood as a rush/rushing through sensory distortion, but one that leads towards an awakening, a rebirth, a turning on, a returning to full consciousness with greater clarity about the nature of one's environment and the structures that threaten to confine it.

The alternative to 'turning on' is musically recreated in the long, resonating E major piano chord that concludes 'A Day in the Life'. Ian MacDonald notes that Lennon wanted 'a sound like the end of the world' (MacDonald, 2005, p. 230), thus making it the final final chord, starkly acknowledging – as in the first verse of the song – that death is the inescapable conclusion of all our lives. The brutal striking of the chord, and the long fade-out to the void, can be understood as an attempt to inject a sense of existential urgency into the listener, encouraging him or her to reflect back on the lyrics of the song, and so upon life itself. The rest may well be silence, but 'A Day in the Life' attempts to shed the scales from our eyes so that life itself is not a rehearsal for death, nor a reflection of it, but rather a state of Being in which we are truly alive both physically and intellectually, and thus able to live more creatively. The almost interminable drone of the fading chord tolls out warningly the dead lives of the 'crowd of people' unable to engage with anything other than superficial experience. As such, it creates a chilling contrast with the *Pet Sounds*-inspired fade-out that marks 'Good Morning, Good Morning'. Here, the irritating refrain based on a cornflakes advert, intercut with farmyard and fox hunting sounds, both reflects and satirizes the growing consumer society, and while the objective is the same, the deliberate superficiality of the exercise amplifies the effect of the final chapter in 'A Day in the Life'.

Harrison's 'Within You, Without You' is a more direct attempt to turn the listener on: groundbreaking for its time in musical terms by rejecting the traditional pop/rock content/context, something which works in parallel with the lyrics to destabilize and challenge both the ear and the imagination. The listener is transported by the Indian sounds beyond the familiar and into a strange, mystical and timeless space – a meditative area rather than narcotic – where we are urged to realize that we are only 'very small' in the universal scheme of things, but that love and wisdom – inner peace – can be achieved through unlocking that which is within, and that the key lies in our own hands. 'No one else can make you change', although clearly Harrison and the other Beatles want to help the listener in his or her own steps to liberate the self through the psychic/psychedelic manifesto playing itself out on the turntable. The fact that they felt the need to add some laughter at the end of 'Within

You, Without You', apparently in a spirit of comic relief after a 'heavy' listening experience, is a testament to just how seriously they both took the message and wanted it to be taken, even if it also betrays an engaging sense of apprehension and self-consciousness about the enterprise. As such, it can also be read as anticipating the laughter of straight society mocking those looking for another way of being and experiencing: one that appears 'awfully funny'[12] to the uninitiated. It is straight society and conventional perception that prevent the kind of enlightenment that Harrison is trying to move us towards. The peace that comes through the capacity to engage with love in a universal sense is lost to those pursuing material satisfaction alone, and so too the message of the song that runs against the ideology of the ever-growing consumer society.[13] These are all subjects that 'we' have been 'talking' about, that the Beatles through *Sgt. Pepper* are discussing in a variety of different and yet interconnected ways. Subjects too that should concern the listener, ever more closely addressed throughout the second half of 'Within You, Without You', and ultimately asked to decide which side of the fence they are on. Think for yourself: are you with us, or are you 'one of them'?

To conclude, we can remark that *Sgt. Pepper's Lonely Hearts Club Band* is a revolutionary album on a number of different levels. It allowed the Beatles to reconstruct themselves and seek to effect similar transformations in the pop-buying public by offering them a musical and lyrical text that both reflected counter-cultural philosophy at the same time as it worked on the process of helping to define it.[14] It elevated pop into a place where it transgressed the high culture/low culture boundary, which led to Kenneth Tynan's comment that the album's release 'was a decisive moment in the history of Western civilization' (cited in MacDonald, 2005, p. 249), giving the Beatles an artistic and intellectual credibility unimaginable when they first started out. Revolutionary too, in marking the high point of their psychedelic experimentation – perhaps the zenith of their career as a band – and yet at the same time there is a sense in which LSD is gradually being exchanged for a more soberly critical and less chemically influenced view of reality. Yes, Lucy and her 'kaleidoscope eyes' are still there, Mr Kite will continue to fly 'through the ring' to a swirl of trippy sounds, but there is all the time a much deeper musical and lyrical canvas being painted. Unlike Tennyson's Lotus Eaters, the Beatles were able to pass beyond frequent moments of physical and intellectual inertia and produce an album in which the listening experience itself became transitional. As well as being a personal – and self-conscious – statement about their musical intentions and desire to give pop/rock greater critical integrity,

Sgt. Pepper is also an album that engages directly with the listener in an attempt to liberate his or her perception of the world. Time and again – in ways that go beyond the original concept for the record – it both reflects upon the vacuous and superficial nature of contemporary 'modern' life, and offers an alternative narrative. Having suffered the limiting experience of being turned into products themselves, *Sgt. Pepper* shows the Beatles to be turning the product against the system from the inside in a celebration of autonomy designed to transcend cultural and political repression. While inviting the record buyer to enjoy Lucy, Rita, Mr Kite, Billy Shears and the eponymous Sergeant himself, the Beatles were not simply interested in guaranteeing a splendid time for all. Beyond this, they encourage the listener to join the psychic revolution, allowing him or her to become an active participant in the deconstruction of all the forces that limit existential freedom and clarity. Even though the Beatles' idealism eventually went pear-shaped – or rather Apple-shaped – as they tried to apply psychedelic/counter-cultural theory to the corporate world, *Sgt. Pepper* – at the very least – enabled both the band and their followers to see a way beyond 'the wall of illusion'.

Notes

1. Although reaching only a fairly lowly position, Ian MacDonald observes that 'Love Me Do' was the 'first faint chime of a revolutionary bell' (2005, p. 205).
2. As Pearson Phillips eulogized in *The Daily Mail* on 11 April 1970: 'Before them there were things called romance and glamour. They injected sincerity, realism, sex. They picked up a pass from D. H. Lawrence, and ran the whole length of the field. They put the sugar on The Pill' (Egan, 2009, pp. 222–3).
3. Paul Gleed, in ' "The rest of you, if you'll just rattle your jewelry": The Beatles and questions of mass and high culture', also understands Lennon's comment to reflect something of the Beatles' position as artists breaking down not only class barriers, but those between popular culture and high culture (Womack and Davis, 2006, p. 162).
4. See MacDonald (2005), p. 153.
5. See *Anthology* (2000), p. 241, and Badman (2002), p. 256.
6. Bernard Gendron states that after the release of *Sgt. Pepper* 'The Beatles were being hailed as *bona fide* artists belonging in the same company as illustrious highbrow creators and not merely as pop cultural proxies or simulacra' (2002, p. 195).
7. See Munice (2000), pp. 50–1, for an alternative point of view.
8. Sheila Whiteley in ' "Tangerine trees and marmalade skies": cultural agendas or optimistic escapism?', concludes that Sgt. Pepper testifies to the fact that both the Beatles and the 1960s were evolving in significant ways and that it is an album 'highlighting the need for cultural change and setting an agenda based on love' (Julien, 2008, p. 22).

9. For a detailed reading of Sgt. Pepper within the wider pyschedelic context and community, see Russell Reising and Jim LeBlanc, 'Within and without: Sgt. Pepper's Lonely Hearts Club Band and psychedelic insight' (Julien, 2008, pp. 103–20).

10. From 'Brainwashed', the title track of George Harrison's *Brainwashed*, released posthumously in 2002.

11. This idea is further explored in 'Good Morning, Good Morning', a more expansive account of a tedious and superficial life dulled by the mass media into passive submission: 'I've got nothing to say, but it's OK.'

12. In a much quoted comment to Sir Joseph Lockwood, Chairman of EMI, and made some time towards the end of 1967, the Queen remarked of her once loyal subjects, 'The Beatles are turning awfully funny, aren't they?'

13. Ian MacDonald wryly observes that the 'accusatory finger' pointed by Harrison in 'Within You, Without You', was certainly felt to be 'bad manners in times of relativism and making-do' (MacDonald, 2005, p. 243).

14. Allan F. Moore makes the point that while Sgt. Pepper gave rise to a variety of critical responses on its release, it is impossible to know how the vast number of ordinary listeners reacted. Moore notes that unlike the general record-buying public, 'Critics and reviewers are paid to respond', and thus their observations are easier to trace. However, there is a general consensus that Sgt. Pepper, if it didn't entirely (and on its own) dictate a future direction, certainly articulated the desires and aspirations of many young people in the second half of the 1960s, and became both a musical and cultural focal point around which counter-cultural ideas and ideology coalesced (2001, p. 65).

Bibliography

Badman, Keith (2002) *The Beatles: Off the Record: The Dream Is Over*, New York: Omnibus.

Beatles, The (1996) *The Beatles Anthology* (DVD), directed by Geoff Wonfor: Apple.

Beatles, The (2000) *The Beatles Anthology*, London: Cassell.

Decker, James M. (2009) "Try thinking more": *Rubber Soul* and the Beatles' transformation of pop', in Womack, Kenneth (ed.) *The Cambridge Companion to The Beatles*, Cambridge: Cambridge University Press.

Egan, Sean (ed.) (2009) *The Mammoth Book of The Beatles*, London: Constable and Robinson.

Gendron, Bernard (2002) *Between Montmartre and the Mudd Club*, Chicago: University of Chicago Press.

Julien, Olivier (ed.) (2008) *Sgt. Pepper and the Beatles: It Was Forty Years Ago Today*, London: Ashgate.

Leary, Timothy, Metzner, Ralph and Alpert, Richard (2008) *The Psychedelic Experience: A Manual Based on 'The Tibetan Book of the Dead'*, London: Penguin Modern Classics.

LeBlanc, Jim and Reising, Russell (2009) 'Magical mystery tours and other trips: yellow submarines, newspaper taxis, and the Beatles' psychedelic years', in Womack, Kenneth (ed.) *The Cambridge Companion to The Beatles*, Cambridge: Cambridge University Press.

MacDonald, Ian (2005) *Revolution in the Head: The Beatles' Records and the Sixties*, London: Pimlico.

Martin, George (1994) *Summer of Love: The Making of Sgt. Pepper*, London: Macmillan.

Moore, Allan F. (2001) *The Beatles: Sgt. Pepper's Lonely Hearts Club Band*, Cambridge: Cambridge University Press.

Munice, John (2000) 'The Beatles and the spectacle of youth', in Inglis, Ian (ed.) *The Beatles, Popular Music and Society: A Thousand Voices*, London: Macmillan.

Womack, Kenneth and Davis, Todd F. (eds) (2006) *Reading The Beatles: Cultural Studies, Literary Criticism, and the Fab Four*, Albany, NY: State University of New York Press.

Womack, Kenneth (ed.) (2009) *The Cambridge Companion to The Beatles*, Cambridge: Cambridge University Press.

10
Preservation Society

Raphael Costambeys-Kempczynski

Introduction: or simulating the transcendence of a potentially isolated subject

In political terms, 1968 began on 5 January with the Prague Spring and was dominated by a growing violence linked to various civil rights movements. On 17 March, 80,000 anti-Vietnam War demonstrators clashed with police outside the American Embassy on London's Grosvenor Square, leading to 200 arrests and nearly 90 injuries. An eye-witness to the event, Mick Jagger was inspired to write the song 'Street-Fighting Man' (1968). On 20 April, Enoch Powell gave his divisive Birmingham speech, more commonly known as the 'Rivers of Blood' speech, which would later be satirized by Paul McCartney in the Beatles' song 'Get Back' (1969). In his book, *Ray Davies: Not Like Everyone Else* (2007), Thomas M. Kitts writes about the reception of the Powell speech:

> Anxious about the radical assault [Powell's supporters] had witnessed on all kinds of social and political issues launched by the young, women, and minorities and frightened that the race riots of America would soon come to Britain, they rallied in support of Powell while others rallied in opposition... Many, besides Powell, believed they were living through the collapse of western culture and its once sustaining traditions and comforting morality.
>
> (Kitts, 2007, p. 105)

The year was also marked by the general strike in France in May and by two assassinations: Martin Luther King on 4 April and Robert F. Kennedy on 5 June.

The soundtrack to the year was dominated by such pop songs as the Beatles' 'Revolution' as well as the Rolling Stones' 'Street-Fighting Man'. Both tracks were recorded in 1968, both tracks were inspired by the political unrest of that year, and both tracks can be considered as the most political songs either group ever released. These songs appeared on albums also released in 1968, The Beatles' *The Beatles* (more commonly known as *The White Album*) and The Rolling Stones' *Beggars Banquet*. Both albums were transatlantic commercial successes with *The White Album* reaching the number one spot in the United Kingdom and the United States, and *Beggars Banquet* climbing to number 3 in the UK charts and number 5 in the Billboard 200.

It would appear, then, that 1968 marked the climax of the decade of protest. Society, however, depends on 'heuristic fictions', that is to say fallacies of commonality such as ethics, religion and culture, which, as codifications, may be seen as simulating the transcendence of a potentially isolated subject. One such heuristic fiction is that the Sixties were a 'decade of protest': in other words, the need to project onto the Sixties subject the qualities of revolution and contestation in order to understand the Sixties (and often revolution and contestation themselves). This feature, however, should not be considered as constitutive of the real. These fictions, heuristic, conceptual or philosophical fictions, do not serve to illuminate some kind of reality, but, in Kurt Vaihinger's words, they are instruments 'for finding our way about more easily in the world' (Vaihinger, 1924, p. 15). The value of heuristic fictions finds itself wrapped up in the full title of this collection: *Preserving the Sixties Britain and the 'Decade of Protest'*. Somewhere along the line we all believe that it is 'as if' the Sixties was a decade of protest, 'as if' the quality of protest is relative to the quality of what were the Sixties. Protest, then, is the thing-in-itself of the Sixties, or the 'Ding ansich' to use the Kantian term. Eva Schaper writes:

> Things-in-themselves can consistently be seen as heuristic fictions, as devices enabling us to account for a given situation in terms of a theory. Things-in-themselves as heuristic fictions permit us to derive and exhibit a complicated set of consequences if we proceed as if they were real.
>
> (Schaper, 1966, p. 236)

It would seem, however, that understanding the Sixties as the decade of protest is more than a noumenon, as it would appear that protest is more than something conceived by thought; indeed, it is something perceived in experience. The question that remains is how putative this may be.

The mutually dependent *modi operandi* of cognitive autonomy and social orientation mean that reality constructions on the cognitive level somehow interact with reality constructions on the social level. In alternative terms, fictionality on a self-referential level interacts with fictionality on a hetero-referential level. In this way, fictions, character-ized by entropy, contingency and autonomy, become functional in the communication of socially useful codifications, of which protest in the Sixties is one.

Irrespective of overt political content, pop music has long been viewed as inherently anti-Establishment, though this is undoubtedly a heuristic fiction. Brian Longhurst reminds us that while rock'n'roll was devel-oping as a musical style in the 1950s, it was already understood as 'something authority didn't like' and explains: 'There is something inherently oppositional about rock. In the 1960s, ideas about the oppo-sitional status of rock were entailed in its characterization as the music of protest, the 'movement' or the underground' (Longhurst, 2007, p. 106).

In *Understanding Rock'n'Roll: Popular Music in Britain, 1955–1964*, Dick Bradley places this development in the context of youth culture:

> The unique position of post-war teenagers, physically adult yet excluded from adult roles and responsibilities, with considerable dis-posable cash, and familiar from early childhood with the products of the modern mass media, healthy, well-fed and energetic, yet involved in less hard physical work than many of their ancestors – this privi-leged, new position seemed merely to throw into sharp relief for them the limitations, frustrations and oppressiveness of their existence in other respects, and to give them the opportunity to respond in new ways to these conditions. Music-use became one of the main chosen instruments of their response.
>
> (Bradley, 1992, p. 96)

Though it is popularly considered that the teenager phenomenon was born in the 1950s along with the advent of rock'n'roll, it is worth underlining that Jon Savage's seminal study of the concept in *Teenage: The Creation of Youth Culture* (2007) begins in 1875 and ends with the death of Anne Frank in 1945. Indeed, for Savage, the development of the teenager is linked to the development of *urban* youth culture in the 1890s. This opposition of the urban to the rural is infused in the very title of The Kinks' album *The Kinks Are the Village Green Preservation*

Society where the preservation society is attempting to safeguard against the encroachment of urban culture upon pastoral serenity. Though this positioning may recall that of the hippie counter-culture, hippies rejected established institutions and middle-class values whereas the title of The Kinks' album suggests an ironic reversal of the ideals of contemporary youth cultures as represented by pop music of the late 1960s with its preservation society emblematic of a bourgeois social club. How then are we to understand the paradoxes posed by the apparently counter-revolutionary voice of The Kinks' 1968 concept album?

British invasion: or knocking your singer out with a hi-hat stand?

An unfortunate commercial coincidence saw *The Kinks Are the Village Green Preservation Society* released on 22 November 1968, the same date as the release of the *The White Album* by the Beatles. Though in 2003 The Kinks' album was ranked 255th in *Rolling Stone* magazine's list of the 500 greatest albums of all time,[1] the album was initially a commercial failure. A concept album filled with conservative vignettes of when England was the country and the country was England, songs such as 'Village Green' and 'Animal Farm' lament a simpler, more mundane village life. This nostalgia for a time when England was still the nation of county grounds, warm beer, invincible green shadows and old maids cycling to Holy Communion through the morning mist,[2] seems to stand as a counter-example of what was happening socially and culturally around the time of the album's release. In his book, *The Kinks Are the Village Green Preservation Society*, Andy Miller writes:

> The Kinks' new album wilfully disregarded anything fashionable in British rock or pop at the time. There were no long guitar solos, no extended freeform jams, no lyrics based on the Tibetan *Book of the Dead* or *The Communist Manifesto*... [Ray Davies] drew on a well of traditional and personal sources to create an album which, although nominally concerned with the characters that lived around a village green, goes deep into territory rarely explored in pop: memory, regret, failure, growing old.
>
> (Miller, 2003, p. 5)

'Memory, regret, failure, growing old' are not the habitual *topoi* that sit comfortably with youthful expressions of independence and liberation, freedom and autonomy, protest and contestation. The genesis of *The Kinks Are the Village Green Preservation Society* was that of a Ray Davies project for the theatre inspired by Dylan Thomas' 1954 radio drama *Under Milk Wood*, and we can recognize in the themes that Davies employs in the album Thomas' obsession with the passing of time. Like a piece of theatre, the album is also inhabited by a number of characters that are at times played and at others directed by the band. Though the tracks were all written by Ray Davies, and this is very much a personal project, ultimately, the group, like a troupe of actors, stage the album which includes in its very title the name of the band: *The Kinks Are the Village Green Preservation Society*. The protagonist, after the postmodern fashion, is a first person plural.

The Kinks had been a major player of the 'British Invasion', the period from 1964 onwards which saw a succession of British acts of the beat boom achieve considerable commercial success in the United States. Long periods of touring far from home have a tendency to amplify underlying tensions among band members. This was no different for The Kinks who took to throwing instruments at each other on stage during concerts, resulting in drummer Mick Avory knocking Ray Davies unconscious with his hi-hat stand during a show at the Capitol Theatre, Cardiff (Kitts, 2007, p. 58). Following their 1965 tour of the United States, the American Federation of Musicians refused to issue permits for the group again until 1969 by which time the height of the British Invasion was over. In his book *Revolution in the Head* (2008), Ian MacDonald concludes:

> Their consequent isolation from American influence steered them away from the blues-based riffing of their early material, producing the determined Englishness of what became their most creative period. Once their exile was over, The Kinks' music almost immediately began to revert to its original transatlantic idiom.
>
> (MacDonald, 2008, p. 189)

Work on *The Kinks Are the Village Green Preservation Society*, began during this period of exclusion with the song 'Village Green' being recorded during the sessions for the group's 1967 album *Something Else by The Kinks*. Regarded by most as a quintessentially English pop record, not only do the lyrical themes draw heavily upon English heritage but the musical themes move away from the blues riffs that The Kinks had hardened on songs like 'You Really Got Me' and 'All Day and All of the Night' and towards the English music hall genre. In fact, one could almost say that Ray Davies reinvented himself as a pop version of George Formby.

Like his father, Formby was a hugely successful music hall comedian who brought his light comical songs played on a banjo ukulele, or 'banjolele', to the masses via the silver screen. As Gordon Thompson writes in *Please Please Me* (2008):

> Davies seems to have relished the comparison with Formby, whose films usually portrayed the triumphs of an honest and simple working-class man over the vicissitudes of life and the advantages available only to those born to privilege.
>
> (Thompson, 2008, pp. 221–2)

On the album *The Kinks Are the Village Green Preservation Society*, Davies sings in favour of a simpler life. Borrowing from such English traditions as music hall and village life, he appears to see, in the restoration of a bygone age, the possibility for stability in the lives of the working class who have found themselves ensnared by urbanization.

The Good Old Days: or the pathological nostalgia of Englishness

As we have already come to understand, central to the concept of the album are the notions of conservation and heteronomous green spaces. In his book, *The English Village Green* (1985), Brian Bailey describes the village green as:

> a little patch of grassland that still strikes a chord in the hearts of most native men and women two hundred years after the Industrial Revolution changed the majority of us to urban dwellers. It represents rural peace and quiet, as well as a community spirit that does not obtain in towns, and sets up in most of us a yearning for that fondly imagined country paradise, lost by the growth of imperialism and capitalism which have made England an over-populated country of noisy and dirty towns and cities where the mass of men, as Thoreau put it, lead lives of quiet desperation.
>
> (Bailey, 1985, p. 13)

It is worthwhile recalling the whole of the quote from Henry David Thoreau's *Walden* (1854) which reads:

> The mass of men lead lives of quiet desperation. What is called resignation is confirmed desperation. From the desperate city you go into

the desperate country, and have to console yourself with the bravery of minks and muskrats.

(Thoreau, 2007, p. 10)

It is important to underline that Thoreau is not simply opposing rural peace and quiet to urban hustle and bustle, as Bailey's quote might suggest. For Thoreau, as we move from the city to the countryside, desperation remains a constant. This ambivalence is not alien to the lyrics of Davies on *The Kinks Are the Village Green Preservation Society*. Though there is an overarching undeniable tone of nostalgia for a pastoral idyll throughout the album, there are times when Davies recognizes that this nostalgia is infused with a sense of desperation. In the song 'Do You Remember Walter', for instance, the singer recognizes the divide in time between the idealism of yesterday and the reality of today:

> I bet you're fat and married and you're always
>   home in bed by half-past eight.
> And if I talked about the old times you'd get
>   bored and you'll have nothing more to say.
> Yes people often change, but memories
>   of people can remain.

('Do You Remember Walter')

The memories in question belong to an imagined territory that is the wont of nostalgia and Davies is knowingly constructing and populating the 'fondly imagined *country* paradise' (my italics) of Bailey's village green.

The village green is not, of course, the country and even less the pre-industrial wild countryside idealized through a prescriptive reading of a 'romantic' Romantic vision (itself, therefore, a heteronomy). The village green is a construct of town planning, a paradigmatic space of village communality, a simulacrum of nature. This inheritance of the notion of the village green finds itself injected into the post-war New Towns Act of 1946 where the 'construction followed conservative anti-urban principles, driven by a nostalgic desire for an idyllic past' (Lupro, 2006, p. 192). Ray Davies and Dave Davies grew up in North London at 6 Denmark Street, and Ray settled with his family just a few hundred yards away at 87 Fortis Green where he wrote most of the material for *The Kinks Are the Village Green Preservation Society*. Having grown up in North London where the New Town model was largely deployed, the Davies brothers were immersed in this anti-urban vision. In his autobiography,

Dave Davies, the younger of the two brothers, writes critically of this town planning:

> When you look around now at the terrible architecture in England...it serves as a constant reminder of how thoughtless and naive post-war Britain was. They tore down lovely Victorian terraced houses all over London and replaced them with cold, ugly office blocks.
>
> (Dave Davies, 1996, p. 107)

Of course, these comments recall the lines 'We are the office block persecution affinity' and 'We are the skyscraper condemnation affiliate' from the song 'The Village Green Preservation Society'.

The track 'Village Green' begins with the singer wishing to escape the trappings of fame and the city by returning to a pastoral romantic utopia:

> Out in the country,
> Far from all the soot and noise of the city,
> There's a village green.
> It's been a long time
> Since I last set eyes on the church with the steeple
> Down by the village green
>
> ('Village Green')

The orchestral backing faintly recalling Bach, combined with unusual rhythms and the wordless 'la-la' backing vocals-come-choruses, conjure up images of what Kitts calls the 'lost domain of carefree childhood' (Kitts, 2007, p. 120). The title track of the album, 'The Village Green Preservation Society' also invokes images of Constable-like Romantic visions of the English countryside dominated by Salisbury Cathedral, and declares: 'I miss the village green / The church, the clock, the steeple.' This may remind us of Jeremy Paxman's exchange with Alan Bennett on the nature of Englishness – Bennett sends Paxman a postcard on which he expresses his hope that Paxman's home village has not changed since he last visited it 30 years ago. Paxman is left to ponder:

> And that final comment about the village and the hope that it hadn't changed: that too was essentially English, the prayer of a people marching backwards into the future, for whom change always meant change for the worse.
>
> (Paxman, 1998, p. 18)

It would appear then that Davies and The Kinks find themselves in the quandary of 'marching backwards into the future'. Though there are moments of savvy ambivalence, somewhere along the line the album still reverberates with Stanley Baldwin's proclamation to the Royal Society of Saint George in 1924 that 'England is the country and the country is England', they echo 'the tinkle of the hammer on the anvil in the country smithy' (Baldwin, 1926, pp. 6–7).

It would appear that part of the enigma of Englishness is its rather conservative 'pathological nostalgia', that is its need to look back ceaselessly from past glory to past glory: 1966, the Second World War, the Empire, the Industrial Revolution, and ultimately, we regress, with a sense of pastoral loss, to a time when the long shadows were not cast by dark satanic mills (see Costambeys-Kempczynski, 2009). Though not all of the songs stay close to the theme of the village green, pre-industrial, stereotypical Romantic view of England from the country lane, they do share a very English preoccupation with the past as Ray Davies appears to be 'mourning a loss, personal and national, in song' (Miller, 2003, p. 26).

A close study of *The Kinks Are the Village Green Preservation Society* requires us to shade this notion of pathological nostalgia with what the historian Norman Davies calls 'anticipatory nostalgia'.[3] This kind of nostalgia is experienced when we begin to regret the present though it has yet to become the past, and this notion seems relevant to 1968 and the decade of protest. Though the verses of 'The Village Green Preservation Society' offer an archival *enumeratio* forcefully demanding our respect for everyday objects and subjects, from draught beer to Mrs Mopp, from the George Cross to custard pies, the chorus also asks us to bear in mind the preservation of modern conveniences:

> Preserving the old ways from being abused
> Protecting the new ways for me and for you
> What more can we do
> God save the village green.

> ('The Village Green Preservation
> Society')

Brought together, the notions of anticipatory nostalgia and Marshall McLuhan's idea of marching backwards into the future help expound Michael Mooradian Lupro's idea of a postmodern time conundrum. In his article, 'Preserving the Old Ways, Protecting the New: Post-War British Urban Planning in *The Kinks Are the Village Green Preservation*

Society', Lupro compares Bernards Heath conservationists attempting to force the city council not to develop the green space behind the fire station to The Kinks' album writing:

> Both Davies's Village Green and the Bernards Heath Village Green Preservation Society express a postmodern time conundrum where the best practices of the present are squeezed between nostalgia for an idyllic past and visions of a Utopian future. This necessarily uncomfortable predicament is further complicated as the Utopian vision and the idyllic nostalgia intermingle – where the future is a regeneration of the past and the past a legacy of antiquated future visions.
>
> (Lupro, 2006, p. 190)

A combination, therefore, of both pathological and anticipatory nostalgia, *The Kinks Are the Village Green Preservation Society* positions itself against the mind-altering drug-induced progressiveness of contemporary Beatles releases and the confrontational antagonism of The Rolling Stones. Though the romantic ideals that find themselves woven through the fabric of The Kinks' album appear to run against the grain of the revolutionary fervour of 1968, let us not forget that Romanticism was a movement that reacted against the Industrial Revolution and fed on the ideologies and events of the French Revolution. There is no doubt that there is a political undercurrent to the nostalgia of this album and Lupro suggests that the subtle commentary of the songs, as opposed to overt rebelliousness, enables them to escape the confines of one particular moment in time: 'Being more oblique, nuanced, and camouflaged as sweet and innocent, his critique of the structures of post-war Britain effectively stretches beyond the heady revolutionary days of 1968 to both the past and the future' (ibid., p. 193). In his autobiography, Davies suggests that he was aware that the revolutionary nature of the post-modern time conundrum of the late 1960s was producing a gap through which would slip a contingent of politically, socially and culturally excluded:

> The Sixties were like a carrot held up to youth to distract us so that we would not rebel against the ruling classes and all the backhanders and corruption that were actually present in politics … I was becoming aware of the thousands of people who would be left behind when the party was over, without a place in society.
>
> (Ray Davies, 1994, pp. 311–12)

Revolution does not seem to be a particularly English quality. Writing in his essay, 'The English People', George Orwell suggests that 'England is the only European country where internal politics are conducted in a more or less humane and decent manner' and claims that the English people 'are not good haters' (Orwell, 2001, pp. 322, 304). Davies was not, therefore, about to abandon the generation that had fought and survived the war or the heritage of an Empire that was on the decline. Following on from Walter Benjamin, Savoj Žižek writes: 'the present appears to a revolutionary as a frozen moment of repetition in which the evolutionary flow is immobilized, and past and present directly overlap in a crystalline way' (2008, p. 115). If anything, what Davies is doing on this album is trying to *make* the past and present overlap in order to avoid the antiquated future visions of office blocks but also to better anticipate an uncertain future brought on by a revolution that is not fuelled by youth culture but is in fact a heteronomy: preserving the old ways, protecting the new, what more can we do?

Picture Book: or the mortification of the living body

Notably, two songs deal with preserving the past, archiving memories for future consultation, through photography: 'Picture Book' and 'People Take Pictures of Each Other'. On the latter, the very last song on the album, photography, as one may expect, offers proof of the existence of the past:

> People take pictures of the Summer,
> Just in case someone thought they had missed it,
> And to prove that it really existed.

('People Take Pictures of Each Other')

Within the logic of the album's concept, the past that is on offer here appears to be one of simpler times:

> Picture of me when I was just three,
> Sat with my ma by the old oak tree.

('People Take Pictures
of Each Other')

It is not solely the physical tangibility of the past, however, that the singer is trying to recapture in these pictures. Indeed, lost emotions and sentiments are also what the singer appears to be trying to regain:

> Fathers take pictures of the mothers,
> And the sisters take pictures of brothers,
> Just to show that they love one another.
>
> ('People Take Pictures of
> Each Other')

In these two songs the central force of the photograph is that the fixed image guarantees the existence of this idyllic past. At least, this is how nostalgia functions. This idea is expressed in Slavoj Žižek's reading of photography, what he calls the 'medium of immobilization' (Žižek, 2008, p. 108):

> in terms of its original phenomenological status, movement equals blindness; it blurs the contours of what we perceive: in order for us to perceive the object clearly, it must be frozen, immobilized – immobility makes a thing visible... it is only immobility that provides a firm visible existence.
>
> (ibid., pp. 108–9)

Žižek does not forget, however, that photography 'was first perceived as involving the *mortification* of the living body' (ibid., p. 108). This appears in line with Ray Davies's obsession, not so much with the good old days, but with the passing of time, or more precisely the inevitability of death. Žižek's paradigm is simple: taking the example of X-rays (and here lies a happy coincidence as Ray Davies's (1994) autobiography is called *X-Ray*), Žižek reminds us that this particular kind of photography allows us 'to see a person who is still alive *as if he were already dead*' (Žižek, 2008, p. 108).

This idea is combined with the notion that clear perception of an object is only possible when that object is 'frozen, immobilized' (ibid., p. 109). This leads Žižek to follow Paul Virilio's idea that 'the person who has stopped being alive exists more fully than when actually alive, moving around before us' (Virilio, in Žižek, 2008, p. 109). Perhaps then, the 'Daviesland'[4] that Ray Davies populates in *The Kinks Are the Village Green Preservation Society* is to be understood as more real to the band leader than the world revolving around him. If one holds as true the old adage to always write about what you know, the gift of the author is to be able to transform personal details into the symbolic, to transform the individual into the universal, and Davies admits that *this* revolution did not occur in his composition of the album:

> It's a very intimate album. That's the problem. Paul Schrader once said to me, 'When you get a good story, you get a personal problem, then you turn it into a metaphor.' I didn't do that. I just got the personal problem.
>
> (Miller, 2003, p. 6)

Perhaps it is here that Ray Davies's radicalism is to be found. Rather than aiming for the universal wherein lies the ideology of revolution, as well as the true potential outreach of pop music, Davies produces an album that is solipsistic. With the global scale of the civil unrest during 1968, the only solution that seems to offer itself to Davies is the life of a reclusive, as Kitts writes:

> With 1960s rock music and radicalism becoming increasingly inter-national, Davies was becoming increasingly private. 'I wanted to be Walt Disney,' says Davies. '"Village Green" meant nothing to me except in my fantasy. It was my ideal place, a protected place. It's a fantasy world that I can retreat to.' Thus Village Green becomes an extended treatment of Davies's dream theme, of escaping the world and himself.
>
> (Kitts, 2007, p. 117)

This understanding of mortification through photography is thickened in the song 'Village Green' where Davies sings:

> American tourists flock to see the village green.
> They snap their photographs and say gawd darn it,
> Isn't it a pretty scene?
>
> ('Village Green')

Through the holiday snaps the village green is here stripped of its primary function and commodified into the dead symbol of quaint Englishness, its social purpose has been reduced to a purely aesthetic value. This is not a critique of American tourists as what they offer here is an outsider's perspective of the village green seen for what it is and not for what it was or should be.

Mortification is also the denial or self-inflicted suppression of desires and passions, of emotions and sentiments. If the people fixed in these images exist more fully than if they were moving around us, the emotions felt remain but a blur. It is impossible to reconcile the physical tangibility of the photograph before our eyes and the emotions that the images recall to mind. Childhood love then becomes something that is forever lost along with the innocence of a time when we were unaware of the obligations that contribute to the lives that we live and of the rules that govern society. This leaves the singer to conclude:

> You can't picture love that you took from me,
> When we were young and the world was free.
> Pictures of things as they used to be,
> Don't show me no more, please.

('People Take Pictures of Each Other')

In the end, the singer finds himself in an ambiguous state where he is unable to look at any more pictures of the past because he is conscious of the fact that this paradise lost can never be regained. These pictures offer but a selective archive of the past, and as with all archives it has no emotional index.

What the singer truly wants to attain through the pictures, the pre-symbolic real life, remains impossibly out of reach. The singer, then, has come to the difficult conclusion that these images but reflect the symbolized gaze which can see only mortified objects. Davies recognizes this and in his autobiography he confirms the idea that photographs simply serve as a reminder of our own mortality, of the ageing process and of our ultimate passing away, and that the personal and emotional are only truly represented in our mind's eye:

> I like to remember people the way they were. Pictures just show the world how much a person has aged, whereas memory renders a person ageless.

> The camera may not lie, but it is not entirely honest. It shows only a small slice, a narrow perspective. It makes events which should be ambiguous turn into absolutes, and it disallows personal interpretation. Why reduce life to a series of images that shows a bias towards the objective when a person has spent his entire lifetime creating subjective, ambiguous images?

(Ray Davies, 1994, pp. 329–30)

For his reading of nostalgia, Simon Reynolds draws on the theories of Svetlana Boym who differentiates between restorative and reflective nostalgia. In restorative nostalgia, we find the ultra-conservative political desire to establish the old order, whereas reflective nostalgia is a personal reverie, the Daviesland of the village green where instants are captured by instant picture cameras:

> Far from wanting to resurrect a lost golden age, reflective nostalgia takes pleasure in the misty remoteness of the past and cultivates the bittersweet pangs of poignancy. The danger of restorative nostalgia lies in its belief that the mutilated 'wholeness' of the body politic can be repaired. But the reflective nostalgic understands deep down that loss is irrecoverable: Time wounds all wholes. To exist in time is to suffer through an endless exile, a successive severing from those precious few moments of feeling at home in the world.
>
> (Reynolds, 2011, p. xxviii)

Though the track 'Last of the Steam-Powered Trains' does not refer to photography or, indeed, a living body, the song is again framed by a sense of mortification. The singer and the steam-powered train are confounded into another inhabitant of the village green Daviesland, personified through the use of the first person and brought to life as a sole survivor: 'I'm the last of the blood and sweat brigade' ('Last of the Steam-Powered Trains'). For all the want of a steam train to romantically race through the countryside taking passengers to distant destinations, the last of the steam-powered trains finds itself protected against its will from such exertions and archived away for memory:

> I'm the last of the good old renegades.
> All my friends are all middle-class and grey,
> But I live in a museum, so I'm okay.
>
> ('Last of the Steam-Powered Trains')

Like a photograph, the transformation of the 'ol' puffer' into a museum-piece marks the death of the train, or rather freezes it in a state of constant decay. The reference to being 'okay' is infused with sarcasm and the train is left to conclude in all honesty that 'all this peaceful living is driving me insane' ('Last of the Steam-Powered Trains'). The nostalgia felt by the train that once could foresee itself 'rollin' till my dying day' is translated into the song's musical composition and in this way becomes analogous to the situation the band find themselves in as they are commercially isolated from America. The central chugging riff from the track is a modified quotation from Howlin' Wolf's (1956) song 'Smokestack Lightnin', thus taking the band back to its early influences and breaking from the rest of the album's musical inspirations, leaving Matthew Gelbart to conclude that the songs ' "dinosaur" quality can hardly be missed' (Gelbart, 2003, p. 239). The insanity expressed by the train in the third verse is followed by the riff looping and increasing in tempo until it appears to snap when a new pattern emerges moving up an octave through a chromatic scale only to be rendered with an e-chord that brings us back to where we began and the continuing frustration of the train that doesn't 'know where I'm going, or why I came' ('Last of the Steam-Powered Trains').

As with all the tracks on this album, this song's subversion positions itself on several levels. 'Last of the Steam-Powered Trains' represents the continuing struggle of the working class where the train is the 'last of the soot and scum brigade' in a world where '[a]ll my friends are middle-class and grey'. This is as close to talk of revolution as Davies comes on this album with the train proclaiming that it will 'Huff and puff till I blow this world away.' As we have already seen, however, this is yet another futile gesture and this is how Davies seems to view the contemporary atmosphere of revolution where the rebellious nature of late-1960s youth culture is, in fact, a 'carrot', in other words something that has already been subsumed by society into a normative frame that constrains and stabilizes the world as we know it.

Conclusion

The songs of Davies on this album are both sincere and mocking, nostalgic but with a knowing sense of wry humour. Undoubtedly at odds with the received norms of the rebellious nature of youth culture, Davies populates his Daviesland with marginal or marginalized characters, from Wicked Anabella, the village witch, to Tom, the grocery boy. As Gelbart writes:

> Rock, with its supposed counter-cultural force and embodiment of alienation, might seem an ideal place to destabilize any central, authoritative persona. In their quietly subversive songs of the late 1960s, the Kinks fulfilled this potential – creating increasing friction between elements under the control of a dominant persona and various 'decentred' voices.
>
> (Gelbart, 2003, p. 204)

In the song, 'The Village Green Preservation Society', the main vocal appears under-produced and stands as part of the harmonic accompaniment of the backing vocals. As Gelbart points out, the vocals, however, continually shift between the stereo right and left channels, they change in pitch and tone. The combination of voice, music and technology reproduce the population of the village green, with its harmonies and discordances. The pop candy style of the music is itself humoristic, and as we have already seen, Davies, aware of the ambivalence of nostalgia, seems to confirm that this past he longs for never really existed.

As one would expect from The Kinks, there is, indeed, much humour on this album, both in the lyrics and the music. The songs on this album, however, remain personal and never attain the universal through metaphor. I would contend, therefore, that this humour is not ironic but reflects more the other typical English humoristic device of self-deprecation. In *Revolution in the Head* (2008), Ian MacDonald compares American rock to its English associate, stating:

> Apart from conceptual in a way which most American pop/rock is not, the pop music made in Britain over the last thirty years, while predominantly gay in the old sense, is also permeated by the wry scepticism of the country's self-deprecating humour. An off-shore adjunct to the often-ruined culture of Europe, Britain – more especially England – is cheerfully inured to failure and decline. As such, the native humour is based mainly on pessimism and self-mockery, while the English notoriously derive pleasure from the prospect of disaster.
>
> (MacDonald, 2008, p. xx)

Revolution leading on to disaster, perhaps, but at least God save The Kinks.

Notes

1. The full list is available from the *Rolling Stone Magazine* website: http://www.rollingstone.com/music/lists/500-greatest-albums-of-all-time-19691231.
2. I am here quoting from John Major's timeless and much satirized vision of Britain published in *The Guardian* on 23 April 1993, St George's Day: 'Fifty years from now, Britain will still be the country of long shadows on county grounds, warm beer, invincible green shadows, dog lovers and pool fillers and – as George Orwell said – "old maids cycling to Holy Communion through the morning mist" '.
3. Norman Davies speaking on *Start the Week*, BBC Radio 4, 14 November 2011.

4. Cf. original liner notes to *Something Else by the Kinks* (1967):

> Welcome to Daviesland, where all the little kinklings in the magic Kinkdom wear tiny black bowlers, rugby boots, soldier suits, drink half pints of bitter, carry cricket bats and ride in little tube trains . . . Gulliver-like Ray Davies stoops to pluck a small mortal from his musical world – turns him upside down to see where he was made – and replaces him gently but firmly in that great class society where all men are equal but some are more equal than others.

Bibliography

Bailey, Brian (1985) *The English Village Green*, London: Robert Hale.

Baldwin, Stanley (1926) *On England, and Other Addresses*, London: Philip Allan.

Bradley, Dick (1992) *Understanding Rock'n'Roll: Popular Music in Britain, 1955–64* Buckingham: Open University Press.

Costambeys-Kempczynski, Raphael (2009) 'A view of Englishmen from street level: Mike Skinner and the geezer', in Reviron-Piegay, Floriane (ed.) *Englishness Revisited*, Newcastle-upon-Tyne: CSP, pp. 79–96.

Davies, Dave (1996) *Kink: An Autobiography*, New York: Hyperion.

Davies, Ray (1994) *X-Ray: An Unauthorized Autobiography*, Woodstock, NY: Overlook Press.

Gelbart, Matthew (2003) 'Persona and voice in the Kinks' songs of the late 1960s', *Journal of the Royal Musical Association*, 128(2), 200–41.

Kitts, Thomas (2007) *Ray Davies: Not Like Everybody Else*, London: Routledge.

Longhurst, Brian (2007) *Popular Music and Society*, Cambridge: Polity.

Lupro, Michael Mooradian (2006) 'Preserving the old ways, protecting the new: post-war British urban planning in *The Kinks Are The Village Green Preservation Society*', *Popular Music and Society*, 29(2), 189–200.

MacDonald, Ian (2008) *Revolution in the Head*, London: Vintage.

Miller, Andy (2003) *The Kinks Are the Village Green Preservation Society*, London: Continuum.

Orwell, George (2001) *Orwell's England*, London: Penguin.

Paxman, Jeremy (1998) *The English*, London: Penguin.

Reynolds, Simon (2011) *Retromania: Pop Culture's Addiction to Its Own Past*, London: Faber and Faber.

Savage, Jon (2007) *Teenage: The Creation of Youth Culture*, London: Viking.

Schaper, Eva (1966) 'The Kantian thing-in-itself as a philosophical fiction', *The Philosophical Quarterly*, 16 (64), History of Philosophy Number (July 1966), 233–43.

Thompson, Gordon (2008) *Please, Please Me: Sixties British Pop, Inside Out* New York: Oxford University Press.

Thoreau, Henry David (2007) *Walden and On the Duty of Civil Disobedience* Rockville: Arc Manor.

Vaihinger, Kurt (1924) *The Philosophy of 'As-If'*, trans. C. K. Ogden, London: Kegan Paul, Trench, Trubner and Co.

Žižek, Slavoj (2008) *The Plague of Fantasies*, London: Verso.

Discs

The Beatles, *The Beatles*. Apple Records/Parlophone PCS (PMC) 7067/68, 1968.2-LP.

The Beatles, 'Hey Jude/Revolution'. Apple Records/Parlophone R 5722, 1968.7".

The Beatles, 'Get Back/Don't Let Me Down'. Apple Records/Parlophone R 5777, 1969.7".

The Kinks, 'You Really Got Me/It's Alright'. Pye 7N 15673, 1964.7".

The Kinks, 'All Day and All of the Night/I Gotta Move'. Pye 7N 15714, 1964.7".

The Kinks, *Something Else by The Kinks*. Pye NSPL 18193, 1967. LP.

The Kinks, *The Kinks Are the Village Green Preservation Society*. Pye NSPL 18233, 1968. LP.

The Rolling Stones, *Beggars Banquet*. Decca SKL 4955 FFSS, 1968.LP.

The Rolling Stones, 'Street Fighting Man'. London 45 LON 909 (US), 1968.7".

Thomas, Dylan, *Under Milk Wood*. Argo Records RG 21/RG 22, 1954. 2-LP.

Wolf, Howlin', 'Smokestack Lightnin'/You Can't Be', 1956. Chess 1618.7".

Conclusion

Trevor Harris and Monia O'Brien Castro

The Sixties today still represent something of an exception: a historical period which is deemed to correspond to a decade. But the latter is, as we know, largely illusory, and appears to have happened by default, in a similar way to the 1970s, the 1980s, the 1990s or the 'noughties', in what is an increasingly marked trend. But none of these other decades has even begun to attain the historical importance of the Sixties. It is possible that the Sixties will slowly merge with the surrounding chronological features, as they are increasingly reassessed over time. But the label, for better or worse, now seems to have stuck fast, and the 'Sixties', as opposed to the 1960s, may well retain their status as a recognised historical period, however difficult it may prove to define.

A certain number of characteristics are said to separate the Sixties from the immediate post-war years, at one end, and from the remaining part of the twentieth century, at the other. But even the nature of these characteristics, as we have seen, and the way they are used as part of a historical interpretation, can run into problems: we are now familiar with the dichotomy between the 'liberal' approach to the Sixties – which underlines the period as bursting at the psychedelic seams with creativity and constructive energy – and the 'New Right' interpretation, which sees the Sixties as the distillation of all that was most decadent and destructive where British society was concerned.

The contributors to this volume, in discussing various aspects of politics, society and culture at this point in post-war Britain, nonetheless show that trends can be discerned and a certain cohesion observed: the rapid expansion of the pop music industry, the tentative convergence of pop music, youth and radical politics; the redevelopment of British cities; controversial social legislation; the tragic deterioration in the situation in Northern Ireland; the emergence of the working class as both a consumer and a producer of art. All of these would tend to support the liberal view that the Sixties were a time of radical engagement with innovative social, political and cultural practices: here was modernity made visible, tangible. Just as, across the Channel the 'new France' was emerging, so there was a 'new Britain' coming into being.

But as one of the most consistently radical figures in post-war Britain, Tony Benn, once pointed out, 'new' is the oldest word in politics. The Sixties as the high point of modernity nonetheless remained affected by a pervasive conservatism – a frequently recurring theme in the pages above. As Matthew Leggett and Sylvie Pomiès-Maréchal show, the victory for women's rights embodied in the Abortion Act of 1967, while not a hollow victory, was hard-won, and even then only partial: the result of hard work, determination, and some profoundly old-fashioned political horse-trading at Westminster, in order to break down entrenched institutional opposition across the political spectrum. Even within the vanguard of this modern, 'new' Britain, there was, in addition, a healthy scepticism. The Beatles themselves, as Ben Winsworth argues, were, from relatively early in their career, keenly aware of the contradictions and limitations of the music industry: as, it seems, were the satirists so prominent on British television at the time. Judith Roof's analysis suggests, indeed, that even the most critical jokes, in spite of themselves, shade towards the conservative, since they must use the same signifying codes that they are criticizing: rather than attacking 'from within', this is more a question of not being able to attack 'from without'.

In short, there were strong personal and institutional limits to breaks with the past: continuity, or the return of a national repressed, were important components of the British Sixties: that perennially absorbing subject in Britain – class – remained one of the most reliable touchstones throughout the Sixties. Indeed, attempts by Britain's radical left to recuperate pop culture met, as we have seen, with only very marginal success. The most contradictory developments came in Northern Ireland, where the civil rights movement – as Martine Pelletier argues – clashed violently with a government lauded by many, then and since, for its open-mindedness and its fearless promotion of change. In what was in many ways a grotesque travesty, modernity seems merely to have contributed to the revival of age-old antagonisms.

Rather than frivolity, youth, peace and love, one of the main preoccupations of the Sixties seems to have been not the future, not even the present, but the past. And it is this paradox which emerges most strongly from the contributions to this volume. The Sixties, supposedly in thrall to the present, to the loss of one's self in the moment, the permanent now of the 'trip', in fact find it decidedly difficult to let go. In a society which, both superficially and spectacularly, was wedded to an almost pathological celebration of the new, there is clear evidence that this was accompanied by a desperate anxiety about the passage of time. The paramountcy of the present was, indeed, an exacerbated, drug-induced/enhanced awareness of the need not to lose that moment, a sense that the present was already in the act of passing and that it had to be preserved.

Is the term 'Sixties', then, ultimately to be set to one side, abandoned as having little or no historical validity or purchase? That would be an unnecessarily sweeping reaction. For the usefulness of the term (which may or may not prove to be a durable one) perhaps lies in this very British notion of rebellion as embodying a fundamental scepticism about the *new*. It is not that the permissive society was ranged against traditional values, but that not all branches of that tradition were able to appreciate how the modern might be, and needed to be, integrated into tradition. Ray Davies' 'Preservation Society' needs, in this context, to be seen as a form of radical nostalgia: the music and lyrics of the Kinks' 'Village Green Preservation Society', in many ways represent an elegy to a particularly English form of simplicity and decency.

In this, the Sixties were following in the steps of some illustrious English predecessors. The 'Preservation Society' clearly lies in a tradition which includes the thought of E. M. Forster, for example, whose militancy expressed itself in the National Council for Civil Liberties, founded in 1934, of which he was the first president. But the 'Preservation Society' also recalls Forster's Abinger, and his impassioned appeal for the preservation of 'England's grass network of lanes', of 'England, green and eternal'. In that same green, eternal England, we can also find William Morris's Kelmscott. Morris, too, was a radical, but one whose vision of the idyllic, democratic future was derived from a re-working of England's decent, democratic past.

It may be, in the end, that one of the most lasting and most significant aspects of the Sixties is that they invented a new way of seeing the present as part of England's intricate evolution and improvement; a new way, as it were, of being old-fashioned. English conservatism had hit upon the most spectacular way yet, the most novel way yet, of absorbing the new and preserving the old.

Index

Note: 'n.' after a page reference refers to a note number on that page.

Printed and bound by CPI Group (UK) Ltd, Croydon, CR0 4YY